# The Suasive Art of David Hume

# The Suasive Art of
# David Hume

*M. A. Box*

PRINCETON UNIVERSITY PRESS

PRINCETON, NEW JERSEY

Library of Congress Cataloging-in-Publication Data

Box, M. A., 1952–
The suasive art of David Hume.
1. Hume, David, 1711–1776—Literary art. I. Title.
B1498.B63   1990   192   89-10848
ISBN 0-691-06828-3

This book has been composed in Linotron Caledonia

Princeton University Press books are printed on acid-free paper,
and meet the guidelines for permanence and durability of the
Committee on Production Guidelines for Book Longevity of the
Council on Library Resources

Printed in the United States of America by Princeton University Press,
Princeton, New Jersey

1 3 5 7 9 10 8 6 4 2

[A]nd then there was Hume: the scepticism of that charming philosopher touched a kindred note in Philip; and, revelling in the lucid style which seemed able to put complicated thought into simple words, musical and measured, he read as he might have read a novel, a smile of pleasure on his lips.
—W. Somerset Maugham, *Of Human Bondage*

# CONTENTS

# PREFACE

THIS BOOK is a literary study with an orientation in intellectual history. Its purpose is not to confirm or confute Hume's philosophy, but to describe his development as a writer over one period of his career. On the other hand, it has been necessary to claim that he held certain tenets and thought others false, and as his tenets are not plain to the view I have endeavored to explain them as the occasion called for it. Over interpretive details there is unending disagreement, and it is not to be hoped that any explanation of Hume's tenets will satisfy everyone. Many more contradictory positions have been attributed to Hume than one would expect from a thinker who, unlike Emerson or Nietzsche, was attempting to build a self-consistent system. A recent trend has been to see him as much more consistent than generally had been supposed, but exegetical unanimity is still nowhere in sight, and the digressions needed to defend every disputable point of interpretation would have crowded my own contributions. For such defenses sometimes the reader is referred in the citations to other commentators. I have had to depend upon those commentators who seem to me most sound and to walk humbly before those who do not. However, I have not used the notes to provide a bibliographic survey of Humean studies, for which there has been no room here and which is better provided, moreover, by Roland Hall's *Fifty Years of Hume Scholarship* (Edinburgh, 1978) together with his supplements in the second number of each volume of *Hume Studies*.

It would be best to state my allegiances outright. My understanding of the moral theory is based primarily upon J. L. Mackie's account. On passional psychology, valuation, and reasonableness I am the pupil of Páll Árdal, while on Hume's sociopolitical views I have found David Miller especially helpful. An important and underappreciated fact is that by his "logic" Hume means a conflation of logic and epistemology (an epistemologic, so to speak) in which the rules for reasoning are determined by the limitations inherent in the process by which we can know things. For Hume's "logic" I am indebted to James Noxon. My own explanations, however, not being mere synopses of these accounts, have no claim to the endorsement of these commentators.

I have also tried to depict in general terms the system into which these tenets fit. It has been necessary to consider Hume's system as a whole in order to relate his behavior as a writer to his aspirations for his philosophy. In historical fact, his system as a totality probably had no effect whatsoever on society since it was never perceived as a cohesive unit. Hume appears to have made his mark on history entirely through individual arguments, usually negative ones viewed in isolation from their contexts. But this was not his intention, and it is with his intentions that we will be concerned.

One can hardly say anything about Hume's philosophy with complete assurance; and the following literary readings are pervaded with the philosophy. I have had to revise my own views of his thought too often to offer these readings otherwise than in the tentative spirit of empirical inquiry, with the hope and expectation that further research will in many respects supersede them.

For various favors thanks are due to Mlle. Tisnes, *bibliothécaire* of Prytanée Militaire de La Flèche, Dr. M. A. Stewart, Mr. A. D. Nuttall, and Dr. Juris Lidaka. I have benefited from the Meyerstein Special Research Fund. Special thanks are due to Rotary International and to the University of Wisconsin at Madison for giving me fellowships, to the late J. C. Hilson, the late J. L. Mackie, Dr. Avril Bruten, Mr. Patrick Gardiner, and Dr. J. D. Fleeman. It is trite but true and needful to say that this monograph could not have been completed without the help of my wife, Elizabeth Shapland, to whom it is dedicated.

# ABBREVIATIONS

LDH       *Letters of David Hume*, ed. J. Y. T. Grieg, 2 vols. (Oxford, 1932)  1: 168 = vol. 1, p. 168

NLDH     *New Letters of David Hume*, ed. Raymond Klibansky and Ernest C. Mossner (Oxford, 1954)

Hist.      *The History of England, from the Invasion of Julius Caesar to the Revolution in 1688*, foreword by William B. Todd, 6 vols. (Indianapolis, 1983)  5: 155 = vol. 5, p. 155

The following will usually be cited parenthetically within the text:

THN      *A Treatise of Human Nature*, ed. L. A. Selby-Bigge, 2d rev. ed., P. H. Nidditch (Oxford, 1978)  2. 3. 3 (414) = bk. 2, pt. 3, § 3, p. 414

Abs.      *An Abstract of a Book Lately Published; Entitled, A Treatise of Human Nature, &c* (quoted from *THN* cited above)

DNR      *Dialogues concerning Natural Religion*, ed. Norman Kemp Smith, 2d ed. (Edinburgh, 1947)  iv (159) = pt. 4, p. 159

Wks.      *The Philosophical Works of David Hume*, ed. T. H. Green and T. H. Grose, 4 vols. (London, 1874–75)  3: 39 = vol. 3, p. 39

EHU      *An Enquiry concerning Human Understanding* (referred to hereinafter as the *Philosophical Essays* and quoted from *Essays Moral, Political, and Literary*, vol. 4 of the *Wks.* cited above)  vii. 2 (62) = § 7, pt. 2, p. 62

EPM      *An Enquiry concerning the Principles of Morals* (referred to hereinafter as the second *Enquiry* and cited from vol. 4 of the *Wks.*)  ix. 1 (252) = § 9, pt. 1, p. 252

| | |
|---|---|
| *LGent.* | *A Letter from a Gentleman to His Friend in Edinburgh (1745)*, fac. repr. ed. Ernest C. Mossner and John V. Price (Edinburgh, 1967) |
| *EMPLit.* | *Essays Morals, Political, and Literary*, ed. Eugene F. Miller (Indianapolis, 1985) |

Page number citations for the following will be from the *EMPLit.* cited above:

| | |
|---|---|
| "A" | "Of Avarice" |
| "BT" | "Of the Balance of Trade" |
| "Comm." | "Of Commerce" |
| "CL" | "Of Civil Liberty" |
| "DMHNat." | "Of the Dignity or Meanness of Human Nature" |
| "DTP" | "Of the Delicacy of Taste and Passion" |
| "E" | "Of Eloquence" |
| "EW" | "Of Essay Writing" |
| "FPGov." | "Of the First Principles of Government" |
| "IM" | "Of Impudence and Modesty" |
| "Int." | "Of Interest" |
| "IParl." | "Of the Independency of Parliament" |
| "IPComm." | "Idea of a Perfect Commonwealth" |
| "LM" | "Of Love and Marriage" |
| "M" | "Of Money" |
| "MSL" | "Of the Middle Station of Life" |
| "NC" | "Of National Characters" |
| "OContr." | "Of the Original Contract" |
| "PDiv." | "Of Polygamy and Divorces" |
| "PGen." | "Of Parties in General" |
| "PO" | "Of Passive Obedience" |
| "PSci." | "That Politics May Be Reduced to a Science" |
| "RPASci." | "Of the Rise and Progress of the Arts and Sciences" |
| "Sceptic" | "The Sceptic" |
| "SE" | "Of Superstition and Enthusiasm" |
| "SHist." | "Of the Study of History" |
| "SRW" | "Of Simplicity and Refinement in Writing" |
| "ST" | "Of the Standard of Taste" |

# The Suasive Art of David Hume

# Chapter I

## THE CLIMATE OF OPINION

> Certain masters of composition, as Shakespeare,
> Milton, and Pope, the writers of the Protestant Bible
> and Prayer Book, Hooker and Addison, Swift, Hume,
> and Goldsmith, have been the making of the English
> language.
> —Newman, *The Idea of a University* II. iii. 3

HUME WAS one of the most celebrated writers of his day. George Birkbeck Hill, who was qualified to judge, reckoned that his European fame was equaled only by Rousseau's and Voltaire's.[1] Thus we find Boswell, before he fell under Johnson's influence, recording in his journal that Hume was "the greatest Writer in Brittain." Upon Hume's death an anonymous biographer wrote that after the publication of the *History* Hume "was considered as the greatest writer of the age: his most insignificant performances were sought after with avidity."[2] We must make allowances for exaggeration here, and acknowledge that some of this celebrity was a *succès de scandale* due to his scepticism. And, as we shall see, his career was by no means a succession of triumphs. One suspects, however, that in Britain the scandal of his scepticism hurt Hume as much as it helped, and among the English any admissions of the literary ability of a Scot were only grudgingly

[1] George Birkbeck Hill, ed., *Letters of David Hume to William Strahan* (Oxford, 1888), 83. For Hume's reputation in France, see the doctoral theses of Laurence Bongie, "Hume en France au dix-huitième siècle" (Université de Paris, 1952); Paul H. Meyer, "Hume in Eighteenth-Century France" (Columbia University, 1954).

[2] 4 Nov. 1762, *Private Papers of James Boswell*, ed. Geoffrey Scott, 18 vols. (n.p., 1928–34), 1: 130; "An Account of the Life and Writings of the Late David Hume, Esq.," repr. *Annual Register* 19, pt. 2 (1776, 4th ed. 1788): 31.

extracted. Yet it remains that his literary stature was equal to, very possibly greater than, Samuel Johnson's during what is now often called the age of Johnson.

Because we now have a much narrower notion of what constitutes literature, this picture of Hume comes as somewhat of a surprise. But the fact that Hume wrote philosophy and history and not poems, plays, or novels did not keep Goldsmith from thinking of him as a competitor in letters. From Boswell we learn that Goldsmith

> lamented . . . that the praise due to literary merit is already occupied by the first writers, who will keep it and get the better even of the superior merit which the moderns may possess. He said David Hume was one of those, who seeing the first place occupied on the right side, rather than take a second, wants to have a first in what is wrong.

A note of envy is detectable in Goldsmith's disapproval. One gathers that from his own professional frustrations he thought he had personal insights into Hume's motives. Goldsmith's competitive feelings are slightly muted in the periodical essay of 3 November 1759, "A Resverie," in which Goldsmith imagined an allegorical coach that delivers worthy writers to the temple of fame. Previous passengers had been Addison, Swift, Pope, Steele, Congreve, and Cibber. Modestly, Goldsmith depicts himself as being refused upon applying for transport. The first to gain admittance is Johnson, the third is Smollett, and between them is none other than Hume. In application Hume first submits for judgment his *Philosophical Essays*:

> "These . . . are rhapsodies against the religion of my country." "And how can you expect to come into my coach, after thus chusing the wrong side of the question." "Ay, but I am right (replied the other;) and if you give me leave, I shall in a few minutes state the argument." "Right or wrong (said the coachman) he who disturbs religion, is a blockhead, and he shall never travel in a coach of mine." "If then (said the gentleman, mustering up all his courage) if I am not to have admittance as

an essayist, I hope I shall not be repulsed as an historian; the last volume of my history met with applause."[3]

The *History* is sufficient for the discriminating coachman. The *Philosophical Essays* is disqualified for its pernicious tendencies and not for being different in kind from the productions of the other passengers. It is evident from the company he will keep in the coach and at the temple that in the eyes of the allegorist Hume was not less of a writer for writing philosophy or history. William Shaw plainly thought of Hume as competition for Johnson:

> His peculiar excentricities and paradoxes, chiefly on moral, philosophical, and religious subjects, procured him an incredible number of votaries in both kingdoms. Nothing appeared in the literary world, about which he was not consulted; and it is well known, the critics of the times, regarded his opinion as sacred and decisive. He mentioned the Rambler, however, with respect; and only regretted there should be so much cant and so much pedantry, in a performance replete with taste, erudition, and genius.
>
> This stricture very obviously marred, though it did not absolutely prevent the success of the book. Johnson, when told of the fact, only acknowledged himself the less surprized that his papers had not been more universally read. *My countrymen,* said he, *will not always regard the voice of a Blasphemer as an oracle.*[4]

Johnson was right, of course, and Hume's reputation became a casualty of the revolution in tastes of the next century and the widening chasm between the objective sciences and the arts. The belletristic qualities that his writings exemplified

[3] See 26 June 1763, *Boswell's London Journal, 1762–1763,* ed. Frederick Pottle, Yale (Trade) Editions of the Private Papers of James Boswell, 13 vols. to date (London, 1950–), 1: 285; *The Bee,* in *Collected Works of Oliver Goldsmith,* ed. Arthur Friedman, 5 vols. (Oxford, 1966), 1: 448.

[4] *Memories of the Life and Writings of the Late Dr. Samuel Johnson . . . ,* ed. Arthur Sherbo (London, 1974), 32. For a discussion of Hume and Johnson as leaders of rival literary coteries, see Ernest Campbell Mossner, *The Forgotten Hume: Le bon David* (New York, 1943), 189–209.

went out of fashion, and philosophy took on a sense of its own dignity that did not accord with his efforts to please. His works were depreciated as being tainted with an element of popularization. Norman Kemp Smith cited, among others, John Stuart Mill and T. H. Huxley as the most notable among this class of Hume's critics.[5] To them must be added Leslie Stephen, who, though perhaps more appreciative of Hume than anyone else at that time, conceded that "Hume, indeed, may be accused of some divergence from the straight path under the influence of literary vanity."[6] Stephen here refers to the fact that Hume disowned his greatest achievement, the *Treatise*, recast its materials into a number of shorter works, and did so for literary rather than philosophical reasons. Hume's divergence was to indulge in popularization instead of forging ahead with the quest for philosophical truth heedless of public neglect, incomprehension, or disapprobation. In philosophy as in literature, the Victorians demanded a high seriousness that Hume did not exhibit.

Since then Kemp Smith, Ernest Campbell Mossner, Antony Flew, James Noxon, and others have come to the defense of Hume's thought, with such success that he is now not infrequently referred to as the greatest philosopher that Britain has produced.[7] There now exists a society of international membership and a semiannually published journal dedicated to furthering our knowledge of Hume's philosophy. But literary scholars, though they have made great progress in helping us to see eighteenth-century literature with clearer, un-Romantic eyes, have not yet given Hume attention nearly com-

[5] John Stuart Mill, rev. of *A History of the British Empire*, by George Brodie, art. 5, *Westminster Review* 2 (1824): 346; T. H. Huxley, *Hume* (London, 1887), 11; both quoted in Kemp Smith's *Philosophy of David Hume* (London, 1941), 514–20.

[6] *History of English Thought in the Eighteenth Century*, 3d ed., 2 vols. (London, 1902), 1: 43.

[7] See Kemp Smith cited above; Ernest Campbell Mossner, "Philosophy and Biography: The Case of David Hume," *Philosophical Review* 59 (1950): 184–201; Antony Flew, *Hume's Philosophy of Belief: A Study of His First "Inquiry"* (London, 1961), *passim*; and James Noxon, *Hume's Philosophical Development: A Study of His Methods* (Oxford, 1973), *passim*.

mensurate with the figure he cut in his day or with the range and depth of his writings. Only two book-length literary studies of Hume have been published.[8] Today we place a higher value on his thought than even his contemporaries did, but they had a better appreciation of him as a man of letters.

To remedy this defect in our appreciation requires some historical reconstruction and sufficient flexibility of mind to see things through eighteenth-century eyes. As much as possible we shall try to see them through Hume's eyes, mindful of the temptation to reduce Hume's individuality so as to fit him to some preconceived eighteenth-century worldview. Unfortunately his statements on the writing of philosophy are few. He did not often record his authorial intentions, and never did so with much specificity. Possibly he did not formulate them in the detail that students of literature are accustomed to discover in the works they examine. And even when he makes pertinent statements it is often risky to take them at face value. As in the interpretation of his philosophy, it is necessary to reconcile apparent contradictions by referring individual statements to the wider contexts of his writings as a whole and of the culture in which he lived. It is necessary to recreate the milieu in which he executed his works, and to adopt a Humean spirit, in order to uncover his unstated, perhaps only vaguely formulated, aesthetic values and aims.

We will confine our study to the period in his career from

---

[8] J. V. Price, *The Ironic Hume* (Austin, 1965); Jerome Christensen, *Practicing Enlightenment: Hume and the Formation of a Literary Career* (Madison, 1987). Price has also written *David Hume* (New York, 1968) for the Twayne's English Authors Series, and a number of articles on works by Hume not covered here. At first glance Christensen's book and the present one might seem to cover some of the same ground, but our approaches are so different that there is no overlap in content whatsoever. Whereas Christensen is, as he says, deeply "suspicious" of Hume and the Enlightenment, I am sympathetic; and whereas he views Hume from a modern theoretical perspective drawn from Gramsci, Foucault, and Greenblatt, I attempt to understand Hume as he understood himself. Portions of Leo Braudy's *Narrative Form in History and Fiction: Hume, Fielding, and Gibbon* (Princeton, 1970) and John Richetti's *Philosophical Writing: Locke, Berkeley, Hume* (Cambridge, Mass., 1983) are devoted to Hume.

the composition of the *Treatise* through its recasting into the two *Enquiries*. It might seem odd to exclude thereby discussion of the *History*, the work for which Hume was best known in his lifetime; but within our chosen period there is a developmental story of a scope that recommends itself to the telling, with a beginning, a middle, and an end. That story can be summarized briefly as follows. The *Treatise* was the fruit of many years of Hume's hardest and best thinking, involving labor and stress that at one point endangered his health. Its failure with the critics and the public was a shock to which the young author reacted with maturity by turning from epistemological and moral philosophy to more popular subjects, to the more popular essay genre, and to a more concentrated effort to improve his literary talent. At this stage he emulated to different extents the periodical papers the *Spectator* and the *Craftsman* as models of elegant and popular writing. The success that he had with the essay genre encouraged him to return to his epistemological and moral philosophies. Having attempted to fashion them anew into more appealing forms, he felt that he had achieved his purpose with the *Philosophical Essays*, and more so with the *Enquiry concerning the Principles of Morals*.

Herein we may observe a noble attempt, a setback, a gathering of forces, and a victorious return to the arena of the initial defeat. Because Hume saw himself as having solved certain identifiable literary problems in the second *Enquiry*, our story ends with that book. Before we can tell this story intelligibly, however, we must pause to set the scene. There are a number of things that must be understood at the start concerning contemporary attitudes toward philosophy, religion, and literature. For this reason the climate of opinion will be the subject of sections 1–3.[9]

---

[9] It is reassuring to find that what I say in this chapter and elsewhere is in agreement with the picture that Price draws in "The Reading of Philosophical Literature," *Books and Their Readers in Eighteenth-Century England*, ed. Isabel Rivers (Leicester, 1982), 165–96.

## Antimetaphysical Sentiment

Can knowledge have no bound, but must advance
So far, to make us wish for ignorance?
—Denham, *Cooper's Hill* (1660 version), 145–46

The explosive growth of information of which we are the recipients and that necessitates our specialization into separate disciplines was not so advanced in Hume's time that it had yet quite killed off the ideal of the Renaissance man. In claiming for his province practically all knowledge and polite letters too, Hume was not behaving hubristically in the eyes of his contemporaries. Nor did they think him naive. Though they were not insensible of the differences between philosophy, history, and belles-lettres, the importance of maintaining diverse criteria for evaluation in these fields was not so evident to them. The ways in which the fields were complementary seemed more important. History weighed and recounted facts; philosophy ascertained of what factual knowledge consists; historical interpretation was applied philosophy; philosophy and history supplied matter for literature and invigorated it; literature disseminated both. The prevailing cultural values, extending often to firm prejudice, were against specialization and the compartmentalization of learning. They were toward an ideal of the evenly developed, well-balanced, erudite but polished performer in society. There was outside of the universities a positive aversion to even the appearance of pedantry, an aversion that is evident throughout the literature and criticism of the day, evident, for example, in Hume's criticism of the *Rambler* quoted above. Society was demanding that learning endeavor to be polite.[10]

The desire for social advancement is not supposed to be a

[10] As a historian of the idea of politeness has observed, " 'Pedantry' had many meanings, but few friends" (Lawrence E. Klein, "The Third Earl of Shaftesbury and the Progress of Politeness," *Eighteenth-Century Studies* 18 [1986]: 203 n. 43). See also Klein's "Berkeley, Shaftesbury, and the Meaning of Politeness," *Studies in Eighteenth-Century Culture* 16 (1986): 57–68.

determining factor in the activities of philosophers, and by itself it would have been an inadequate incentive for philosophers of real merit to attend to the tastes of society. But for the new breed of philosophers of the seventeenth and eighteenth centuries there was a more compelling reason to learn to write like gentlemen for gentlemen, and this was simply the need to find a more responsive audience than that provided by the scholars of the universities. The stimulating influence of mathematics and experimental science on their thinking had led the more adventurous into tracks where the universities were slow to follow. The natural audience for philosophy, those in the universities and the churches who had studied its questions, was insufficiently responsive to suit the ambitions of the rationalist and empiricist thinkers for the advancement of knowledge. It appeared worth the trial to bypass an unappreciative audience and lay this new philosophy directly before the literate public. From the Restoration age through the eighteenth century the identity of this literate public, like the identity of the "gentleman," came to exchange somewhat its aristocratic for a bourgeois character; but this difference is less important for understanding Hume than that between the literate gentleman, upper or middle class, and the "schoolman."

The universities, then, were more of an obstacle to be surmounted than a theater in which to perform. A more promising theater for the rationalists and empiricists seemed to be that of the world of men of affairs, where, precisely because it was untrained, the audience might be expected to be more receptive. What was lost in the sophistication of the audience stood to be recovered in impartiality and freshness of eye. Of course this lack of sophistication presented certain literary problems to the philosophers. Most philosophers today would look upon the requirement to address their thoughts to the uninformed and untrained as an impracticable compromise. But as it happened, certain philosophers of the Enlightenment not only made do in the face of these problems; they actually produced works that transformed Western civilization and are still centuries later the focus of important discussion.

It has been noted that Descartes wrote the *Discours de la methode* (1637) in French rather than in Latin, just as Galileo when he wrote in Italian, intending "to aim over the heads of the academic community and to reach educated men of *bon sens*, among whom he hoped to get a favorable hearing," and that consequently he developed a prose style that "has always been regarded as a model for the expression of abstract thought in that language."[11] Locke composed his works likewise under the difficulty of having to reach educated men with no expertise in his subject, for he had a low opinion of the impartiality of pedagogues and expected only carping from them.[12] Though not now often lauded as a highly readable book, his *Essay concerning Human Understanding* (London, 1690) enjoyed a popular success unprecedented for a work of epistemology. With this example before them it would not seem impossible to Berkeley and Hume that their philosophical writings could reach a wide audience and attain for them considerable fame. Thus the revolution in thought that has been characterized as the Enlightenment was attended with a change in literary manner to suit a new taste. It is a commonplace of literary history that during this period English prose changed in the direction of the gentlemanly virtues of simplicity and clarity. Remarkably, philosophy was able to partake in this change toward simplicity at a time when it was in ferment. This stylistic change not only did not hamper the new philosophy, but actually seems to have complemented it. The success with which these philosophers dealt with their literary problems is of a high order of cultural significance, and, with Berkeley, Hume stands at the summit of this achievement.

This stylistic change is the literary aspect of the Enlightenment repudiation of scholasticism. Disdain for the "school-

---

[11] Bernard Williams, "Descartes, René," *Encyclopedia of Philosophy*, ed. Paul Edwards et al., 8 vols. (New York, 1967), 2: 344–45.

[12] See, e.g., *An Essay concerning Human Understanding* 4. 20, § 11. For Locke's intentions and projected audience, see Neal Wood, *The Politics of Locke's Philosophy: A Social Study of "An Essay concerning Human Understanding"* (Berkeley, 1983), 41–64.

man" is a theme common to the writings of Bacon, Hobbes, Locke, Berkeley, and Hume. Under the rubric of "the schools" the empiricists tended to lump together that large and various body of medieval and Renaissance theological philosophy with the disputation taught then at Oxford and Cambridge. Locke called this disputation "Hogshearing."[13] To distinguish between Scotism and Thomism, or between them both and what went on in the modern universities, did not serve the new philosophers' polemical purposes. Hume, having no personal quarrel with Oxford or Cambridge, and being an alumnus of a university not given over to scholastic disputation, usually alluded only to the neo-Aristotelians and Neoplatonists of the Middle Ages and Renaissance when he disparaged the "dreaming and captious philosophy of the schools."[14] For their own reasons the empiricists took up the Renaissance humanists' criticisms of the schools, prominent among which was the charge of barbarous writing. Cowley thus described the corruption of Aristotelianism into scholasticism:

> And in the *School-mens* hands it perisht quite at last.
>     Then nought but *Words* it grew,
>     And those all *Barb'arous* too.
>   It *perisht*, and it *vanisht* there,
>   The *Life* and *Soul* breath'd out, became but empty *Air*.[15]

The preoccupation of philosophers with disputes over meaningless words is to be deplored by anyone who cares about the state of the language: it is a misfortune for culture in general. "Every science, as well as polite literature, must be con-

---

[13] Peter Laslett's introduction to his edition of *Two Treatises of Government* . . . , by John Locke, 2d ed. (London, 1967), 23. Cf. Locke, *Essay* 3. 10, § 2; 20 Jan. 1693, *Correspondence of John Locke*, ed. E. S. DeBeer, 8 vols. to date (Oxford, 1976–), 4: 627.

[14] *Hist.* 3: 229 (A.D. 1536). For the comparative freedom of Edinburgh University from "scholastic jargon," see Goldsmith, *An Enquiry into the Present State of Polite Learning*, in *Collected Works* 1: 333.

[15] "To Mr. Hobs," st. 2, *Poems*, ed. A. R. Waller (London, 1905), 188. For Hume's assessment of Cowley's writings, see *Hist.* 6: 152.

sidered as being yet in its infancy," wrote Hume of the Jacobean age. "Scholastic learning and polemical divinity retarded the growth of all true knowledge."[16] What progress Europe had made was possible only to the extent that scholastic philosophy had lost its influence over society. The unintelligibility complained of was treated in society as a failure of taste as well as of clear reasoning. For the new philosophers to censure the schoolman was, as well as a genuine expression of protest, an implicit appeal to the gentleman's distaste for the pedantic. This gentlemanly distaste was reflected in and probably given some vogue by the second Earl of Rochester's famous "Satyr against Reason and Mankind" (London, 1679), in which the poet pillories philosophical pride:

> This busy, puzzling stirrer-up of doubt
> That frames deep mysteries, then finds 'em out,
> Filling with frantic crowds of thinking fools
> Those reverend bedlams, colleges and schools;
> Borne on whose wings, each heavy sot can pierce
> The limits of the boundless universe. . . .
>
> (lines 80–85)[17]

It may seem foolish of philosophers to seek an audience in people with such an attitude, but in important ways the empiricists concurred with the views Rochester expressed. They held that proud reason unchecked by reference to experience was abusive and often ridiculous. Hence the empiricists looked upon rationalists, deluded into a false sense of certainty by a priori reasoning, as little better than the schoolmen; and they had some success in bringing the public to share this opinion. As scholastic legerdemain had been satirized in the character of Hudibras, so now was a prominent strain of rationalism in the characters of Mr. Square and Pangloss. The empiricist stress on experience as against ratioci-

---

[16] *Hist.* 5: 155 (app. to the Reign of James I).

[17] *Complete Poems of John Wilmot, Earl of Rochester*, ed. David M. Vieth (New Haven, 1968), 97. For Hume's assessment of Rochester's poems, see *Hist.* 6: 543–44.

nation was appealingly analogous to the gentlemanly stress on worldly experience as against book-learning. Both were seen as means of keeping one's feet firmly on the ground.

By the eighteenth century the preeminent figure of empiricism was Locke, whose influence reached deep into popular culture.[18] Of course Locke repeatedly and in no uncertain terms disavowed the mixing of literature and philosophy,[19] but there is no question that to many he represented an example of the grooming of philosophy for society. Locke's famous declaration of purpose was that he had employed himself

> as an Under-Labourer in clearing Ground a little, and removing some of the Rubbish, that lies in the way to Knowledge; which certainly had been very much more advanced in the World, if the Endeavours of ingenious and industrious Men had not been much cumbred with the learned but frivolous use of uncouth, affected, or unintelligible Terms, introduced into the Sciences, and there made an Art of, to that Degree, that Philosophy, which is nothing but the true Knowledge of Things, was thought unfit, or uncapable to be brought into well-bred Company, and polite Conversation.[20]

This hint was taken up by Locke's sometime educational charge, the third Earl of Shaftesbury, who, characteristically emphasizing taste, maintained that "[t]o philosophise, in a just signification, is but to carry good-breeding a step higher." Philosophy, he lamented,

> is no longer active in the world, nor can hardly, with any advantage, be brought upon the public stage. We have immured her, poor lady, in colleges and cells, and have set her servilely to such works as those in the mines. Empirics and pedantic soph-

[18] See Kenneth MacLean, *John Locke and English Literature of the Eighteenth Century* (New Haven, 1936).

[19] See *Essay* 3. 10, § 34; the letter of 5 Apr. 1696; and the draft of a letter dated 1698/99, *Correspondence* 5: 596, 6: 539.

[20] *Essay*, ed. P. H. Nidditch, Clarendon Edition of the Works of John Locke (corr. repr. Oxford, 1979), 10.

ists are her chief pupils. The school-syllogism and the elixir are the choicest of her products. . . .

It may be properly alleged perhaps, as a reason for this general shyness in moral inquiries, that the people to whom it has principally belonged to handle these subjects have done it in such a manner as to put the better sort out of countenance with the undertaking. The appropriating this concern to mere scholastics has brought their fashion and air into the very subject. . . . We can give no quarter to anything like it in good company. The least mention of such matters gives us a disgust, and puts us out of humour. If learning comes across us, we count it pedantry; if morality, 'tis preaching.

Philosophy is discredited by association with tasteless pedants, and the leaders of society injudiciously turn from it. Shaftesbury feared that writing on substantial subjects would be left to languish with the schoolmen:

If the formalists of this sort were erected into patentees with a sole commission of authorship, we should undoubtedly see such writing in our days as would either wholly wean us from all books in general, or at least from all such as were the product of our own nation under such a subordinate and conforming government.[21]

Good relations between philosophy and literature, then, are a matter of some importance. Philosophy without tasteful presentation is vitiated for society, and society without philosophy is undiscerning and directionless. To restore a balance was imperative. Hume would say, further, that familiarity with social life is essential to reasoning accurately about human nature: "We must . . . glean up our experiments . . . from a cautious observation of human life, and take them as they appear in the common course of the world, by men's behaviour in company, in affairs, and in their pleasures" (THN, xix). In "Of Essay Writing" Hume welcomes the progress that

---

[21] *Characteristics of Men, Manners, Opinions, Times, etc.*, ed. John M. Robertson, 2 vols. (London, 1900), 2: 255, 4–5; 1: 216. "Empirics" here does not mean empiricists, but quacks.

had been made in striking such a balance since Shaftesbury's day. Bad relations between society and the intelligentsia rendered society insipid, and

> Learning has been as great a Loser by being shut up in Colleges and Cells, and secluded from the World and good Company. By that Means, every Thing of what we call *Belles Lettres* became totally barbarous, being cultivated by Men without any Taste of Life or Manners, and without that Liberty and Facility of Thought and Expression, which can only be acquir'd by Conversation. Even Philosophy went to Wrack by this moaping recluse Method of Study, and became as chimerical in her Conclusions as she was unintelligible in her Stile and Manner of Delivery. And indeed, what cou'd be expected from Men who never consulted Experience in any of their Reasonings, or who never search'd for that Experience, where alone it is to be found, in common Life and Conversation? (*EMPLit.*, 534–35)[22]

We might guess that Hume has in mind the Cambridge Platonists and the *Port-Royalistes*.[23] But though people like Locke, Shaftesbury, and Hutcheson had restored the good name of philosophy to an extent, the climate of opinion was still not propitious to it, as we shall see. To the cultivation and maintenance of good relations Hume wanted to contribute. Thus when he proclaimed to Montesquieu, "*J'ai consacré ma vie à la philosophie et aux belles-lettres,*" he was not confess-

---

[22] Cf. Frances Hutcheson, *Inquiry into the Original of Our Ideas of Beauty and Virtue*, 3d corr. ed. (London, 1729), xv–xvi: "*I doubt we have made* Philosophy, *as well as* Religion, *by our foolish management of it, so austere and ungainly a Form, that a Gentleman cannot easily bring himself to like it; and those who are strangers to it, can scarcely bear to hear our Description of it. So much it is changed from what was once the delight of the finest Gentlemen among the* Ancients *and their Recreation after the Hurry of publick Affairs!*"

[23] I say this notwithstanding the extent to which the Cambridge Platonists influenced Shaftesbury and thereby, possibly, Hume (see Ernst Cassirer, *The Platonic Renaissance in England*, trans. James P. Pettegrove [Austin, 1953], 157–202), and the extent to which unacknowledged Cartesian notions underlay Hume's thinking (see John P. Wright, *The Sceptical Realism of Hume* [Minneapolis, 1983]).

ing to having separate and unrelated ambitions;[24] philosophy and belles-lettres he regarded as complementary and even interdependent. Grooming philosophy for acceptance in society meant much more than writing it well. It involved adjusting the topics to the concerns of a sensible man of the world. Philosophy had to be made to turn from topics merely curious. Philosophers must not be pedants, but rather wise men helping people to live constructive, moral lives. Mr. Spectator's well-known statement of purpose was

> It was said of *Socrates*, that he brought Philosophy down from Heaven, to inhabit among men; and I shall be ambitious to have it said of me, that I have brought Philosophy out of Closets and Libraries, Schools and Colleges, to dwell in Clubs and Assemblies, at Tea-Tables, and in Coffee-Houses.[25]

The idea here is not to trivialize philosophy, but to raise the moral sophistication with which people conduct their daily lives. Philosophy that shows people how to get along better is much more valuable than that which squares the circle. What it meant for Socrates to bring philosophy down to earth is made clearer in the source of Addison's sentiment. Cicero

[24] 10 Apr. 1749, *LDH* 1: 138.

[25] Addison, no. 10, *Spectator*, ed. Donald Bond, 5 vols. (Oxford, 1965), 1: 44. Cf. Gay's statement that Mr. Tatler "has indeed rescued [learning] out of the hands of Pedants and Fools, and discover'd the true method of making it amiable and lovely to all mankind: In the dress he gives it, 'tis a most welcome guest at Tea-tables and Assemblies, and is relish'd and caressed by the Merchants on the Change" ("Present State of Wit," *John Gay: Poetry and Prose*, ed. Vinton A. Dearing and Charles E. Beckwith, 2 vols. [Oxford, 1974], 2: 452). Cf. also John Ramsay: "Being written in a charming style, equally remote from pedantry and flimsiness, [the *Tatler, Spectator*, and *Guardian* papers] were read with great avidity by the fair and the gay, who were amazed and delighted to see philosophy brought down to the level of common-sense, the cobwebs of metaphysics being carefully kept out of sight" (*Scotland and Scotsmen in the Eighteenth Century*, ed. Alexander Allardyce, 2 vols. [Edinburgh, 1888], 1: 6); and "Socrates brought philosophy down from heaven to earth; I have brought it even into games, informal conversations, and drinking parties" (*Colloquies of Erasmus*, trans. Craig R. Thompson [Chicago, 1965], 630).

wrote, "Socrates . . . was the first to call philosophy down from the heavens and set her in the cities of men and bring her also into their homes and compel her to ask questions about life and morality and things good and evil."[26] Socrates made philosophy responsible. "Hence it was," wrote one contributor to the *Spectator*,

> that the Oracle pronounced *Socrates* the wisest of all Men living, because he judiciously made Choice of humane Nature for the Object of his Thoughts; an Enquiry into which as much exceeds all other Learning, as it is of more Consequence to adjust the true Nature and Measures of Right and Wrong, than to settle the Distance of the Planets, and compute the Times of their Circumvolutions.[27]

In the seventeenth and eighteenth centuries, this Ciceronian portrayal of Socrates was taken to mean that there are limits (1) to what philosophy *should* examine, and (2) to what it *can* examine successfully. According to Thomas Stanley, both the "inconveniences and imperfections" of philosophy led Socrates to conclude

> First, That it was improper to leave those affairs which concern Mankind, to enquire into things without us. Secondly, That these things are above the reach of Man, whence are occasioned all disputes and oppositions, some acknowledging no God, others worshipping Stocks and Stones; some asserting one simple Being, others infinite. . . . And thirdly, that these things, if attained, could not be practised, for he who contemplating divine Mysteries, enquires by what necessity things were made, cannot make himself any thing. . . . Thus esteeming speculative knowledge as far only as it conduceth to practice, he cut off in all Sciences what he conceived of least use. . . .[28]

---

[26] *Tusculan Disputations*, trans. J. E. King, rev. ed. (London, 1945), 435 (5. 4. 10–11). D. F. Bond identifies this as Addison's source.

[27] [?Pope,] no. 408, *Spectator* 3: 523.

[28] "Socrates," *History of Philosophy: Containing the Lives, Opinions, Actions, and Discourses of the Philosophers of Every Sect*, 3d ed. (London, 1701), 77.

If philosophy becomes engrossed in problems of no consequence or that it cannot solve, it is a fit object of contempt
among men of sense. But it can also be pernicious. European
history showed that disputes over mysteries were not always
contemptible: sometimes, particularly when they involved religion, they shook nations. In the context of modern European
history, then, the program to limit philosophy to constructive
inquiries took on great significance.

At the lowest levels of understanding, rejection of "school
philosophy" was simply the rejection of the pedantic, a matter
of good taste. At the higher levels it was a coherent and sophisticated view of the purposes and limitations of philosophy. With these attitudes Hume had to contend. But empiricism, especially sceptical empiricism, could assimilate these
attitudes rather than oppose them. Hume's philosophy of human limitations reflects his own complete agreement with antimetaphysical sentiment at both the levels of taste and of conviction. It is against this background that we may understand
the nuances of Hume's often quoted clarion call for the new
philosophy:

> If we take in our hand any volume; of divinity or school meta-
> physics, for instance; let us ask, *Does it contain any abstract
> reasoning concerning quantity or number?* No. *Does it contain
> any experimental reasoning concerning matter of fact and exis-
> tence?* No. Commit it then to the flames: For it can contain
> nothing but sophistry and illusion.          (*EHU* xii. 3 [135])

Hume is here proposing to remove the rubbish that lies in the
way to knowledge by delimiting knowledge, exposing all philosophies that purport to offer knowledge humanly impossible
to possess. But as Antony Flew has pointed out, this statement is not so iconoclastic as it sounds to the modern reader.[29]
Hume is appealing to his contemporaries' prejudice against
the schoolman, giving a philosophical justification to act on
their inclination and condemn the old philosophy as worse
than worthless. He is playing his own variation on the familiar

---

[29] Flew, *Hume's Philosophy of Belief*, 272.

humanist theme that man should be "lowly wise," as Raphael advised Adam, and content himself with the knowledge suited to his capacities and station.[30]

## Scriblerian Humanism

Faith, Gospel, all, seem'd made to be *disput'd,*
And none had *Sense enough to be Confuted.*
—*Essay on Criticism,* 442–43

In literary taste Hume was not a rebel. His manner was an affirmation of the literary movement described above, which was in full vogue in his formative years. To Hume the great names of this movement were Addison, Congreve, Prior, Pope, Swift, and Bolingbroke.[31] Congreve and Prior seem to have been of negligible influence. Bolingbroke seems to be on this list largely for his contributions to the *Craftsman* and for his association with Pope and Swift. Upon the publication of his collected works under David Mallet's editorship, he took a precipitous drop in Hume's esteem.[32] But Addison, Pope, and Swift had a deep and lasting influence on Hume's tastes. In the sphere of philosophical writing the great predecessors were Locke, Shaftesbury, Mandeville, Hutcheson, Butler, and Berkeley.[33] Their names, combined with those of the great triumvirate of wit, represented the standards of composition and thought for Hume and his compeers in the Scottish Enlightenment. It was their successes that he would set himself to match or surpass. The influence on Hume of Addison, Pope, and Swift has received fairly little notice,

[30] In "The Tendency of Hume's Skepticism," *The Skeptical Tradition,* ed. Myles Burnyeat (Berkeley, 1983), 409–10, Robert J. Fogelin briefly touches upon the humanist strain in Hume's scepticism.

[31] I take this list from Hume's statements in *The Scots Magazine* 4 (1742): 119; repr. in Robert C. Elliot, "Hume's 'Character of Sir Robert Walpole': Some Unnoticed Additions," *Journal of English and Germanic Philology* 48 (1949): 369.

[32] See 24 Sept. 1752 and 24 Oct. 1754, *LDH* 1: 168, 208.

[33] The primary source of this list is *THN,* xvii, n. 1. For Berkeley's inclusion, see 1. 2. 7 (17 n. 1).

but within its channel that influence was deep. I will maintain that this influence, particularly of the two Scriblerians, was related to the contemporary antagonism to the old philosophy. Addison's influence (full discussion of which must wait for chapter 3) was most notable in providing models for the writing of popular essays. Pope's and Swift's influences, being more general and deeply assimilated, are less apparent. An indication of Hume's admiration for Pope is his statement that "*England* must pass thro' a long Gradation of its *Spencers, Johnsons, Wallers, Drydens*, before it arrive at an *Addison* or a *Pope*." Addison and Pope represented for Hume the culminations of English prose and poetry. Three paragraphs below this statement we find that, to Hume's mind, the greatest English poets are Milton and Pope ("MSL," 549–50).[34] Pope was still alive when these remarks appeared in print (*Essays, Moral and Political*, vol. 2 [Edinburgh, 1742]), and it is true that Hume was a little given to flattery. G. B. Hill thought that he "was a thorough Frenchman in his love of paying pretty compliments."[35] But the indications are that these critical judgments do not exaggerate Hume's esteem for the poet. We know that he sent Pope a complimentary copy of the *Treatise*, in which he had entered the errata corrections by hand.[36] In print and in letters Hume occasionally quoted from Pope, and to the refutation of the idea of one couplet he devoted the entire essay "That Politics May Be Reduced to a Science." More significantly, Popean phrases appear in Hume's writings, so naturally at times that it is difficult to tell whether an instance is an allusion or an unconscious echo. This is not uncommon among the literati of that time: Johnson

[34] Cf. "E," 99: "A hundred cabinet-makers in LONDON can work a table or a chair equally well; but no one poet can write verses with such spirit and elegance as Mr. POPE." The "Johnson" mentioned is, of course, Ben Jonson.

[35] *Letters to Strahan*, 260 n. 16.

[36] See Maynard Mack, "Pope's Books: A Biographical Survey with a Finding List," *English Literature in the Age of Disguise*, ed. Maximilian E. Novak (Berkeley, 1977), 209–305; David Yalden-Thomson, "More Hume Autograph Marginalia in a First Edition of the *Treatise*," *Hume Studies* 4 (1978): 73–76.

and Boswell could quote Pope as the occasion arose, and there is no reason for surprise that Hume was an equally proficient votary. When, for instance, Hume confessed that the "Love of literary fame" was his "ruling Passion," he assumed that his readers would recognize the allusion to Pope's concept of the Ruling Passion as set out in the *Moral Essays* (i. 174–265). When he wrote that the *Treatise* "fell *dead-born from the Press*," he alluded to dialogue 2, line 226 of the "Epilogue to the Satires."[37] Hume was able to recite from memory to Thomas Blacklock the "Elegy to the Memory of an Unfortunate Lady";[38] it appears that this was only one of many verses that he had memorized.

Swift also loomed large in Hume's literary consciousness, though Hume's esteem for him was not unqualified. Allusions to Swift's writings can be found in Hume's letters and in his recorded conversations. On the few occasions when he attempted political satire, such as his pamphlet *The Bellman's Petition* (Edinburgh, 1751), Hume adopted a recognizably Swiftian manner. (We shall examine in chapter 4 Hume's Swiftian use of a persona when dealing with religion.) It appears, however, that only grudgingly did he give Swift a high station on Parnassus. He disliked the personality evinced in Swift's writings, finding him an "author, who has more humour than knowledge, more taste than judgment, and more spleen, prejudice, and passion than any of these qualities" ("BT," 633). Johnson might have inserted the same judgment into his "Life of Swift" without discontinuity with his own statements. Both men were the more willing to be severe with a writer whose works they knew would remain standards of composition no matter what critics said. Swift's place in literary history was secure. In "Of Civil Liberty" Hume wrote,

---

[37] "My Own Life," *LDH* 1: 7 (cf. p. 1), 2. G. B. Hill identified these allusions in *Letters to Strahan*, xviii, n. 2; xx, n. 2. See also Oct. 1754; Nov. or Dec. 1768, *LDH* 1: 210, 2: 194.

[38] See 15 Oct. 1754, *LDH* 1: 200. More allusions are identified in J. C. Maxwell, "Hume: A Reference to Pope," *Notes and Queries* 204 (1959): 404; John W. Yolton, "Hume's Ideas," *Hume Studies* 6 (1980): 1; Mossner, "Pope, Alexander," *Encyclopedia of Philosophy* 5: 398.

The elegance and propriety of style have been very much neglected among us. . . . The first polite prose we have, was writ by a man who is still alive [i.e., Swift]. As to SPRAT, LOCKE and, even TEMPLE, they knew too little of the rules of art to be esteemed elegant writers. The prose of BACON, HARRINGTON, and MILTON, is altogether stiff and pedantic; though their sense be excellent. (*EMPLit.*, 91–92)

Hume agreed with the common opinion, reiterated by James Beattie, that "[o]ur tongue was brought to perfection in the days of Addison and Swift."[39] Whatever their other merits might be, the writers of the Restoration era or earlier were for Hume inappropriate as models of elegance and correctness. He was like Goldsmith and Joseph Warton in holding that politeness in English writing had only appeared with the great figures of the immediately preceding generation.[40] If Swift had failings, then, they were to be seen in proportion to the overall contribution that everybody credited to him, that of initiating an age of refinement in prose.

Irregularity, stiffness, and pedantry were not the only flaws of the seventeenth-century writers. Refinement also involves moral and intellectual balance. Hume wrote:

The reign of Charles II. which some preposterously represent as our Augustan age, retarded the progress of polite literature in this island, and it was then found that the immeasurable licentiousness, indulged or rather applauded at court, was more destructive to the refined arts, than even the cant, nonsense, and enthusiasm of the preceding period.[41]

[39] [Beattie,] *Scoticisms, Arranged in Alphabetical Order, Designed To Correct Improprieties of Speech and Writing* (Edinburgh, 1787), 5.

[40] "An Account of the Augustan Age in England," *The Bee*, in *Collected Works of Oliver Goldsmith* 1: 498–505. On p. 498 n. 4 the editor cites Warton's *Essay on the Writings and Genius of Pope*, 2 vols. (London, 1756, 1782), 1: 160–61.

[41] *Hist.* 6: 543 (A.D. 1689). Cf. Swift, "Thoughts on Various Subjects," *A Proposal for Correcting the English Tongue, Polite Conversation, Etc.*, ed. Herbert Davis and Louis Landa, *Prose Works of Jonathan Swift*, gen. ed. Herbert Davis, 13 vols. (Oxford, 1939-59), 4: 249: "the End of King *Charles*

Hume held enthusiasm in particular abhorrence, and thought that religious fervor during the Civil War had been culturally disastrous in creating a climate in which ostentatious piety became obligatory. He also subscribed to the commonplace notion that in reaction to this ostentation Charles II's court set a standard at the opposite extreme of license. According to this commonplace it was Addison's distinction to strike a balance and show that morality was consistent, and even had an affinity, with elegance. Here, once again, Hume and Johnson concurred in critical judgments; and this is not a coincidence. Both, in critical principle, gave considerable weight to general opinion. The judgment of individuals, however expert, was to be regarded as limited and partial, and always to be checked in due humility against the judgment of the many.[42]

Hume, then, was quite conventional in his critical opinions and in accepting Addison's, Pope's, and Swift's writings as standards of good taste. This standard was not merely stylistic, but extended to a general aesthetic and cultural outlook. It is the nature of satire to deal with espoused norms and deviations from them: such deviations are the object of attack and by contrast illustrate the norms advocated. The dominance of satire in the literature of this period suggests, then, that the society of that time was highly concerned with norms of behavior and thought. As the foremost satirists of the time, Pope and Swift had great influence on the normative attitudes of the time in which Hume matured as a writer. Of course they did not create norms and impose them; they espoused and gave sharper formulation to existing norms, gave them a new turn and increased strength. Particularly significant to Hume was the role of Pope and Swift in the great current debate over the proper limits and ends of human knowledge. On the level of philosophy, where it is usually studied in connection with Hume, this debate took the form of the controversy over deism and its claims for human reason. But the literary and

the Second's Reign; which is reckoned, although very absurdly, our *Augustan Age*."

[42] See Jean Hagstrum, *Samuel Johnson's Literary Criticism* (1952; repr. Chicago, 1967), 27–31.

cultural level of this debate was also important to Hume, and in the form of Scriblerian writings had a discernible influence on his work. Scriblerian writings more than any others would have provided him with useful touchstones for popular sentiment. It was to the standards here provided that Hume would look in projecting what would please and what would not. And Pope and Swift had a good deal to say about whether, or in what ways, philosophy would please or displease.

The literary manifestation is familiar to students of literature in the Scriblerian works concerning the "Quarrel between the Ancients and the Moderns." In Pope's writings this is sometimes referred to as the war of the Wits and Dunces, the Wits being those adhering to the Scriblerian view of things. At its shallowest this quarrel was simply over whether classical or modern writers and thinkers were superior. More significantly, the quarrel was over the ends of education and what the thinking, inditing man should be like. As such the quarrel had its place in the continuum of this debate stretching back to that between Renaissance humanism and scholasticism. It is not possible here to present a balanced account of the different sides of this debate; nor is it desirable to try here to set out fully all the various kinds of duncery that Pope and Swift satirized. We will confine ourselves to those aspects of the Scriblerian view that would most directly concern Hume as a sceptical empiricist. Therefore, admittedly, as a treatment of Scriblerian satire what follows will be a bit imbalanced. But our present concern is strictly with what would have been salient to Hume as an inditing philosopher.

As the Scriblerians portrayed them, the Moderns closely resembled the schoolmen in being intellectually sterile, or duncical. A continuum between Modern and scholastic dullness is overtly implied in the epithet "dunce," with its derivation from Duns Scotus's name, which the humanists and Protestant Reformers had made into a synonym for "caviling sophist."[43] The aspect of humanist tradition that Pope and

---

[43] See Aubrey Williams, Pope's "Dunciad": A Study of Its Meaning (London, 1955), 104–30. I am particularly indebted to this chapter for my under-

Swift stressed was the application of knowledge to man's state on earth. Schoolmen and their modern counterparts were to be deplored for misdirecting intellectual curiosity into frivolous or improper topics. If such inquiries yielded knowledge at all, it was irrelevant to life and therefore an encumbrance. Or worse, these inquiries were such as in their nature could yield no knowledge to men, as in the probing of Christian mysteries. This latter folly was not to be considered merely as benign trifling; it could be downright harmful. Inquiries that necessarily could attain no definitive results foster an indefinite multitude of theoretical systems, each equally chimerical and each engendering its own apologists. Disputation naturally foments partisan contention; and as the ensuing controversies cannot be argued upon clear evidence toward a resolution, they can only take place in terms of carping and wrangling. Education along these channels will produce in the student only a "trifling head, and a contracted heart."[44] Under its direction knowledge degenerates into quiddity, and the thinker into (in Rochester's phrase) a thinking fool.

Probing Christian mysteries could yield no knowledge simply because mysteries are by definition incomprehensible to human reason. "[S]ince Providence intended there should be Mysteries," Swift wrote, "I do not see how it can be agreeable to *Piety, Orthodoxy,* or good *Sense,* to go about such a Work. For, to me there seems to be a manifest Dilemma in the Case: If you explain them, they are Mysteries no longer; if you fail, you have laboured to no Purpose."[45] To the fortunate few elect who enjoy personal revelations, the mysteries comprehended remain ineffable: prophets do not compose disserta-

---

standing of Scriblerian humanism. See also Austin Warren, *Alexander Pope as Critic and Humanist,* Princeton Studies in English 1 (Princeton, 1929), esp. chaps. 1 and 9.

[44] *Dunciad* iv. 504, in *The Poems of Alexander Pope,* ed. John Butt (London, 1963). All quotations from Pope's poems will be from this text, the one-volume version of the Twickenham Edition, and (normally) cited within the text parenthetically.

[45] *A Letter to a Young Gentleman, Lately Entered into Holy Orders,* in *Irish Tracts 1720–1723 and Sermons,* ed. Louis Landa, vol. 9 of *Prose Works* (Oxford, 1948), 77.

tions. The writing or studying of dissertations could offer no hope of advancement in such areas, but could easily create disquiet. This scholastic impiety ends up weakening faith, and for this reason Pope connected it with scepticism in the character of the gloomy Clerk of the *Dunciad*, book 4 (1742), who was a "Sworn foe to Myst'ry, yet divinely dark" (line 459). He is gloomy because his scepticism denies him the consolations of religion; he is dark in that his syllogizing is a tissue of obfuscation. In contrast to the empiricist's painstaking inductive reasoning up from particulars observed in nature to general principles, the Clerk's rationalist method is to "take the high Priori Road, / And reason downward, till we doubt of God" (lines 471–72). Reason is insubordinate to try to examine God other than through his manifestation in nature (and, of course, through biblical revelation, though Pope does not mention it). Insubordinate reason is portrayed in the Clerk's blasphemous phrasing. His word-play conflating the technical phrase "a priori" with the common expression "to take the high road" suggests that the rationalist foolishly imagines a priori reasoning to be an easy, direct route to knowledge of the godhead. To deduce from one's own fallible principles *down* to God is to put human reason above God, the very source and standard of truth.

Until 1748, when in the *Philosophical Essays* Hume knocked the legs out from under empirical theism, it was not unreasonable to think that Newton and Locke had shown definitively that the surest and sanest way to affirm providence was through observation of nature, that is, inferring from the effect, which is observable, to the cause, which is not. Just as the design of the artifact indicated the existence of a purposive, intelligent artificer, so the apparent design of the world suggested the same qualities in the First Cause. This line of reasoning seemed at once so simple, salutary, and obvious that one could feel justified in questioning the intellectual or moral soundness of any who were dissatisfied with it. Admittedly this analogical reasoning promised only limited results because analogy consists of only a general parallel and not a perfect similitude between things. But, as one of Pope's sources said, "This analogical knowledg of God's Nature and Attributes is all of which we are capable at present; and we must either be contented to know him thus, or sit down with an entire Ignorance and Neglect of God, and finally despair of future Happiness."[46] Naturally one would wish to know more, but there is no problem with living within our limitations since man is afforded light enough to tell right from wrong and to live in sufficient correctitude. Right Reason was still possible.[47] To have held man to a moral standard that he had not the means to descry would be inconsistent with God's goodness and wisdom.

To be sure, Pope was not simply an empiricist. His theodicy contains disparate strands, not all of which may be consistent with empiricism or with each other. The empiricism is prominent, though, and undoubtedly appealed greatly to Hume. True, Pope's humanist emphasis on usefulness kept him from appreciating the experimental activities of the virtuosi, who he thought resembled the schoolmen in pursuing worthless investigations. The attraction of empiricism for him seems to have been largely its consistency with common sense, its chastening of proud reason. Pope scorns the rationalist Clerk for disdaining to

> creep by timid steps, and slow,
> On plain Experience lay foundations low,
> By common sense to common knowledge bred,
> And last, to Nature's Cause thro' Nature led.
>
> (lines 465–68)[48]

In his *Essay on Man* (1733–34) Pope had called for empirical limitations on theological reasoning:

[46] William King, *Divine Predestination and Fore-knowledg, Consistent with the Freedom of Man's Will* (Dublin; repr. London, 1709), 14.

[47] Cf. Pope and Warburton's note to *Dunciad* iv. 471 with Locke, *Essay* 4. 10, § 1.

[48] It has been suggested that the Clerk is the rationalist Samuel Clarke (see the editor's notes to iv. 459, 471). But although Pope might have punned on Clarke's name so as to bring him to our minds, the gloomy Clerk cannot be taken as a caricature of any one person; rather he is a composite of rationalist arrogance and dullness.

> Say first, of God above, or Man below,
> What can we reason, but from what we know?
> Of Man what see we, but his station here,
> From which to reason, or to which refer?
> Thro' worlds unnumber'd tho' the God be known,
> 'Tis ours to trace him only in our own.
>
> (i. 17–22)

The implications of these lines would have cried out to Hume. As Pope told Spence, "The rule laid down . . . of reasoning only from what we know . . . will go a great way toward destroying all the school metaphysics. As the church-writers have introduced so much of those metaphysics into their systems, it will destroy a great deal of what is advanced by them too."[49] Neither Pope nor Hume was a misologist. They just thought that placing limitations on inquiry could put an end to many futile disputes premised upon dubious a priori principles. Inferring from this happily limited data, it was generally thought, we can still possibly, even presumptively, ascribe to the First Cause all of the characteristics fundamental to Christian doctrine: eternity, immateriality, omnipotence, omniscience, and providence. The latter three characteristics were taken as necessary to account for the apparent physical and moral order in the observable world.

The ideas of order and design were not only important premises in the popular theodicy; they had a profound influence on aesthetic assumptions.[50] Order, design, harmony, symmetry, and artifice were elevated to become necessary components of the good and beautiful. To the theist of the first half of the eighteenth century, the conscious imposition of form on a work was not mere shallow craftsmanship; it was emblematic of divine creativity. The conscious imposition of

---

[49] Joseph Spence, Dec. 1743, *Observations, Anecdotes, and Characters of Books and Men, Collected from Conversation*, ed. James M. Osborn, 2 vols. (Oxford, 1966), 1: 134.

[50] I am indebted throughout this paragraph to Martin Battestin, *The Providence of Wit: Aspects of Form in Augustan Literature and the Arts* (Oxford, 1974), esp. chap. 1.

form on the void was the principal evidence of God's intelligence, power, and beneficence. Artistic control was hence a quasi-moral condition devoutly to be striven for, described as follows by Edward Young:

> Weighty the subject, cogent the discourse,
> Clear be the style, the very sound of force;
> Easy the conduct, simple the design,
> Striking the moral, and the soul divine.[51]

In works that had been well conceived and executed, with all parts in proportion and service to the whole, the lucidity of the plan would be plain to see. Clarity and simplicity were signs that the whole was in proper order.

A result of this system of aesthetic values was a critical disposition in which whatever works lacked simplicity or lucidity of parts and plan were seen as not a little suspect. In Swift the presumption against complicated and abstruse writing was stronger even than in Pope. The *Dunciad* and *A Tale of a Tub* (London, 1704) are among the most complicated and abstruse writings in English literature, but they are abstruse largely because they are parodies of tasteless and obscure writing in all its varieties and causes: illogic, ignorance, stylistic ineptitude, pedantic distortion of emphasis, encrustations of notes and digressions, pretentiousness, and plain perverseness. Of most significance to Hume would have been the condemnation in these writings of obscurity as it arises from the corruption of philosophy. He, too, worried about the health of philosophy, and hoped to fortify it against corruption by introducing into it the "experimental Method of Reasoning" (*THN*, title page).

We have seen that while Pope cannot accurately be characterized simply as an empiricist, the strains of empiricism in his poems are distinct and, we can presume, would have been salient to Hume. In Swift's works the distinction between em-

---

[51] "Epistles to Mr. Pope Concerning the Authors of the Age," ii. 201–4, in *The Complete Works . . . of the Rev. Edward Young, LL.D.*, 2 vols. (London, 1854), 1: 43.

piricism and rationalism is less applicable. Phillip Harth has shown that the epistemological premises beneath the apologetics in *A Tale of a Tub* are, in fact, largely rationalist in orientation.[52] But he sees this orientation not as an adherence to one methodology in opposition to another—indeed, Swift seems to have been unaware of any such opposition. His rationalism, if it may be called that, derived from his reading in preparation for ordination, largely in the apologetics of Cudworth, More, Stillingfleet, and others whom historians have placed within the rationalist camp. It appears that at the time of this reading and of the composition of the book (the late 1680s and early 1690s) Swift simply was unalive to the new vogue for Lockean empiricism. For him the important distinction was not between empiricism and rationalism, but between those arguments that served to support the established church and those that did not. Theological argumentation and its epistemological presuppositions are barely visible in the background of Swift's satire. It took the concerted diggings of a first-rate scholar to find them at all. Although Hume was familiar with the writings of the Cambridge Platonists, it is doubtful that he would have recognized a rationalist strain in Swift's writings, especially since Swift specifically attacked Descartes.[53] What he would have been impressed by, as most of Swift's readers have been, is the broadly anti-intellectual and pro-common sense thrust of the satire.

By the time of Hume's childhood, common sense had become associated with unsceptical, Lockean empiricism, which, in limiting knowledge to ideas gained from experience, seemed to give convincing reasons why speculation could not reach very far without falling into absurdity. Locke's tenets seemed, quite literally, to be designed to bring men back to their senses. Swift seems to have been immune to Locke's influence; but given his pronounced distrust of any-

[52] *Swift and Anglican Rationalism: The Religious Background of "A Tale of a Tub"* (Chicago, 1961), esp. chaps. 4 and 5.

[53] For which, see Michael R. G. Spiller, "The Idol of the Stove: The Background to Swift's Criticism of Descartes," *Review of English Studies*, n.s. 25 (1974): 15–24.

thing in the least contradicting common sense, it is not surprising that scholars have tended to see the Dean not as rationalistic, but as anti-Cartesian, antischolastic, and in the last analysis, antiphilosophical. His persona in *A Tale of a Tub*, an impersonation of a Modern writer, poses the question, Whence philosophy?

> LET us next examine the great Introducers of new Schemes in Philosophy, and search till we can find, from what Faculty of the Soul the Disposition arises in mortal Man, of taking it into his Head, to advance new Systems with such an eager Zeal, in things agreed on all hands impossible to be known: from what Seeds this Disposition springs, and to what Quality of human Nature these Grand Innovators have been indebted for their Number of Disciples.[54]

This section is a piece of mock philosophizing on philosophy itself. It is (to coin a term in keeping with Swift's spirit of burlesque) meta-metaphysics. The persona speaks in the pompous manner of a pretentious minute philosopher and, after thus preparing the reader for a profound answer, anticlimactically proposes that the origin of philosophy is in vapors rising to the head. In refusing to find the origin more obviously in curiosity or love of truth, the satirist turned against contemporary philosophers what he saw as their tendency to reduce human motives and behavior to mechanical principles. As philosophy dehumanizes man in finding the principle of behavior beneath the level of conscious moral will, so the philosopher too is dehumanized. Knowledge that dehumanizes, if indeed it is knowledge, is yet not wisdom because it hinders the moral life: it nullifies the nobility of good actions and excuses bad ones. And as the inquiry is corrupt, so the presentation of it will be tainted. The presentation cannot be clear because it deals with what cannot be known, nor can it be tasteful because it is adverse to morality. If obscurity is ob-

[54] *A Tale of a Tub, to Which Is Added The Battle of the Books and The Mechanical Operation of the Spirit*, ed. A. C. Guthkelch and D. N. Smith, 2d ed. (corr. repr. Oxford, 1973), 166.

jected to, the Modern invokes "certain common Privileges of a Writer" according to which where he is "not understood, it shall be concluded, that something very useful and profound is coucht underneath."[55] Systems thus created (to speak in terms of Swift's fable of the bee and the spider) are like a cobweb palace, intricate to the last degree, dusky, insubstantial, spat and spun entirely from the innovator's entrails, and compounded of the poisonous pride of reason referring only to itself and not to external reality.

It now seems to be a generally accepted interpretation of Pope's and Swift's attitudes toward intellectual inquiry to see them as deriving ultimately from the Christian humanist tradition, though neither writer ever overtly invoked the Renaissance movement or, to my knowledge, ever even uttered the word "humanism." Simply to give these attitudes the name of Scriblerian humanism is not very helpful, of course; the benefit is in placing these attitudes within the context of their cultural precedents. This cultural reconstruction allows us to make some sense of what otherwise might appear to be their merely idiosyncratic and unaccountable prejudices, just as looking back on Scriblerian humanism through Hume's eyes will help make sense of his writings. No simple equation of Scriblerian and Renaissance humanism will hold because in particulars the parallel breaks down, as in, for example, their differences over the worth of philological and textual criticism. Scriblerian humanism is nonetheless a recognizable descendant of Renaissance humanism in looking back through the immediate past to the classics for a source, after Christianity, of enduring principles of value. The principles that the Scriblerians feared modernity was losing were those of practical wisdom serviceable to the active man. Knowledge conducive to moral action had not to do with the enumerating of insect species or Latin cases. It certainly had not to do with the controversies over transubstantiation, the paradox of trinal unity, the qualities of spiritual substance, or the reconciliation of divine foreknowledge with human free will. Hume showed

[55] *Tale*, 46.

himself aware of how silly philosophy can look when he jest-
ingly offered to write essays on "the Deiform Fund of the
Soul, the passive Unions of Nothing with Nothing, or any
other of those mystical Points, which I wou'd endeavour to
clear up, & render perspicuous to the meanest Readers."[56]
Hume must have been uncomfortably aware that the Scriblerian notion of wisdom had not to do with the divisibility of
space and time, with the basis for causal reasoning, with
whether a priori knowledge was restricted to questions of
quantity and number, or with whether values are inherent in
external reality or projected by the mind. Questions like
these, Hume admitted more than once, have no obvious or
direct effect on men's behavior and moral choices. By contrast
the Scriblerian humanist wisdom had to do with the pressing
questions of active life, with the understanding and cultivation of those virtues like eloquence and discretion that aid
man in serving God and society more effectively.

Whether or not Hume agreed with this notion of wisdom,
he had to contend with it. When in his ode "On the Refinements in Metaphysical Philosophy" Thomas Blacklock included a complimentary line on Hume, he immediately undercut it with the following note:

> The Author's intention will be ill understood, if he is thought
> here to recommend universal scepticism; for which reason, he
> may, with all decorum, declare what authors and sentiments he
> approves. The philosophy useful to man consists, not in abstract
> and uncertain propositions, but, being designed to regulate his
> conduct and ascertain his happiness, must not only be founded
> on his nature, but comprehend all the principles of an active and
> percipient being.[57]

Berkeley, too, had been found wanting in this respect. An
anonymous critic wrote:

> It were to be wish'd that his lordship had always employed
> his fine genius (as indeed he has done of late) in teaching man-

[56] 14 Nov. [1742], *LDH* 1: 45.
[57] *Poems on Several Occasions* (Edinburgh, 1754), 64, n. to st. 17, line 4.

kind useful truths, and not taken so much delight in displaying its subtilty by astonishing the world with paradoxes, and making impossibilities plausible.[58]

Hume conceded that there was an abyss between the metaphysician and the active man. Even the metaphysician himself forgets his conclusions when business calls. Philosophy "vanishes when the philosopher leaves the shade, and comes into open day" (*EHU* i [4]). But Hume also knew that as unnatural as philosophy might seem it was integral to life, being only an extension, albeit more rigorous, of normal daily problem solving. Philo says

> that every one, even in common life, is constrained to have more or less of this philosophy; that from our earliest infancy we make continual advances in forming more general principles of conduct and reasoning; that the larger experience we acquire, and the stronger reason we are endowed with, we always render our principles the more general and comprehensive; and that what we call *philosophy* is nothing but a more regular and methodical operation of the same kind.          (*DNR* i [134])

Rigorous thinking is just an attempt to deal with life more realistically. It is of great practical concern to act on truth and not falsity. One cannot act with confidence without some reasonable assurance that one's judgment is at least likely to be sound. This is one of the paradoxes for which Hume has been disparaged, that though philosophy at times seems to be an artificial, even ineffectual refinement on thought, it inevitably returns importunately upon the mind, arising from reflections upon the exigencies of life and not from an unruly imagination. Responsible people cannot altogether avoid it. Life seems alternately to deny and demand it. Like most of Hume's paradoxes, this is not contrived and paraded to impress the reader. It presented itself to Hume as a problem, appearing unbidden in the course of living thoughtfully.

In trying to win over the wits, Hume might well have urged

[58] "Anti-Berkeley," letter of 14 Nov. 1751, *Gentleman's Magazine* 22 (1752): 13.

that philosophy is not an intellectual perversion, that any notion of wisdom excluding rigorous thinking is untenable; but
he did not stress this argument. The reason is that the win-
ning over of an audience with misologist tendencies is much
more a matter of rhetoric than logic. It is less easy to disdain
Hume's belletrism after considering the attitudes and tastes
of the audience that he aimed to convert. A kind of anti-intellectualism had found compelling expression in the most popular and sophisticated literature of the day. Hume accepted
certain of these values, even, in his fashion, the suspicion of
unconstrained reason. But an audience with Scriblerian notions clearly would not welcome Hume's contributions to the
republic of letters, for these were both heterodox and abstruse. There can be little doubt that in the Scriblerian
scheme of things Hume must be found to be a duncical, Modern innovator. William Warburton indicated as much when in
editing Pope's *Dunciad* he added Hume to the dunces.[59]
Against this complex of values Hume ran head on with the
*Treatise*, and, not surprisingly, he failed to make his book accepted. The rest of his career can be seen as a series of adjustments to these circumstances. If he wished to be heard
and given due consideration, he needed to avoid the odious
literary faults associated with dark systematizers and write
with something like an Addisonian or Scriblerian elegance.
About the heterodox and innovative aspects of his material he
could do very little without compromising his own intellectual
integrity. Consequently any success that he could hope to
have would depend greatly upon whether his manner could
mitigate the readers' predictable negative reactions to the
oddity and unpalatability of the material. Fortunately Hume
did not have to imitate a literary manner that was uncongenial
to him. The empiricist tradition ran parallel to the humanist
tradition in arraigning futile and ill-expressed reasonings. As
an empiricist Hume shared many values with eighteenth-century humanism, and these he could and did pointedly empha-
size in his writings. One effect of this emphasis would be to

[59] See Mossner, *The Life of David Hume*, 2d ed. (Oxford, 1980), 290.

offset somewhat the tendency of readers to take him for a Modern schoolman.

In this light we can understand Hume's experimentation after the *Treatise* with genres and different subjects. He was working for the requisite simplicity and lucidity of style, argument, and plan. These experiments will be the subject of later chapters. For the moment it is important to consider Hume's general strategy of accommodating the expectations of his readers. As has been said, the great issue of current humanism was the end, uses, and limits of human knowledge. Knowledge was not generally considered to be an end in itself. That which did not promote practical wisdom was the scorn of the man of sense. The first step to wisdom, then, was to know where inquiry should stop. This step was a kind of mental discipline; or, to judge from Pope's and Swift's extreme disgust with impertinent inquiry, we might say that it was regarded as a kind of mental hygiene. Pope's famous dictum was, "Know then thyself, presume not God to scan; / The proper study of Mankind is Man" (*Essay on Man* ii. 1–2). To try to scan God beyond what he had made observable is contrary to his will and therefore wrong and futile. If man had been meant to know certain things, he would have been given the means: "In Pride, in reas'ning Pride, our error lies; / All quit their sphere, and rush into the skies" (i. 123–24). Society had suffered much from the pretensions of individual enthusiasts to have exceptional insights into God's nature and will. The best countervailing standard of what was or was not knowable in God seemed to be consensus, or common sense. Lockean empiricism seemed to support common sense by confining knowledge to what could be observed and therefore commonly known. For the rest, what man could and should know was himself, that is, his capacities, his duties, and his best means of fulfilling those duties. To know one's limitations was to know one's place. An appreciation of how little one knows all told is conducive to Christian humility and civic sanity.

Humanism shared this theme of man's limitation with empiricism, and not surprisingly we find Hume adopting the theme and making it quite his own. He made it no less than the raison d'être of his epistemology, reiterating frequently that philosophy had gone astray in probing the unprobeable. Like Locke's, his epistemology was an attempt to establish the boundaries of possible knowledge. He hoped to settle vain disputes by showing them to be undecidable, and thereby to turn man's inquisitiveness into constructive channels. If God could not be known, man could at least profitably explore his own nature. It is likely that it was in this regard that Hume supposed Pope would appreciate the *Treatise.* "The *imagination* of man," Hume wrote,

> is naturally sublime, delighted with whatever is remote and extraordinary, and running, without controul, into the most distant parts of space and time in order to avoid the objects, which custom has rendered too familiar to it. A correct *Judgement* observes a contrary method, and avoiding all distant and high enquiries, confines itself to common life, and to such subjects as fall under daily practice and experience; leaving the more sublime topics to the embellishment of poets and orators, or to the arts of priests and politicians.          (*EHU* xii. 3 [133])

That is, Hume implies with delicate sarcasm, we should leave such topics to those orders from whom, due to the character of their professions, we do not expect strict truth. He says that

> if men attempt the discussion of questions, which lie entirely beyond the reach of human capacity, such as those concerning the origin of worlds, or the oeconomy of the intellectual system or region of spirits, they may long beat the air in their fruitless contests, and never arrive at any determinate conclusion.
>
> (viii. 1 [66])

But a little scepticism can deflate reasoning pride. Philosophers "will never be tempted to go beyond common life, so long as they consider the imperfection of those faculties which they employ, their narrow reach, and their inaccurate operations" (xii. 3 [133]). Of course Hume's program for self-knowledge was not so restricted to the pragmatic as Pope's. And by placing the limit of theological knowledge at a place commensurate with agnosticism, he gave such a turn to the theme of intellectual humility that it was unacceptable to theists. Much of Hume's notorious irony consists of his twisting of this Christian humanist theme against theism. But it should not be concluded from this fact that this theme was for Hume merely a prop for irony. He sincerely held with the humanists the conviction that the primary desideratum for culture was to fix the frontiers of inquiry and thus put an end to the wrangling and stalemate that disgraced philosophy. Kant, another admirer of Pope, recognized the importance in Hume's system of philosophical retrenchment when he wrote that Hume looked to "the negative utility that the moderation of the exaggerated claims of speculative reason would have, in completely putting an end to so many endless and troublesome disputes that confuse the human species."[60] And Boswell responded to Hume's humanism when he wrote that "David Hume, who has thought as much as any man who has been tortured on the metaphysical rack, who has walked the wilds of speculation, wisely and calmly concludes that the business of ordinary life is the proper employment of man."[61]

So it was that Hume, like the apologists for theism whom he scandalized, preached intellectual humility. And while he did so in all sincerity, the rich irony of the situation colors his exhortations, as we shall see in chapter 4. James Beattie, doubtless with Hume foremost in mind, urges his readers not to be tempted by sceptics into intellectual arrogance:

> O then renounce that impious self-esteem,
> That aims to trace the secrets of the skies:
> For thou art but of dust; be humble, and be wise.[62]

"Well said," Hume might retort, "but do you now practice what you preach. It is the religionists, not the sceptics, who

---

[60] *Prolegomena to Any Future Metaphysics that Will Be Able to Present Itself as a Science*, trans. Peter G. Lucas (Manchester, 1953), 6 n.

[61] 9 July 1764, *Boswell in Holland, 1763–1764*, ed. Frederick A. Pottle, vol. 2 of Yale Eds. (London, 1952), 303.

[62] *The Minstrel; or, the Progress of Genius. A Poem* (London, 1771), bk. 1, st. 52.

pretend to have knowledge unavailable to man, and who, insisting that all conform to their conflicting, fantastical systems, foment disputes throughout mankind" (cf. "PGen.," 62–63 [penult par.]). Of course Hume could not prudently say such things outright. His need to state them only by implication led him to write some of the most subtly ironic passages in English literature.

## HUMEAN HUMANISM

But I really do not like such abstruse kind of
speculation. I wish to reason upon such principles as
experience furnishes, and not to go too far from the
common and ordinary train of thinking. To speculate
for instruction, or for amusement, is wise; but to
distend our faculties by ineffectual stretches is both
unwise and painful.
—Boswell, *Hypochondriack* 22

The place where Hume most openly discussed the relationship between belles-lettres and philosophy is "Of the Different Species of Philosophy," the first of the *Philosophical Essays concerning Human Understanding* (London, 1748).[63] It has the significance of being introductory to the work in which he tried again to set forth his "logic," eight years after the episode of the *Treatise*. It is a valuable statement of Hume's intentions in the writing of philosophy, and in it he directly addresses the expectations of readers adhering to the humanist values discussed above.

He begins by contrasting two types of philosophers and their ways of writing. One type considers man chiefly as born for action and hence endeavors to paint virtue in "the most amiable colours; borrowing all helps from poetry and eloquence, and treating their subject in an easy and obvious manner, and such as is best fitted to please the imagination, and engage the affections." By making us feel the difference between vice and virtue, they excite and regulate our passions

---

[63] Now known as the *Enquiry concerning Human Understanding*.

in order to "bend our hearts to the love of probity and true
honour" (*EHU* i [3]). The other type does not cultivate virtue
directly, but instead seeks to establish the foundations of
moral values and truth. The procedure of these philosophers
is to infer "from particular instances to general principles,"
moving empirically to ever greater generalities until "they arrive at those original principles, by which, in every science,
all human curiosity must be bounded" (p. 4). Recognition that
there are bounds to science does not move them to abjure
speculation altogether in favor of the "easy," reformative philosophy. Unfortunately this abstract and painstaking line of
philosophy often seems unintelligible to readers. But (to
adopt an expression of Bishop Butler's) everything is what it
is and not another thing: to require of "accurate and abstruse"
philosophy that it be "easy and obvious" is to require it to be
something other than it is. Thus Hume gently disengages a
level of philosophy from the commitment that humanism im-
posed upon it to be immediately improving, much as the Aes-
thetes of the 1890s did for art when they tried to free it from
the constraining principle of utility. But Hume did not go so
far as to proclaim, Philosophy for Philosophy's sake.

The easy, obvious philosophy is clearly something that today would generally be taken for a branch of literature. Remarkably, Hume gives a kind of precedence to this belletristic
philosophy. It has, he says, a more immediately salutary effect
on men's behavior, and furthermore, it has a greater claim to
universal value if such claims are to be judged by the durability of the fame of its productions. Cicero's popularity had out-
lived Aristotle's, and La Bruyère and Addison would be more
highly valued in the long run than Malebranche and Locke.
It was not merely a concession of the moment when Hume
gave precedence to literature, for it appears again elsewhere:

> No English author in that age [the Commonwealth] was more
> celebrated both abroad and at home than Hobbes: In our time,
> he is much neglected: A lively instance how precarious all rep-
> utations, founded on reasoning and philosophy! A pleasant com-
> edy, which paints the manners of the age, and exposes a faithful

picture of nature, is a durable work, and is transmitted to the latest posterity. But a system, whether physical or metaphysical, commonly owes its success to its novelty; and is no sooner canvassed with impartiality than its weakness is discovered.[64]

To be durable a work must present a picture that posterity will recognize as true to nature, and philosophers are more likely to fall into absurdities than belletrists. A philosophical system, though not true to nature, or not easily recognizable as such, can still give the quite genuine pleasure of novelty: "At worst, what [abstruse thinkers] say is uncommon; and if it should cost some pains to comprehend it, one has, however, the pleasure of hearing something that is new" ("Comm.," 253). But the pleasure of novelty is transient, decidedly second-rate.

Furthermore, novelty is an outright flaw when writers pursue it as an end in itself. For this reason people of Hume's generation were inclined to be suspicious of it. This critical presumption against novelty is worth dwelling upon because novelty is endemic to accurate and abstruse philosophy, and to Hume's especially. We should distinguish between three kinds of novelty. The first is unintentional, following incidentally upon an author's efforts to achieve his purposes, as in the case of Hobbes, whom Hume did not accuse of setting out to be novel. To a candid judge incidental novelty should not reflect one way or another upon an author, though it would be fair to observe, as Hume does above, that a work cannot endure for long on the merits of its novelty alone. Secondly there is gratuitous novelty, such as Johnson had in mind when he depreciated Voltaire, Rousseau, and Hume: "All infidel writers drop into oblivion, when personal connections and the floridness of novelty are gone." Infidelity is so obviously untrue to nature, Johnson supposed, that it can only succeed with the public on the insubstantial basis of its novelty. But the novelty of infidelity is not innocently incidental:

[64] *Hist.* 6: 153 (A.D. 1660). Cf. *EHU* i (5 n.) and "ST," 242–43.

Hume, and other sceptical innovators, are vain men, and will gratify themselves at any expense. Truth will not afford sufficient food to their vanity; so they have betaken themselves to errour. Truth, Sir, is a cow that will yield such people no more milk, and so they are gone to milk the bull.[65]

Hume himself was alert to the danger of falling into gratuitous novelty, warning us that the "endeavour to please by novelty leads men wide of simplicity and nature, and fills their writings with affectation and conceit" ("SRW," 196).[66] The cultivation of novelty for its own sake is a mistake, not only because its pleasures are transient, but also because a plethora of novelties is intrinsically distasteful. Such is the thinking behind Hume's criticism of Laurence Sterne's novel: "*Tristram Shandy* may perhaps go on a little longer; but we will not follow him [it was appearing in installments]. With all his drollery there is a sameness of extravagance which tires us. We have just a succession of Surprise, surprise, surprise."[67] Surprise is at best only a fleeting pleasure, and when the attempt at surprise is so regular as to become predictable, it is in a sense surprise no longer. For these reasons "productions, which are merely surprising, without being natural, can never give any lasting entertainment to the mind" ("SRW," 192).

None of this means that writers should strive to be commonplace. If they can manage to be both novel and natural, holding the two in balance, they will have attained in great

[65] 10 June 1784; 21 July 1763, *Boswell's Life of Johnson* . . . , ed. G. B. Hill, rev. L. F. Powell, 6 vols. (Oxford, 1934–50), 4: 288, 1: 444.

[66] Cf. Henry Home, Lord Kames, *Elements of Criticism*, 3d ed. 2 vols. (London, 1765), 1: 255: "But the man who prefers any thing merely because it is new, hath not this principle [curiosity] for its justification; nor indeed any good principle: vanity is at the bottom, which easily prevails upon those who have no taste, to prefer things odd, rare, or singular, in order to distinguish themselves from others."

[67] Quoted by Boswell, 4 Nov. 1762, *Private Papers* 1: 127. Cf. Johnson's remark: "Nothing odd will do long. 'Tristam Shandy' did not last" (20 Mar. 1776, *Life of Johnson* 2: 449).

measure that elusive quality of elegance.[68] This balance will produce in the reader at once a stimulating sense of newness and a sense of truth to nature, of rightness. We will develop the notion of this third kind of novelty in connection with Hume in chapters 3 and 4. For the moment we may observe simply that two ways to achieve it are (1) to express familiar sentiments in a new way, putting old ideas into a novel form so that "the novelty of the manner may compensate the triteness of the subject" (*DNR*, par. 3 [127]); or (2) somehow to enunciate new, unfamiliar ideas so that they seem natural. The former procedure would be followed by an easy, obvious philosopher such as Addison. The crucial passages, familiar to students of the period, are the following. In *Spectator* 253 Addison seconded Boileau in saying

> that Wit and fine Writing doth not consist so much in advancing things that are new, as in giving things that are known an agreeable Turn. It is impossible, for us who live in the later Ages of the World, to make Observations in Criticism, Morality, or in any Art or Science, which have not been touched upon by others. We have little else left us, but to represent the common Sense of Mankind in more strong, more beautiful, or more uncommon Lights.[69]

Hume could not have agreed with this strikingly extreme limitation on the possibilities for natural novelty, for it is premised upon the impossibility of new knowledge. Pope's formulation of the notion in his *Essay on Criticism* also follows Boileau:

> *True Wit* is *Nature* to Advantage drest,
> What oft was *Thought*, but ne'er so well *Exprest*,

---

[68] See Hagstrum's discussion of this notion (*Samuel Johnson's Literary Criticism*, 154–72). Richetti puts his finger on Hume's problem of natural novelty (*Philosophical Writing*, 189). In "The Rationale of Hume's Literary Inquiries" (*David Hume: Many-Sided Genius*, ed. Kenneth R. Merrill and Robert W. Shahan [Norman, 1976], esp. 108–15), Ralph Cohen discusses Hume's criterion of naturalness, though not in connection with the writing of philosophy.

[69] *Spectator* 2: 483–84.

*Something*, whose Truth convinc'd at Sight we find,
That gives us back the Image of our Mind. . . .

                                    (lines 297–300)

Certainly Hume did not believe (and we may doubt that Pope really believed[70]) that all truths in nature had been thought before, and that the expression of new truth could not partake of wit. The second couplet gives a more flexible formulation that can be construed so as to allow elegance to accurate, abstruse writing: things previously unthought could be naturally novel if expressed so that they give the reader back the image of his mind. Johnson's formulation cannot be improved upon: wit is that "which is at once natural and new, that which though not obvious is, upon its first production, acknowledged to be just; . . . that, which he that never found it, wonders how he missed."[71]

Here is a possibility, if only a slim one, of attaining elegance in accurate and abstruse philosophy. It was in terms of these attitudes toward novelty that Hume saw the rhetorical problem of writing abstruse philosophy. If abstruse philosophy is not false wit, it certainly resembles false wit in its highly perishable fame. It naturally tends to conclusions that shock common sense. It ages badly. A thing of beauty may be a joy forever, but truth is not necessarily a thing of beauty. Abstruse philosophy is much more prone to superannuation than the easy variety because in thought so subtle it is difficult not to err, one error invalidating perhaps a whole system. An accurate philosopher cannot allow the sense of what seems natural to enter into his reasoning. He resolves not to be deterred by the singularity or disagreeableness of any conclusion to which his reasoning leads him (*EHU* i. [4–5]). He puts himself out on a limb, venturing his reputation with posterity on tenuous

[70] See Edward Niles Hooker, "Pope on Wit: The *Essay on Criticism*," *The Seventeenth Century: Studies in the History of English Thought and Literature from Bacon to Pope*, by Richard Foster Jones et al. (Stanford, 1951), esp. 243–46.

[71] "Cowley," *Lives of the English Poets . . .* , ed. G. B. Hill, 3 vols. (Oxford, 1905), 1: 19–20; hereinafter cited as *Poets*.

chains of reasoning, leading often to apparent or actual absurdity. Others will diligently search for errors, as of course they should. The likelihood then is that sooner or later, and probably sooner, the speculator will be shown to have held extravagant opinions for flawed reasons. In this event the sensible man is confirmed in having adhered to the consensus and gainsaid the philosopher's claims, though the abstruse arguments had appeared unanswerable.

The easy philosopher is protected from this embarrassment by choosing his positions beforehand from among the old and tried verities. His challenge is not to discover new truth, but to present old truths in an entertaining way. He must, in Johnson's words, overcome in his readers "that inattention by which known truths are suffered to lie neglected."[72] This is a great challenge, but in restricting his vision the easy philosopher gains a great advantage:

> [A] philosopher, who purposes only to represent the common sense of mankind in more beautiful and more engaging colours, if by accident he falls into error, goes no farther; but renewing his appeal to common sense, and the natural sentiments of the mind, returns into the right path, and secures himself from any dangerous illusions.                        (*EHU* i [5])[73]

With foregone conclusions, his individual errors of reasoning inflict no telling damage and remain only minor faults of the whole. This belletristic philosophy is also more in keeping with the dictates of human nature. Nature commands:

> Indulge your passion for science . . . but let your science be human, and such as may have a direct reference to action and society. Abstruse thought and profound researches I prohibit,

---

[72] "Swift," *Poets* 3: 52.

[73] Cf. *Abs.*, 645: "Most of the philosophers of antiquity, who treated of human nature, have shewn more of a delicacy of sentiment, a just sense of morals, or a greatness of soul, than a depth of reasoning and reflection. They content themselves with representing the common sense of mankind in the strongest lights, and with the best turn of thought and expression, without following out steadily a chain of propositions, or forming the several truths into a regular science."

and will severely punish, by the pensive melancholy which they
introduce, by the endless uncertainty in which they involve
you, and by the cold reception which your pretended discoveries shall meet with, when communicated. Be a philosopher; but,
amidst all your philosophy, be still a man. (p. 6)[74]

This passage could serve as a diagnosis of the failings that
doomed the *Treatise* and can give us insights into Hume's disowning of his first book. Hume had come to believe that the
science of the *Treatise* had not been quite "human" enough.
He had allowed many speculations in it to end in uncertainty.
Uncertainty is intrinsically unpleasant, and if the book often
registers the author's perplexity, what effect should he have
expected it to have on its readers? The effect on a commonsensical reader going through it might be described as "surprise, surprise, surprise." And for his considerable labors in
working through the book, not only was the reader not sent
back "among mankind full of noble sentiments and wise precepts, applicable to every exigence of human life" (p. 5); it is
arguable from the humanist perspective that it sent him back
less equipped for the business of life, newly hampered by
doubts.

Having given a kind of precedence to the easy philosophy,
and having granted in some degree the validity of the objections of the worldly wise against abstruse philosophy, Hume
now proceeds to defend the kind of philosophy in which he
excelled. In this defense he is not, as might be expected, in
the least aggressive. He does not sally forth to smite the Philistines, though it would have been easy enough for someone
of his argumentative powers. But a refutation of philistinism
would not change people's minds, especially since the people
were suspicious of rigorous argument. It could not win over
an audience. What is more, there is no evidence to show that
Hume thought of the anti-intellectualism he faced as simply
philistine. The indications are that he respected it and even
accepted it in part. Accordingly he is careful in this introduc-

[74] Cf. Pope, "Epistle to James Cragg . . . ," lines 12–13: "But candid, free,
sincere, as you began, / Proceed—a Minister, but still a Man."

tory essay to give due consideration to all sides of the question. He pleads only that abstruse philosophy be allowed a place in letters. Hume grants the humanist argument everything except the "absolute rejecting of all profound reasonings, or what is commonly called *metaphysics.*" One reason to spare abstruse philosophy is "its subserviency to the easy and humane" variety (p. 6). Though the immediate object of abstruse philosophy is not to promote virtue, a more accurate knowledge of what constitutes virtue must help those who undertake to promote it. Though it is not the purpose of abstruse philosophy to create beauty, such philosophy can help the artist to know better the nature he attempts to dress to advantage: "Accuracy is, in every case, advantageous to beauty, and just reasoning to delicate sentiment. In vain would we exalt the one by depreciating the other" (p. 7).

Another indirect but no less real benefit of this philosophy for society is that it helps foster a healthier cultural climate. It does so by setting an example of rigorous thinking that, when emulated, will redound to the advantage of all departments of active life: "And though a philosopher may live remote from business, the genius of philosophy, if carefully cultivated by several, must gradually diffuse itself throughout the whole society, and bestow a similar correctness on every art and calling" (p. 7). This is similar to the argument that Newman and Arnold made for the place of the humanities in education, according to which a liberal education is not replaceable by vocational training: though it has no obvious immediate benefit, it trains the mind generally so that it can apply itself more effectively to any particular problem. It is not difficult to draw from Hume's own writings illustrations of how accurate philosophy can indirectly benefit society after diffusing itself. For example, to ascertain through a process of abstruse reasoning that we have no more genuine idea of spiritual substance than we do of material substance does not seem to offer any clear advantage in solving daily problems. But to be made aware of how little can be known in such matters can make us more cautious in asserting ourselves or contradicting others, thereby reducing tensions between individuals and sects. For another example, it might be said (and it was) that to hold that justice is not founded on an immutable moral code inherent in situations or actions is to subvert the rule of law. It appears that this item of knowledge is not only useless, but even pernicious. Hume could point out, however, that a recognition of the conventional and arbitrary nature of governmental structures can free the mind of the ideological cant of political parties. Knowing that government need not in the nature of things be one form or another, we are freed from Tory doctrines of passive obedience and royal prerogative as well as from Whig doctrines of constitutional liberty. Once doctrinal contentions are dispelled, a compromise between parties is much more attainable. A philosophical temper diffused throughout society would help curtail the disease of faction in the body politic. Where there are genuine differences, a spirit of accuracy can help people to identify the crucial issues and keep to the point. In such ways abstruse philosophy encourages the increase of practical wisdom, though it does not address itself directly to that end as do belles-lettres.

Another value of this philosophy, and no contemptible one, is simply that, in Bishop Butler's words, it can "render life less unhappy, and promote its satisfactions."[75] It does so by providing one more amusing pastime to mankind's store. Though to the majority of people it seems painful and fatiguing, there are always certain minds for which this effort is an enjoyable exercise. Though this philosopher enters into the intrinsically displeasing areas of uncertainty and confusion, the challenge to surmount these obstacles keeps him eagerly striving for success and competing for preeminence: "Obscurity, indeed, is painful to the mind as well as to the eye; but to bring light from obscurity, by whatever labour, must needs be delightful and rejoicing" (*EHU* i. [8]). This is the rarefied aesthetic delight of the performing mind, glorying in its power. It is, in Yeats's phrase, the fascination of what is difficult.[76]

[75] *The Works of Joseph Butler, D. C. L.*, ed. W. E. Gladstone, 2 vols. (Oxford, 1897), 2: 228.

[76] Cf. Locke, *Essay*, 6–7.

It is objected, however, that this is not an innocent "accession to those few safe and harmless pleasures, which are bestowed on human race [*sic*]" (p. 7). More often it is a source of error. This is the charge that Hume took most seriously. In his view it was not at all ridiculous to claim that prying inquiry had done mankind harm and that sensible people therefore might leave abstruse topics alone:

> Here indeed lies the justest and most plausible objection against a considerable part of metaphysics, that they are not properly a science; but arise either from the fruitless efforts of human vanity, which would penetrate into subjects utterly inaccessible to the understanding, or from the craft of popular superstitions, which, being unable to defend themselves on fair ground, raise these intangling brambles to cover and protect their weakness.
>
> (p. 8)

Those having read Hume's "Of Superstition and Enthusiasm" will recognize in this passage his psychology of religious corruption. He is not just paraphrasing a commonsensical objection to "metaphysics," but is incorporating his own views that philosophy, like religion, is subject to enthusiasm and superstition, that is, to overreaching itself through reasoning pride and to abasing itself before fallible authorities (cf. *THN* 1. 4. 7 [271–72]). But allowing that abstruse philosophy can be and had been corrupted, what was to be done about it?

It seems unlikely that Hume could make peace at all with those who felt that "metaphysics" should be shunned as pernicious, yet this is precisely what he tried to do, conceding that certain orders of investigation are unfit for man. Men, he felt, should be dissuaded from these investigations and turned to better employments. His answer to the problem of misguided investigation, however, is not to denigrate abstruse philosophy, but to show men that certain kinds of investigation are necessarily futile. Philosophy must come to know itself and presume not to scan where its vision cannot be clear:

> The only method of freeing learning, at once, from these abstruse questions, is to enquire seriously into the nature of human understanding, and shew, from an exact analysis of its pow-

ers and capacity, that it is by no means fitted for such remote
and abstruse subjects. We must submit to this fatigue, in order
to live at ease ever after: And must cultivate true metaphysics
with some care, in order to destroy the false and adulterate. . . .
Accurate and just reasoning . . . is alone able to subvert that
abstruse philosophy and metaphysical jargon, which, being
mixed up with popular superstition, renders it in a manner impenetrable to careless reasoners, and gives it the air of science
and wisdom. (p. 9)

The cure for bad philosophy is its exposure by good philosophy. What Hume thought was good philosophy was empiricism kept rigorous by the constant challenge to it of scepticism. Here he appropriates the humanist antimetaphysical
theme for his own polemical use. He also attempts to avert
charges of duncery against his own philosophy by adopting
the stance of an ally in the war against adulterate philosophy.
How far this maneuver was a result of calculated strategy is a
question admitting of no definite answer. It seems clear,
though, that in voicing the theme of man's limitations Hume
was not merely being ironic. He took the theme quite to
heart, fully expecting certain benefits to accrue to mankind if
it could be persuaded to close the book on many questions
and disputes. Perhaps it will be thought that Hume was trying
to trick Christian humanists into not recognizing him as their
enemy. It is possible, on the other hand, to think of this maneuver as a politic effort to direct attention toward areas of
agreement and away from areas of disagreement. What accords could ever be reached if the opposing parties were so
outspoken as always to put each other in mind of the points of
their contention?

But there is another way in which Hume tried to accommodate himself to the expectations of his projected audience.
He declares that in his *Philosophical Essays* he will attempt
to make abstruse philosophy less abstruse. His essays, then,
will not be of the abstruse *or* the easy kind, but will be a hybrid, something combining as far as possible the clarity and
elegance of an Addison with the accuracy of a Locke:

> But as, after all, the abstractedness of these speculations is no
> recommendation, but rather a disadvantage to them, and as this
> difficulty may perhaps be surmounted by care and art, and the
> avoiding of all unnecessary detail, we have, in the following en-
> quiry, attempted to throw some light upon subjects, from which
> uncertainty has hitherto deterred the wise, and obscurity the
> ignorant. Happy, if we can unite the boundaries of the different
> species of philosophy, by reconciling profound enquiry with
> clearness, and truth with novelty!                       (pp. 12–13)

If Hume were to ally himself successfully with the Wits
against duncery, then he would somehow have to remedy the
obscurity for which "metaphysics" was generally disparaged.
He would have to reconcile what strikes the reader as true to
nature with the new knowledge that is the subject of abstruse
philosophy. If he could not do these things, then his bid for a
coalition would fail. In this context the popularization of abstruse philosophy is not a vulgarization of it. It did not in
Hume's view adulterate philosophy to render it approachable
to men of *bons sens*; it adulterated philosophy to becloud it
with occult qualities and incoherent jargon. To Hume, as to
Locke, Shaftesbury, Berkeley, and others, it was of immense
importance to the welfare of both philosophy and society to
achieve a reconciliation between them. Characteristically,
Hume was diffident of claiming that the welfare of society depended on the success of the arbitrator. He made the more
modest claim for the popularizer that he would introduce
many men to an entertainment they would not otherwise have
enjoyed: "The sweetest and most inoffensive path of life leads
through the avenues of science and learning; and whoever can
either remove any obstructions in this way, or open up any
new prospect, ought so far to be esteemed a benefactor to
mankind" (pp. 7–8). Hume might easily have argued instead
that for society to spurn philosophy is calamitous. It was more
like him, though, to make philosophy more appealing and to
entice the reader to "those noble entertainments" (p. 5) of the
life of mind. It was more like an artist thus to wed instruction
with entertainment.

# Chapter II

## THE *TREATISE*

I borrowed today out of the Advocates' Library, David
Hume's *Treatise of Human Nature*, but found it so
abstruse, so contrary to sound sense and reason, and so
dreary in its effects on the mind, if it had any, that I
resolved to return it without reading it.
—*Boswell, Laird of Auchinleck*

*Il est quelquefois malheureux d'avoir trop d'esprit & de
pénétration.*
—Anon. rev. of the *Treatise*, art. 8, *Bibliothèque
raisonnée des ouvrages des savans de l'Europe* 26, pt. 2
(April–May–June 1741): 412–13

### PROMULGATING THE SCIENCE OF MAN

We have seen that Hume regarded philosophy as an entertainment, a noble and salutary one, but an entertainment
nonetheless. He did not in the least regard it as frivolous, yet
he was eager that it should be neat and elegant in its presentation. It was precisely because it was important that it should
be advantageously dressed. "[A]ny author who speaks in his
own person," and who merely states his case without regard
for the refinements of language, "may be correct; but he
never will be agreeable" wrote Hume ("SRW," 192), explicitly
including philosophers in his pronouncement. In his wish to
be agreeable he reflected the attitude of the culture to which
he belonged. In George Campbell's view, "even the most
rigid philosopher, if he choose that his disquisitions be not
only understood but relished (and without being relished they
are understood to little purpose), will not disdain sometimes
to apply to the imagination of his disciples, mixing the pleas-

ant with the useful."[1] This mixture involved much less of a concession from the philosophers of that age than might be supposed. If ever there was in British literary history a time when tastes were suited to the requirements of philosophy, it was that which Goldsmith and Joseph Warton designated as the Augustan. A vigilance against intellectual humbug, a strong presumption against the subjectivism of enthusiasm, a predilection for the clear and factual—these were literary values in which philosophers could acquiesce without great discomfort. Like Berkeley before him, Hume embraced them wholeheartedly.

Putting aside considerations of cultural history, one still might ask why a philosopher should have to divert some of his energy from the pursuit of truth to the elegant presentation of it. Is not the former enough to attempt? For Hume's purposes it was not enough because, aside from ascertaining the truth and informing and convincing his readers of it, he had a second and broader program. He hoped not only to win concurrence to a set of tenets, but also to convert his readers to what in his early writings he called variously the science of man or of human nature. About this intention he was forthright:

> For my part, my only hope is, that I may contribute a little to the advancement of knowledge, by giving in some particulars a different turn to the speculations of philosophers, and pointing out to them more distinctly those subjects, where alone they can expect assurance and conviction. Human Nature is the only science of man; and yet has been hitherto the most neglected.
>
> (*THN* 1. 4. 7 [273])

Hume here describes his program in terms of the humanist dictum that the only proper study of mankind is man; but he plainly intended it to have the farther reaching implication that the natural sciences would be restricted to empirical procedures. If men would adopt the experimental method of reasoning, it would "*alter from the foundation the greatest part*

---

[1] *The Philosophy of Rhetoric*, 2 vols. (London, 1776), 2: 163.

*of the sciences"* (*Abs.*, 643). It would redirect inquirers from unanswerable questions to those that might be answered; and, as science depends upon the asking of the right questions, it would lead philosophy out of its discreditable stagnation and into areas where it could succeed. Moral and natural philosophy, for example, would be relieved of occult qualities and of the extrascientific requirement of evidencing God's providence. That the public should witness the sciences advancing was imperative. The unhealthy alternative would be the drifting of the inquisitive into adulterate philosophy and of the practical minded into misology. Indecisive, profitless disputation over abstruse topics would encourage the public to reject all profound inquiry as duncical and Laputan. Hume espoused empiricism as the *via media* between adulterate philosophy and reactionary antimetaphysics. As well as concurring with his system, Hume's readers were themselves supposed to adopt the experimental method of reasoning. However he may have lowered his expectations after the tepid reception of the *Treatise*, he did not appreciably change the direction of the cultural reform he worked for.

It might be asked why, if he wanted to engage his readers in the science of man, Hume did not stress its utility rather than its attractions as an entertainment. Surely this would have been more comfortable to the seriousness of the undertaking, and Hume did believe that a successful science of man would be "much superior in utility to any other of human comprehension" (*THN*, xix). A Humean answer to this question must come in two stages.

First, it should not be supposed that by stressing utility rather than entertainment Hume would have thought he was appealing to our reason rather than our feelings. According to his psychology of action (*THN* 2. 3. 3), moving people to act requires moving them affectively.[2] Mere apprehension as

[2] See Mackie, *Hume's Moral Theory* (London, 1980), 44–50; Páll Árdal, *Passion and Value in Hume's "Treatise"* (Edinburgh, 1966), 93–108; and Árdal, "Some Implications of the Virtue of Reasonableness in Hume's *Treatise*," *Hume: A Re-evaluation*, ed. Donald Livingston and James King (New York, 1976), 91–106.

such is not a sufficient cause of animal behavior. Reason by itself is inert, and we require the impetus of passion in order to act on our knowledge, indeed, in order to act to acquire knowledge. When we behave in ways that we call reasonable, we really are acting on what Hume called (with no paradox intended) a calm passion, that is, on a preference for what we believe are remoter but greater goods over more immediate but lesser ones. The role of reason in reasonable behavior is only to ascertain what the greater good is and what the means of achieving it are. Without a passional preference for the greater good, people act foolishly, however well they know what the greater good is. So even when Hume did appeal to our sense of utility, as in the first of the *Philosophical Essays* discussed above, he was in his view appealing to our desires, though with a superaddition of reasoned argument to establish the usefulness of abstruse philosophy. To move an audience to adopt experimental habits of reasoning themselves, even to get them to read the *Treatise* through, would involve more than argument and conviction. Everything would depend upon the author's success in exciting a motivating passion.

All this might appear more familiar if considered in light of the conventional rhetorical distinction between argument and persuasion, to which Hume's tenets might serve as a philosophical analogue. As one standard rhetoric has it, the "end of argument, strictly conceived, is truth—truth as determined by the operation of reason. The end of persuasion, on the other hand, is assent—assent to the will of the persuader."[3] Successful argument produces reasoned conviction; successful persuasion, assent and action. To get people to conduct themselves wisely requires both argument and persuasion. This distinction was not unknown to Hume's society. Here it is as drawn by Hume's friend and portraitist, Allan Ramsay the younger:

[3] Cleanth Brooks and Robert Penn Warren, *Modern Rhetoric*, 3d ed. (New York, 1970), 240.

Whenever a truth is to be investigated, the understanding alone
is concerned; and therefore eloquence applies itself to the understanding only, with intention to convince. Whenever an action is to be promoted, eloquence applies itself to the two
springs of human action, the understanding and the passions,
alternately; endeavouring both to convince and persuade.[4]

Ramsay's distinction is recognizably the same as the modern
one, though he confuses things somewhat by introducing eloquence into reasoning (for Ramsay, the proper level of the
belletristic in reasoned discourse is higher even than for
Hume). A rather Ciceronian version of the distinction appears
in Hugh Blair's rhetoric: "Conviction affects the understanding only; persuasion, the will and the practice. It is the business of the philosopher to convince me of truth; it is the business of the orator to persuade me to act agreeably to it, by
engaging my affections on its side."[5] Hume was preeminently
a philosopher but, as a good Ciceronian, amidst all his philosophy he was still a benevolent and public-spirited citizen. In
arguing for the tenets of his system, Hume was acting as a
philosopher; in urging empiricism as an intellectual program
he was acting as a rhetor.

But we still have not answered the question, Why did
Hume prefer to stress the pleasures of philosophy rather than
its utility? We now come to the second stage of our answer.
Hume might have tried to arouse calm passions to which utility appeals, such as regard for self-interest or altruistic feelings. But one good reason not to stress utility is the unlikeli-
hood of satisfying people that abstruse philosophy is useful.
We have seen that Hume thought philosophy to be serviceable only in circuitous and subtle ways. As Hume's Sceptic
says, "the chief benefit, which results from philosophy, arises

---

[4] *An Essay on Ridicule* (1753), as collected in his *Investigator* (London,
1762), 10. I think that Hume refers to this essay in his letter to Ramsay of
spring 1755, *LDH* 1: 221.

[5] No. 25, *Lectures on Rhetoric and Belles Lettres*, 2 vols. (London, 1783),
2: 3; hereinafter cited as *Rhet*.

in an indirect manner, and proceeds more from its secret, insensible influence, than from its immediate application" ("Sceptic," 170). The fruits of philosophy are too distant a prospect to make a sufficiently deep impression on the practical minded. Much more promising is pleasure, which in contrast is direct and has the force of immediacy. Enticement was just better rhetorical strategy. Since there was little prospect of arousing a compelling sense in his audience of their own benefit from philosophical reform, however real that benefit would be, Hume opted for trying to excite the calm passion of curiosity.

Hume's rhetorical task, then, was to excite curiosity in his readers and thereby to inculcate in them a habit of experimental reasoning. Mill and Huxley would have preferred him to appeal to loftier passions such as dedication to truth for its own sake or to the advancement of mankind: Hume's pursuit of reform wanted the reformer's zeal. But a prime target of Hume's reform was precisely the spirit of zealotry, which he associated with fanaticism and social disruption. The indirect utility of philosophy to mankind's advancement could make only a weak appeal to what altruistic feelings readers had, and, moreover, Hume considered dedication to truth for its own sake as inefficacious in itself to inculcate scientific ways of thinking. This he makes plain in "Of Curiosity, or the Love of Truth" (THN 2. 3. 10), where may be found his reflections on the psychology of accurate and abstruse inquirers. An unsentimental examination of the psychology of accurate inquirers shows that the principal incentive to their activities is nothing more lofty than the fascination of what is difficult. That the discovery of truth in itself does not motivate inquiry is obvious from the fact that there are truths so trivial we do not care to search them out. The attractions of philosophy, Hume believed, much more resemble the pleasures of hunting and gaming than the fervors of reformation (pp. 451–52). If Hume were right, his only chance to get his readers philosophizing themselves was for them to enjoy the experience of the investigation. Hume's own books were to provide this experience.

Hume says that a sense of philosophy's utility is "requisite to fix our attention," but a very slight sense of it will suffice, fortunately since a strong sense of its utility is difficult to sustain. The "exercise of genius" (pp. 451, 449) remains the chief motivation. It is curious, then, that Adam Smith imagined that Hume reduced all values to utility. Examining the value we place upon abstruse inquiries, Smith concluded (as he mistakenly thought, against Hume) that utility was only a secondary factor. He proposed instead the sense of "propriety" satisfied in us by the justness and accuracy of superior reasoning—in other words, an aesthetic response. Utility "was but little insisted upon, till it became necessary to make some reply to the reproaches of those, who, having themselves no taste for such sublime discoveries, endeavoured to depreciate them as useless."[6] Actually Hume and Smith were substantially in agreement, as Hume must have seen.[7] Both believed that, given the facts of psychology, abstruse inquiries are an acquired taste first and a means to social good only secondarily and indirectly. Someone of this opinion would be inclined to suppose that books intended to cultivate this taste in their readers should be agreeable. The frequency with which teachers of philosophy employ Hume's writings as texts for introductory classes suggests the extent to which Hume succeeded in providing pleasant stimulation for the interested but uninitiated.

There is another reason that Hume could give for his concern to write entertainingly, though it is uncertain how willing he would be to advance it. I have maintained that Hume's intentions were two-tiered: to convince his readers that his tenets were true, and, more broadly, to persuade them to adopt an empirical way of thinking, the latter purpose neces-

[6] *The Theory of Moral Sentiments*, ed. D. D. Raphael and A. L. Macfie, Glasgow Edition of the Works and Correspondence of Adam Smith, 6 vols. in 7 (Oxford, 1976–80), 1: 189.

[7] This might be why, confining himself to substantial disagreements in his letter to Smith about the *Theory*, Hume did not mention the question of utility, though Smith had raised the issue in his book specifically as a challenge to Hume. See 28 July 1759, *LDH* 1: 312–13.

sitating an attractive presentation. But this does not mean that were he only hoping to win concurrence for his tenets he would have had no reason to write pleasingly. His psychology of belief did not allow him the luxury of writing inelegantly. According to Hume, belief consists in the liveliness with which an idea presents itself to the mind (*THN*, 1. 3. 7–8). This is what he meant when he wrote, with some exaggeration,

> 'Tis not solely in poetry and music, we must follow our taste and sentiment, but likewise in philosophy. When I am convinc'd of any principle, 'tis only an idea, which strikes more strongly upon me. When I give the preference to one set of arguments above another, I do nothing but decide from my feeling concerning the superiority of their influence.          (§ 8 [103])

Readers who believe in the veridicalness of Hume's tenets simply are conceiving them in a livelier way than readers who do not believe them. The most philosophically respectable means for Hume to make his tenets livelier would be, of course, to present cogent arguments for them, but there remains a serious problem. Simple, cogent arguments have great force, but insofar as arguments increase in subtlety and complexity they become more difficult to grasp and appear in a less lively manner. However cogent once grasped, abstruse arguments are inherently hard to believe. We feel that they are tenuous, wiredrawn. Hume held that

> the conviction, which arises from a subtile reasoning, diminishes in proportion to the efforts, which the imagination makes to enter into the reasoning, and to conceive it in all its parts. Belief, being a lively conception, can never be entire, where it is not founded on something natural and easy.    (1. 4. 2 [186])

Hume would have to make his abstruse inquiries as natural and easy as he could. Beyond this, there are other ways of making ideas livelier, one being to express them in a lively style. Such is the theoretical background to Hume's left-handed praise of Voltaire's style: "He has the Art of couching his Determinations in such lively Terms, that they often carry

Conviction, as much as if they were supported by the strongest Arguments."[8] Included in this kind of liveliness would be
the various classical critical notions, like Aristotle's and Quin-
tilian's, of stylistic force, or energy.[9] The greatest achievement, and Hume's goal, would be to combine the strongest
arguments with the art of couching them in lively terms,
thereby compensating somewhat for the reader's natural resistance to abstruse reasoning.

### THE SMALL DECENCIES OF PRESENTATION

Given his rhetorical purposes, then, Hume was in a measure
committed by his epistemology and psychology of action to
treating his readers as an audience to be entertained. Doubtless he did not reach his conclusions about the psychology of
inquiry and belief first and then consciously adopt an appro-
priately belletristic manner in adjustment. More likely his
conclusions and his personal tastes were mutually reinforcing
in steering him toward belletrism. We have Hume's own testimony that the origin of his own philosophizing was the pursuit of pleasure (*THN* 1. 4. 7 [271]). Someone of Hume's
tastes, inspecting himself and generalizing from that data concerning the psychology of inquirers, *would* come to those conclusions. Those conclusions in turn would support, or seem to
support, his authorial instincts.

It should be noted that this commitment was as applicable
to the composition of the *Treatise* as to the later works in
which it is generally supposed that Hume deviated from philosophy into· literature. His attentions to his literary manner
were not born of the public failure of his first book; the effect
on him of that failure was only to intensify the efforts in that
direction that he had made from the beginning. The *Abstract*
was an advertisement as well as an aid to study for the *Treatise*, and so the terms in which Hume advertised the *Treatise*
in it are instructive as to how he viewed the work and its pro-

---

[8] 24 Oct. 1754, *LDH* 1: 208.
[9] See Hagstrum, *Samuel Johnson's Literary Criticism*, 50–51, 187 n. 25.

spective audience. Clearly he viewed the *Treatise* as having some potential for popular appeal. Writing anonymously, he informed readers that the *Treatise* belonged to the "vogue" for empiricism that had prevailed of late years (that is, roughly since Locke's lionization). Works of the "new kind of philosophy," he told them, promise much to both "the entertainment and advantage of mankind" (p. 645). In other words, the work had been designed so as to please and instruct. Soon after its appearance Hume concluded that he had failed in this design and came to view the work with some distaste. We need not agree with him; but whether or not the work has succeeded with posterity, it did not with Hume's contemporaries.

Against this eventuality, as he informed Lord Kames, Hume had taken the precaution of publishing the *Treatise* anonymously.[10] Anonymous authorship is as uncommon today as it was common then, and we no longer view it in the same light as Hume. It was often used as a way of disclaiming responsibility for what one had published, a practice not thought blameworthy provided that it was not made a screen for slander. Rather, it was considered a legitimate means by which an author could exempt himself from personal criticism for a failure at inditing. After the *Treatise* Hume continued thus to exempt himself until he had achieved a popular success.[11]

This attitude toward anonymous authorship explains Hume's annoyance at those of his critics who cited the *Treatise* when attacking him, something that to us seems perfectly unexceptionable. His objections to this practice appear in the advertisement that he sent to Strahan for prefixing to the two *Enquiries* and the dissertation "Of the Passions." Here he

---

[10] 13 Feb. 1739, *NLDH*, 4.

[11] Hume published anonymously the *Treatise*, the *Abstract* (London, 1740), the *Letter from a Gentleman to His Friend in Edinburgh* (Edinburgh, 1745), and the first two editions of *Essays, Moral and Political* (Edinburgh, 1741, 1742). In the first edition of the *Philosophical Essays* the writer is identified only as the "Author of the *Essays Moral and Political*," but by then this was enough to give away the secret. Thereafter, as far as we know, Hume published anonymously only politically partisan writings and literary reviews.

makes explicit the disclaimer of the *Treatise* that, in his opinion, his anonymity and his omission to own the work for thirty-five years should have made unnecessary:

> Yet several writers, who have honoured the Author's Philosophy with answers, have taken care to direct all their batteries against that juvenile work, which the Author never acknowledged, and have affected to triumph in any advantages, which, they imagined, they had obtained over it: A practice very contrary to all rules of candour and fair-dealing, and a strong instance of those polemical artifices, which a bigotted zeal thinks itself authorised to employ. (*Wks.* 4: 5)[12]

From a modern point of view this complaint seems unreasonable and petulant. Hume's Victorian editor, Thomas Hugh Grose, called the advertisement "the posthumous utterance of a splenetic invalid."[13] Strahan, who promptly inserted the advertisement into unsold copies of the 1772 edition of *Essays and Treatises*, called the utterance "a very proper one."[14] The author and his printer were judging proprieties according to rules of candor and fairness no longer acknowledged or even remembered by Grose's time, rules that allowed certain privileges to anonymity. Addison had given the rationale for these privileges:

> It has been proposed, *to oblige every Person that writes a Book, or a Paper, to swear himself the Author of it, and enter down in a Publick Register his Name and Place of Abode.*
> This, indeed, would have effectually suppressed all printed Scandal, which generally appears under borrowed Names, or under none at all. But it is to be feared, that such an Expedient would not only destroy Scandal, but Learning. It would operate promiscuously, and root up the Corn and Tares, together. . . .
> There are few Works of Genius that come out at first with the Author's Name. The Writer generally makes a Tryal of them in

---

[12] Hume has in mind Thomas Reid and "that bigotted silly Fellow," James Beattie (see 26 Oct. 1775, *LDH* 2: 301).

[13] "History of the Editions," *Wks.* 3: 39 n.

[14] 30 Oct. 1775, quoted in *LDH* 2: 304 n. 1.

the World before he owns them; and, I believe, very few, who are capable of Writing, would set Pen to Paper, if they knew, before Hand, that they must not publish their Productions but on such Conditions.[15]

The privilege of surrendering a work to oblivion, leaving one's reputation untouched by its failure, was thought a valuable encouragement to aspiring writers. Thus protected, they could indite unintimidated by the prospect of living down for the rest of their lives a public humiliation. Anonymous writers also were freer to experiment, to take risks of looking foolish. In the *Treatise* Hume took full advantage of this freedom of extravagance, with the result, as we shall see, that the work pleased neither its first readers nor, in hindsight, its author.

Before discussing the nature of what Hume took to be the failings of the *Treatise*, it would be best to sharpen our idea of what he had wished to achieve rhetorically. First, we should not be misled by the statement quoted above that in philosophy, as in poetry and music, we must follow taste and sentiment. Hume was not an irrationalist. Those literary qualities that tend to lead the mind into mistaking fancy for reason were in his view improper for philosophy. For example, the scholastic enormities of postulating faculties and occult qualities Hume attributed to the pathetic fallacy:

> There is a very remarkable inclination in human nature, to be-stow on external objects the same emotions, which it observes in itself; and to find every where those ideas, which are most present to it. This inclination, 'tis true, is suppress'd by a little reflection, and only takes place in children, poets, and the an-tient philosophers. It appears in children, by their desire of beating the stones, which hurt them: In poets, by their readi-ness to personify every thing: And in the antient philosophers, by these fictions of sympathy and antipathy. We must pardon children, because of their age; poets, because they profess to follow implicitly the suggestions of their fancy: But what excuse shall we find to justify our philosophers in so signal a weakness?
>
> (*THN* 1. 4. 3 [224–25])

---

[15] No. 451, *Spectator* 4: 86–87.

If the poet appeals to the child in us, the philosopher is to appeal to the adult. The literary qualities that are consistent with unadulterate philosophy do not tempt us into anthropomorphism. Applying Hume's philosophy of the passions, we must take it that only such qualities could be acceptable as were likely to arouse calm passions like curiosity. Calm passions pertain to feelings like "the sense of beauty and deformity in action, composition, and external objects" (2. 1. 1 [276]), to the milder emotions of aesthetic response. Certainly the feelings that he would wish to arouse would be calm and free of distortions of vision. These calm passions are so subtle that we confuse them with reason (2. 3. 3 [417]). They not only are compatible with reason, but reason actually depends upon their motivating power. They can serve to get the reader's attention, arouse his interest, involve and keep him avid in the hunt. This low but steady level of intensity is fit to keep the reader intent on protracted reasonings. As the object of eloquence, on the other hand, is to arouse the violent passions, it had no place in philosophical writings: "Eloquence, when at its highest pitch, leaves little room for reason or reflection; but addressing itself entirely to the fancy or the affections, captivates the willing hearers, and subdues their understanding" (*EHU* x. 2 [96]). But genteel entertainment added to abstract argument does leave room for reflection, and in fact can incite us to it.

Such was the finely gauged visceral effect that Hume sought. It would be possible to speculate in some detail concerning the style that he hoped would achieve that effect, into matters of figurative language, syntax, diction, and so on; but we will not here go into stylistic minutiae. Suffice it to say that foremost, and obviously, Hume would require of himself perspicuity, "a quality," Blair admonishes, "so essential in every kind of writing, that, for the want of it, nothing can atone."[16] Against this may be set the hyperromantic attitude of Blake, who felt that what "can be made Explicit to an Idiot" was not worth his care.[17] In this context an idiot was anyone lacking a

[16] No. 10, *Rhet.* 1: 185.
[17] Letter of 23 Aug. 1779, *William Blake's Writings*, ed. G. E. Bentley, 2

vision of Eternity, and possibly also any seer whose vision did
not square with Blake's. This attitude plainly brings all constructive discussion to a halt by precluding criticism: " 'Tis
impossible to refute a system, which has never yet been explain'd. In such a manner of fighting in the dark, a man loses
his blows in the air, and often places them where the enemy
is not present" (*THN* 3. 1. 1 [464]). The debates of the republic of letters should not be carried out as though on a dark-
ling plain where ignorant armies clash by night. Hume would
diagnose Blake's attitude as a symptom of the communicable
distemper enthusiasm and would seek to discredit it. He
would press Blake for elucidation and when denied would
pronounce that a "man who hides himself, confesses as evidently the superiority of his enemy, as another, who fairly delivers his arms" (1. 2. 4 [44]).

Hume's attitude shows less tolerance for obscurity than
might be expected from an abstruse inquirer, but this intolerance was the result, once again, of taste and epistemology
in mutual reinforcement. And it was not a mere idiosyncrasy
of Hume's. This reciprocity in taste and epistemology is evident in Blair's adamance about perspicuity:

> Authors sometimes plead the difficulty of their subject, as an
> excuse for the want of Perspicuity. But the excuse can rarely, if
> ever, be sustained. For whatever a man conceives clearly, that,
> it is in his power, if he will be at the trouble, to put into distinct
> propositions, or to express clearly to others: and upon no subject
> ought any man to write, where he cannot think clearly. His
> ideas, indeed, may, very excusably, be on some subjects incom-
> plete or inadequate; but still, as far as they go, they ought to be
> clear; and, wherever this is the case, Perspicuity, in expressing
> them, is always attainable. The obscurity which reigns so much
> among many metaphysical writers, is, for the most part, owing
> to the indistinctness of their own conceptions. They see the ob-

---

vols. (Oxford, 1978), 2: 1526. Bertrand Russell contrasts Hume and Blake in
the eponymous essay of *Mysticism and Logic, and Other Essays* (London,
1917), 1.

ject but in a confused light; and, of course, can never exhibit it in a clear one to others.[18]

Blair's insistence here on clear and distinct ideas evinces the influence of notions about language that came to British writers and readers from Descartes and the Cartesian Port-Royal *Logique* (1662) by way of Locke.[19] The injunction is typical of critics living in "an Age," as Locke described it, "that is not much disposed to admire, or suffer themselves to be deceived, by . . . unintelligible ways of speaking."[20] Its epistemological support is Lockean and is familiar to all students of the age as a pervasive influence on the intellectual life of the time. Epistemologies do not normally enjoy a popular vogue. That Locke's did can be attributed to its fulfilling a popular yearning for the definite and publicly verifiable.

An elaboration on this combination of taste and epistemology might run as follows. Possible knowledge is derived ultimately from our original ideas (impressions, Hume would say) and is for that reason determinate. Anyone who will bother to inspect his ideas and trace them to their original appearances in the mind will have clear and distinct thoughts to express. Jonathan Bennett's useful term for this tenet is "meaning-empiricism," reflecting the conviction of Locke, Berkeley, and Hume that meaning can be determined by demanding the birth certification in experience of an idea.[21] Here is one statement from the *Treatise* of the meaning-empiricist thesis:

[18] No. 10, *Rhet.* 1: 185–86.
[19] See Peter Jones, *Hume's Sentiments: Their Ciceronian and French Context* (Edinburgh, 1982), 143–48.
[20] *Essay* 2. 23, § 21.
[21] *Locke, Berkeley, Hume: Central Themes* (Oxford, 1971), *passim*. The passage concerning the birth certificate of an idea is on p. 300. Páll Árdal has shown that Bennett's account of Hume's meaning-empiricism needs qualification (see "Convention and Value," *David Hume: Bicentenary Papers*, ed. G. P. Morice [Edinburgh, 1977], 51–68). Bennett and others believe that Hume equates the meaning of a word with its original impression as an image in the mind. Árdal holds that for Hume the meaning of a word is not identical with an impressed image, but derived from it. The meaning of words like "negotiation" cannot be reduced to images, but to assure ourselves that they have bases in experience we can trace them to impressions that originally

> 'Tis impossible to reason justly, without understanding perfectly
> the idea concerning which we reason; and 'tis impossible per-
> fectly to understand any idea, without tracing it up to its origin,
> and examining that primary impression, from which it arises.
> The examination of the impression bestows a clearness on the
> idea; and the examination of the idea bestows a like clearness on
> all our reasoning.                              (1. 3. 2 [74–75])

Hume spoke of his version of this procedure as "a new microscope or species of optics" (*EHU* vii. 1 [52]). By likening it to
an invention he was far from saying that no one had ever before had a firm grasp of his ideas; he meant simply that the
new kind of philosophy had been the first to recognize and
formulate what intelligent people had always done more or
less well. It was not an esotericism of the schools and was
available to everyone who would discipline himself; it is,
Hume would say, nothing more than common sense "methodized and corrected" (*EHU* xii. 3 [133]).

Perspicuous writing accordingly becomes a matter of keeping words and their denotations firmly wedded to their origins
in the mind. Divorce yields confusion. Locke wrote that "so
far as Words are of Use and Signification, so far is there a constant connexion between the Sound and the *Idea*; and a Designation, that the one stand for the other: without which Application of them, they are nothing but so much insignificant
Noise."[22] Such is the reasoning behind Hume's disparagement
of the "scholastic way of talking, rather than thinking" (*THN*
1. 4. 5 [243]) and his statement in a letter to Joseph Spence
that " '[t]is certain we always think in some language, viz. in
that which is most familiar to us; and 'tis but too frequent to

---

taught us their meanings. Or if memory fails we can at least reasonably suppose some such experience to have been had. This being a more accurate
interpretation of Hume, his meaning-empiricism becomes only a guiding
principle, or rule of procedure (Noxon, *Hume's Philosophical Development*,
48). It will be convenient for me to appropriate Bennett's term "meaning-
empiricism," but it should be understood that I use it in connection with
Hume as here amended.

[22] *Essay* 3. 2, § 7.

substitute words instead of ideas."[23] So long, then, as in the private world of his own mind each man has ideas roughly corresponding to those in other men's minds, as has happily been the case to date, and so long as men observe the conventions of language, mutual understanding is within reach. Averting a babel-producing divorce between words and their cognitive originals is not always easy, but it is attainable. Thus clear writing, putting proper words in proper places, is not a result of a mysterious authorial inspiration so much as of plain hard work. And an author who will not work hard does not deserve to be read.

Perhaps it will be wondered how, as Blair claimed, an idea can be incomplete or inadequate and still be clear and distinct. Hume would agree with Blair. A notorious example taken from the *Treatise* (1. 4. 6) is the following. We have clear and distinct experience of our own sensory and mental impressions, yet we have no experience to take us beyond the whirl of fleeting impressions to the spiritual substance in which they supposedly cohere. We may have very lively impressions of transient moments of consciousness, but our experience of our enduring personal identities is quite incomplete and inadequate. In other words, we have no impressions of ourselves having impressions, which would be rather like an eye seeing itself. Our idea of self is irremediably inadequate for philosophical or theological purposes.

Hume deals regularly in the *Treatise* with irremediably incomplete and inadequate ideas. As part of his program to delimit possible knowledge he repeatedly brings his reader through difficult reasonings to a halt at man's impressional limits. Few of his readers realized that this was his intention. They only knew that it was not agreeable. In coming to this halt within our impressional limits Hume was following the meaning-empirical procedure, which, according to empiricist ideology, should have led him to a clear and distinct conception and thence to a perspicuous expression of it. But even if he had achieved perspicuity, his conclusion was a negative

[23] 15 Oct. 1754, *LDH* 1: 201.

one concerning what cannot be known. Most readers were well enough pleased not to know that there were problems with their personal identities. They did not feel as though the anonymous author had led them into the light—quite the contrary. An important lesson for Hume to learn from this reaction was that meaning-empiricism was an incomplete recipe for the perspicuity that popular taste demanded. It could not, as many believed, make philosophical exactness equivalent to literary perspicuity. To believe so was wishful thinking. This is more obvious today when philosophers frequently resort to artificial, quasi-mathematical languages for an increased exactness quite incompatible with literary perspicuity. But as late as the publication of Blair's lectures it was not unusual for European and American intellectuals to believe that the disjunction between philosophical prose and literary taste was simply the result of negligent thinking and writing. Right thinking and hard work would solve the problem. Empiricism was good sense, and good sense was good taste.

Hume did not leave us much evidence in his writings concerning the importance that he placed upon perspicuity of style, but what he did write on it is to the point. He wrote to Thomas Reid that the talent of perspicuous expression, "above all others, is requisite in that species of literature which you have cultivated."[24] Doubtless this statement truly reflects his scale of literary values. It has always been for perspicuity more than anything else that Hume's style has been praised. In view of Hume's distinction as a lucid writer, then, it is odd that one of the major complaints against the *Treatise* was that it was difficult to understand. To an extent these complaints followed from readers' failure to recognize that Hume was deliberately looking for the places where our ideas can no longer be clear and distinct. Another contributing factor was that the popular Lockean theory of ideas had created unrealistic public expectations for the simplicity and clarity of philosophy. W. Somerset Maugham thought that, whatever problems might occur, a minimally educated reader should be

[24] [25 Feb. 1763,] *LDH* 1: 375.

able to understand Hume's individual sentences; and this does seem to be the level at which Hume is most lucid.[25] But this leaves the possibility of obscurity at other levels. Later we shall see that there are other reasons for these complaints, and that Hume cannot entirely escape blame for being misunderstood.

## THE DIFFICULTY OF BEING EASY

This reasoning, it must be confest, is somewhat abstruse, and difficult to be comprehended. . . .
—*THN* 1. 4. 2

I was expressing my aversion to disputes: Mr. Hume
. . . said with great surprise, "Why what do you like, if you hate both disputes and whisk?"
—Walpole, 3 Oct. 1765, *Yale Ed. Corr*. 35: 112

Hume attributed the failure of the *Treatise* with the public largely to literary weaknesses. "I had always entertained a Notion," he recorded in "My Own Life," "that my want of Success, in publishing the Treatise of human Nature, had proceeded more from the manner than the matter; and that I had been guilty of a very usual Indiscretion, in going to the Press too early."[26] Hume meant that he should have heeded Horace's advice and put the manuscript aside for some years so as to revise it with the benefit of increased maturity and objectivity; he could not have meant that he had composed the *Treatise* too hastily. To take the measure of what his disappointment must have been at the work's neglect, we should remember how long and under what a variety of circumstances he had toiled over it. He had spent his postgraduate adolescence in private study at the family estate at Ninewells or in Edinburgh, preparing himself, like the young Milton, for the great work he had projected. At about the age of eighteen began his depressions of spirit and the psychosomatic ail-

---

[25] *The Summing Up* (1938: repr. London, 1944), 21.
[26] *LDH* 1: 3.

ments resulting from his overapplication. In one letter he says
that at twenty years he began to "consider seriously" how to
proceed with the work, while in another letter he says that at
that age he planned the work. The actual composition of the
*Treatise*, therefore, can be dated as beginning in 1731. In the
next three years he "collected the rude Materials for many
Volumes," but was vexed at his inability to put them into pre-
sentable order. He sought recovery from his illnesses in the
spring of 1734 by immersing himself in the "more active Life"
of trade in Bristol. By September the young man had left
trade and gone to Rheims, where presumably his annuity
could accommodate more of his living expenses and would let
him devote himself to his writing again. The following year he
moved to La Flèche, where he could live still less expensively
and where the Jesuit college offered an excellent library. It
was here chiefly that he composed the work. At twenty-six
years of age he was in London revising the first two books for
the press. As late as March 1740 he was revising book 3 in
accordance with Hutcheson's criticism. Ignoring the years of
gestation, and dating the composition of the *Treatise* from the
time Hume planned it, one finds that the production of his
first work was the object of his labor for about nine years.[27]
He faced the public indifference, which must have been severely disappointing, with remarkable equanimity. Disappointment at the reception of his work quickly turned into
discontent with the work itself, which, he readily admitted
(speaking of himself in the third person), "on more mature
Consideration, he might have rendered . . . much less imper-
fect by further Corrections and Revisals" (*LGent.*, 33).

[27] The chronology can be pieced together by consulting the following:
Advt., *Essays and Treatises* (*Wks.* 4: v); spring 1734 and spring 1751, *LDH* 1:
12–18, 158; 2 Dec. 1737, *NLDH*, 1–3; letter of 29 Sept. 1734, in Michael
Morrisroe, "Did Hume Read Berkeley? A Conclusive Answer," *Philological
Quarterly* 52 (1973), 310–14; letter of 18 May 1735, in Mossner, "Hume at
La Flèche, 1735: An Unpublished Letter," *Texas Studies in English* 37 (1958):
30–33; letter of 26 Aug. 1737, in Tadeusz Kozanecki, "Dawida Hume'a Niez-
nane Listy W Zbiorach Muzeum Czartoryskich (Polska)," *Archiwum Historii
Filozofii I Mysli Spotecznej* 9 (1963): 133–34; and "My Own Life."

An indication of the depth of Hume's discontent is his decision not to revise the *Treatise*, but rather to forsake it and to "cast the whole anew" in the form of the two *Enquiries* and the dissertation "Of the Passions," where, he tells us, "some negligences in . . . reasoning and more in the expression, are . . . corrected."[28] One way of guessing what Hume's dissatisfactions were is to compare the original with the recastings, as we shall do in Chapter 4. Another is to compare Hume's remarks about the *Treatise* with the criticisms to be found in its reviews. Both procedures show that two of the imperfections in the *Treatise* that displeased Hume were his abstruseness and his egotism. A want of perspicuity, as has been said, was a serious offense. To be egotistical in writing was to adopt the wrong tone with the readers, a clear failure in elegance.

Of the reviews so far uncovered only one was certainly read by Hume, article 26 in *The History of the Works of the Learned* (Nov./Dec. 1739). We learn from the letter to Hutcheson of 4 March 1740 that Hume had originally intended his *Abstract* to appear in that journal but was put off by the "somewhat abusive" article.[29] Mossner believed, justly I think, that Hume would have read the reviews in French published in Dutch journals. At the least it seems unlikely that Hume would not have looked at those appearing in journals with which Pierre Desmaizeaux was connected.[30] While none of the reviews was quite deprecatory, a pattern of complaint does emerge: the *Treatise* was bewildering, and one reason was the author's ostentatious paradoxicality. Even if Hume had not read all of the reviews, this pattern of complaint provides us with a sample of the general response to the *Treatise* of the European intelligentsia, to whose judgments Hume was very sensitive.

---

[28] *Essays and Treatises* (*Wks.* 4: v).

[29] *LDH* 1: 37–38. Kemp Smith thought that the anonymous reviewer was probably Warburton (*Philosophy of David Hume*, 523 n.), but Robert M. Ryley argues to the contrary in "Did Warburton Review Hume's 'A Treatise of Human Nature'?" *Notes and Queries* 221 (1976): 354–55.

[30] "The Continental Reception of Hume's Treatise, 1739–1741," *Mind* 56 (1947): 31–43.

The lightest censure came from the reviewer for the *Nou-velle bibliothèque*, who remarks on the author's custom of rejecting the opinions generally held by philosophers.[31] Later the reviewer excuses himself from relating Hume's theory of external reality, saying that it is so involved that it would be necessary to reprint the whole section for the reader, and that "perhaps even then one would not understand a great deal of it, so singular are the anonymous author's notions and so much does he give an air of singularity to the most common ideas." At another point he suggests that Hume's explanation of solidity is less clear than that which it was intended to explain.[32] These comments are similar to those in the *Biblio-thèque britannique*:

> This is a system of logic, or rather of metaphysics, as original as can be, in which the author claims to correct the most expert philosophers, particularly the famous Mr. Locke, and in which he advances the most unheard-of paradoxes, even to holding that the operations of the soul are not free.[33]

The reviewers had no trust that Hume's paradoxes were justified by his reasonings because they could not follow those reasonings. Paradoxes in such frequency as the anonymous author served them up aroused suspicion that they derived more from the author's predilections than from the state of the subjects discussed. The reviewers saw the paradoxes in the same light as they did the supposed irreverence to Locke, as a symptom of the author's egotism.

A critic dealing with a very difficult book must judge whether the difficulty proceeds from profundity or, less innocently, ineptness, or worse, obfuscation. As we have seen, the critical presumption of the age, supported by Lockean meaning-empiricism, was against abstruse writing. Authors gener-

---

[31] Pt. 1, *Nouvelle bibliothèque, ou histoire littéraire des principaux écrits qui se publient* 6 (July 1740): 312.

[32] My translation. Pt. 2, *Nouvelle bibliothèque* 7 (Sept. 1740): 59, 61.

[33] My translation. Art. 6, *Bibliothèque britannique, ou histoire des ouvrages des sçavans de la Grand-Bretagne* 14 (Oct.–Nov.–Dec. 1739): 216.

ally were to be held accountable for their obscurity. One rebutter of the *Treatise* wrote,

> [I]ndeed, I should have taken no Notice of what he has wrote,
> if I had not thought his Book, in several Parts, so very abstruse
> and perplex'd, that, I am convinced, no Man can comprehend
> what he means; and as one of the greatest Wits of the Age has
> justly observed, this may impose upon weak Readers, and make
> them imagine, there is a great Deal of *deep Learning* in it, be-
> cause they *do not understand it*.[34]

This is a blunt accusation that Hume had thrown dust in his
readers' eyes against the likelihood that, were his positions
clearly descried, they would be scorned as preposterous.
(One might ask how an incomprehensible position can be believed, much less have a *"mischievous* Effect upon the Opinions or Morals of Mankind," as the rebutter feared.)

Along with the influence of meaning-empiricism, the Chris-
tian-humanist tradition exerted its influence over Hume's
readers, inclining them to think that those subjects which in
their nature could not be handled clearly and decisively probably should not be handled at all. This inclination is evinced
in the reviewer for the *Bibliothèque raisonnée*, who wrote
that

> [p]erhaps it will be found that in wishing to investigate the in-
> most nature of things, the anonymous writer sometimes uses a
> language a little unintelligible to his readers. Again I fear that
> his paradoxes favour Pyrrhonism and lead to consequences that
> the author appears to disown. Metaphysics has its [arrogance?]
> as well as the other sciences. When it passes certain limits, it
> obscures the objects that it searches out. Under pretence of
> yielding only to evidence, it finds difficulties in everything. Re-
> ligion itself suffers in many instances: it sometimes makes the
> first principles too recherché, too difficult, in working to dem-
> onstrate and clarify them.[35]

[34] Anon. letter, *Common Sense: or, the Englishman's Journal* 2, no. 178 (5
July 1740): 220. Perhaps the witticism alluded to was Swift's, quoted above,
chap. 1, p. 33.

[35] All except the last sentence and the conjectural reading is Mossner's

Hume's chagrin must have been deep to be lectured thus on the limits of metaphysics. To establish these limits and redirect man's inquisitiveness had been his express purpose, and yet he had failed to communicate this to the reviewer. When faced with such misunderstanding, as he frequently was, Hume tended to take a large portion of the blame on himself. "Where a man of Sense mistakes my Meaning, I own I am angry: But it is only at myself: For having exprest my Meaning so ill as to have given Occasion to the Mistake," he wrote to one detractor of the *Treatise*. He wrote to Hutcheson, "You have mistaken my Meaning in some Passages; which upon Examination I have found to proceed from some Ambiguity or Defect in my Expression." About "Of the Balance of Trade" he wrote to James Oswald, "My expression in the Essay needs correction, which has occasioned you to mistake it."[36] In these remarks Hume was not merely being gracious or patronizing; he seems always to have been genuinely glad to be alerted to defects that he could rectify in subsequent editions, even by people like David Mallet, for whom he did not much care.

Hume did not want his writings to be recherché, least of all for his manner of expression. He shared with his contemporaries the humanist suspicion of the recherché and esoteric. Modern literature tends to be highly esoteric, and the reading public today is fairly resigned to the unapproachability of the best authors. But Hume and his contemporaries saw language as a public instrument, the effectiveness of which is dependent upon everyone's respecting the conventions of usage. They did not think of convention as constricting, but rather acknowledged it as the means by which communication is made possible. If his philosophy had to be difficult, Hume wished that at least it would not be so as a result of his language.

---

translation ("Continental Reception of Hume's *Treatise*," 36). The type for the bracketed word was broken in the copy that I saw. My best guess for the word is *orgueil*. Mossner, who perhaps saw a cleaner copy, translates the word as "stumbling blocks." Art. 5, *Bibliothèque raisonnée des ouvrages des savans de l'Europe* 24, 2d pt. (Apr.–May–June 1740): 328.

[36] [Feb. 1754,] 17 Sept. 1739, 1 Nov. 1750, *LDH* 1: 187, 32, 143.

Unintelligibility might possibly be an innocent failing, but so much could not be said for egotism. The reviewer for the *Bibliothèque raisonnée* was entertained even less than he was instructed by the *Treatise*:

> What is the most offensive is the confidence with which he delivers his paradoxes. Never has there been a Pyrrhonian more dogmatic. . . . The author is on all this as positive as can be. The Lockes and the Clarkes are often, to his eyes, but paltry and superficial reasoners in comparison with himself; and, if it be permitted to speak his language here, it is easy to see that habit and custom have already so framed him to believe that he believes nothing except in a very lively manner.[37]

An accusation of dogmatic Pyrrhonism is tantamount to an accusation of hypocrisy. Hume shows himself in the *Treatise* to be aware that perhaps he had presented his opinions immodestly, and attempts to mollify any readers who might be annoyed. He confesses to having used such immoderate expressions as

> 'tis evident, 'tis certain, 'tis undeniable; which a due deference to the public ought, perhaps, to prevent. I may have fallen into this fault after the example of others; but I here enter a *caveat* against any objections, which may be offer'd on that head; and declare that such expressions were extorted from me by the present view of the object, and imply no dogmatical spirit, nor conceited idea of my own judgment, which are sentiments that I am sensible can become no body, and a sceptic still less than any other.                          (1. 4. 7 [274])

One can see why this caveat did not pacify the reviewers. Experience teaches us that what men claim they or their intentions are is untrustworthy and that a more reliable measure of character is their behavior. If in print Hume had behaved dogmatically and conceitedly, no mere disavowal such as the above could change the reviewers' minds.

Public displays of egotism fairly invite puncturing by the

---

[37] Mossner's translation, 37. *Bibliothèque raisonnée*, 353–54.

first wit who happens along, and this is what happened to the anonymous author at the hands of the writer of the "abusive" article for the *History of the Works of the Learned.* It is true, as Kemp Smith said, that the reviewer was not only unequal to the task of criticizing the *Treatise,* but also was fatuously unaware of his inadequacy;[38] it is also true that his raillery is of no mean quality and makes his review the most entertaining of the lot. Most of his raillery is too closely connected to passages of the *Treatise* to be susceptible of quotation, but the substance of his dissatisfaction with the work is the same as the other reviewers'. He complains of "innumerable" inscrutabilities. He objects to the egotism of the author's references to himself, which could not have been more frequent "if he had written his own Memoirs."[39] No less frequent are the paradoxes, of which he counts enough in book 1, part 4, section 5 to "stagger any Man who has not a strong Head-piece." He rallies Hume for his combativeness: "Our admirable Author must expect to be nibbled at, as all great Genius's have been, by a . . . Parcel of stupid Impertinents." Equally risible is the author's conceit: "Let these Simpletons talk thus if they please, our Author despises their Attacks as he ought."[40]

Hume could not have despised the criticisms of his reviewers since his own opinion of his first work came to be remarkably consistent with theirs. Even before book 3 was published Hume was beginning to think that he had allowed himself to get carried away. He wrote to Kames, "My Fondness for what I imagin'd new Discoveries made me overlook all common Rules of Prudence; & having enjoy'd the usual Satisfaction of Projectors, tis but just I shou'd meet with their Dissappointments."[41] He felt that he had appeared before the world too

[38] Smith, *Philosophy of David Hume,* 522.

[39] Art. 26, *History of the Works of the Learned,* 362 n., 357 n. Cf. no. 562, *Spectator* 4: 519–20: "The Gentlemen of *Port-Royal* . . . banished the way of speaking in the First Person out of all their Works, as arising from Vain-Glory and Self-Conceit. To shew their particular Aversion to it, they branded this Form of Writing with the Name of an *Egotism.*"

[40] *History of the Works,* 393, 380–81.

[41] 4 June 1734, *NLDH,* 5.

early and shown himself to be a brash youth. But for the cover of his imperfectly kept anonymity, he would have been personally exposed to all Europe. In the political and literary world of Georgian Britain, to call oneself a projector would suggest two things. First, projectors were promoters of or spectators in "bubble" stocks. In this context Hume's remark indicates that the investment in the *Treatise* of his time and effort, and his high expectations of renown from it, were foolish. Second, projectors were speculators, like the Projectors of Lagado, whose misconceived innovations were sterile. Both kinds of projector, in the Scriblerian view of society, were pernicious and ridiculous.[42] Years later Hume disowned the *Treatise*, seriously regretting that he had published the work at all. It was, he said,

> a Book, which pretended to innovate in all the sublimest Parts of Philosophy, & which I compos'd before I was five and twenty. Above all, the positive Air, which prevails in that Book, & which may be imputed to the Ardor of Youth, so much displeases me, that I have not Patience to review it.

He goes on to wish that he had always confined himself "to the more easy Parts of Erudition."[43] The work did innovate in all the sublimest parts of philosophy and Hume must have known it. His distaste for the work was not preponderantly for having failed to deliver on this claim, but for having put himself forward as an innovator in a society in which innovation was unwelcome.

If with his caveat Hume had acknowledged in the *Treatise* that perhaps he had been a bit forward, he acknowledged even more readily that he had been abstruse. He had anticipated the complaints of abstruseness, as he had those of ego-

---

[42] Cf. " 'Tis enough that I submit to the ridicule sometimes, in this age, attached to the character of a philosopher, without adding to it that which belongs to a projector" and "Of all mankind there are none so pernicious as political projectors, if they have power; nor so ridiculous, if they want it . . ." ("M," 632; "IPComm.," 647).

[43] [Feb. 1754,] *LDH* 1: 187. Hume's memory failed him when he said that he had completed the *Treatise* when he was twenty-five.

tism, and tried to prepare the readers of the *Treatise* for the unavoidable difficulties ahead:

> For if truth be at all within the reach of human capacity, 'tis certain it must lie very deep and abstruse; and to hope we shall arrive at it without pains, while the greatest geniuses have failed with the utmost pains, must certainly be esteemed sufficiently vain and presumptuous. I pretend to no such advantage in the philosophy I am going to unfold, and would esteem it a strong presumption against it, were it so very easy and obvious.
> (Introd., xiv–xv)

In the end—there is just no getting around it—abstruse inquiries will be abstruse; and this being no less so for the *Philosophical Essays*, in which Hume was more determined to be popular, he there repeated the same caveat:

> What though these reasonings concerning human nature seem abstract, and of difficult comprehension? This affords no presumption of their falsehood. On the contrary, it seems impossible, that what has hitherto escaped so many wise and profound philosophers can be very obvious and easy. (*EHU* i [12])

It might seem odd for a philosopher to state so emphatically what is obvious to us, that what is abstract and difficult is not necessarily false and that the truth is deep. But to Hume's prospective audience this was not obvious at all. Mindful of their prejudices, and also of the natural tendency of our conviction to decrease proportionately as the subtlety of supporting argument increases, Hume warned his readers to keep reason sovereign: "Just reasoning ought still, perhaps, to retain its force, however subtle; in the same manner as matter preserves its solidity in the air, and fire, and animal spirits, as well as in the grosser and more sensible forms." He acknowledged the readers' presumption in favor of common sense:

> I am sensible how abstruse all this reasoning must appear to the generality of readers, who not being accustom'd to such profound reflections on the intellectual faculties of the mind, will be apt to reject as chimerical whatever strikes not in with the

common receiv'd notions, and with the easiest and most obvious
principles of philosophy.          (*THN* 1. 3. 12 [135, 138–39])

Sometimes he nearly apologizes for having indulged in intricacies and abstractions; at other times he gives fair warning
that he is about to "take the matter pretty deep" (1. 2. 5 [55],
3. 3. 1 [575]), as though to allow the reader opportunity to
gird up his loins. In reaction to the complaints that books 1
and 2 were too difficult, Hume prefixed to book 3 a reassur-
ance: "*I am hopeful it may be understood by ordinary readers, with as little attention as is usually given to any books of
reasoning*" (advt.). Yet he was not confident of holding that
requisite attention. He expresses reservations about venturing "upon a third volume of such abstruse philosophy, in an
age, wherein the greatest part of men seem agreed to convert
reading into an amusement, and to reject every thing that requires any considerable degree of attention to be comprehended" (3. 1. 1 [456]).

The charge that Hume obfuscated so as to hide his inade-
quacies has not been credited by serious readers for a long
time. If nothing else does, his attempts to prepare his readers
for abstruseness plainly show that he was deeply concerned
from the start with the problem of making his rather intrac-
table material "*intelligible to ordinary capacities*" (*Abs.*, 643).
But the level of abstraction at which he worked left little room
for simplification. An abstraction is in its nature difficult to
communicate to someone to whom it is new. "General reasonings seem intricate, merely because they are general," Hume
wrote; "nor is it easy for the bulk of mankind to distinguish,
in a great number of particulars, that common circumstance
in which they all agree, or to extract it, pure and unmixed,
from the other superfluous circumstances" ("Comm.," 254).
Some possible tactics are to restate a concept or argument
several times, or to elaborate upon or illustrate it, so as to
familiarize the reader with it and reduce its strangeness for
him. A disadvantage of these tactics is the danger of being
tedious and, in getting involved in intricacies, of losing the
reader anyway. Adequate explanation leads toward prolixity,

but prolixity is itself likely to hamper understanding. Hume felt both the necessities to be copious and to be brief. He excused himself to Kames from summarizing the *Treatise*, saying, "[M]y Opinions are so new, & even some Terms I am oblig'd to make Use of, that I cou'd not propose by any Abridgement to give my System an Air of Likelyhood, or so much as make it intelligible."[44] But when the first two books of the *Treatise* were *"complained of as obscure and difficult to be comprehended,"* Hume did write an abstract, which was necessary, he said, because

> *those who are not accustomed to abstract reasoning, are apt to lose the thread of argument, where it is drawn out to a great length, and each part fortified with all the arguments, guarded against all the objections, and illustrated with all the views, which occur to a writer in the diligent survey of his subject.*
>
> (*Abs.*, 643)

One conclusion that he drew from the reception of the *Treatise* was that it is better to err on the side of brevity than of prolixity. Thenceforth his philosophical ideas appeared only in short works. In the *Treatise*, though, he paid the public the compliment of thinking them up to its length and complexity. The result was a work that Hazlitt affectionately described as "that completest of all metaphysical *choke-pears*, . . . to which the *Essays*, in point of scholastic subtlety and close reasoning, are mere elegant trifling, light-summer-reading."[45]


## OBSCURITIES OF PLAN

Together with the danger of being tedious and too involved for those unaccustomed to abstract reasoning, a work like the *Treatise* presents its writer with a problem of ordonnance. We know that in the early years of composition Hume had produced the basic materials for many volumes, and well he

---

[44] 2 Dec. 1737, *NLDH*, 1.
[45] "My First Acquaintance with Poets," in *The Complete Works of William Hazlitt*, ed. P. P. Howe, 21 vols. (London, 1933–34), 17: 113.

might on a topic so broad as that of human nature. Finding a good way to organize these materials would not have been easy. John Hill Burton's opinion was that Hume had in fact failed to put his thoughts into order for his reader. The scope of Hume's topic, he said, was left too vague to admit of a satisfactory plan.

> The author, therefore, very discreetly allowed his matter to be arranged as the subjects of which he treated had respectively suggested themselves, and bestowed on his work a title rather general than comprehensive,—a title, of which all that can be said of its aptness to the subject is, that no part of his book can be said to be wholly without it, while he might have included an almost incalculable multitude of other subjects within it.[46]

It is an exaggeration to say that the *Treatise* is without a logical arrangement, but it is true to say that the work is open-ended. Actually its title and scope are rather comprehensive than general. Virtually anything *might* be included in a discussion of human nature as Hume thought of it, even those subjects like physics that are not conventionally numbered among the humanities; for the science of man, in one meaning that Hume gave it in his introduction, is the base upon which all other sciences are erected. It sets the rules by which any knowledge whatsoever may be accepted as authentic; it is an epistemology centered in man's sentience and percipience, allowing no knowledge that is not humanly conditioned.[47] Hume more moderately said only that "almost all the sciences are comprehended in the science of human nature" (*Abs.*, 646), but it is hard to see which could be exempt. Geological, astronomical, and meteorological knowledge cannot be ex-

---

[46] *Life and Correspondence of David Hume*, 2 vols. (Edinburgh, 1846), 1: 66–67.

[47] Noxon points out that Hume uses the term "science of man" variously to mean (1) all of the four moral sciences (logic, morals, criticism, and politics) when conducted empirically, and (2) the epistemological foundations of all sciences (logic). It is with the latter meaning that we are here concerned (Noxon, *Hume's Philosophical Development*, 1–8). My discussion of the organization of the *Treatise* owes much to Noxon.

cepted, being as much as any other knowledge shaped by the nature of the human mind. Hume himself hints that, though he had not chosen to give mathematics, natural philosophy, and natural religion their own books in the *Treatise*, he might have done so (*THN*, xv). This anthropocentrism is why Hume has been said to have in a sense conducted an anti-Copernican counterrevolution: whereas Copernicus had removed man from the center of the cosmos, Hume was returning him to that position.[48] The very "cement of the universe," the association of ideas, is provided by the human mind (*Abs.*, 662). All the universe, therefore, could conceivably find a place in a work setting forth the science of man.

On the other hand, Hume did have some notion of where he wished to go in his work and where he wished to stop. His original plan was to cover the following agenda, and probably in this order: logic, morals, criticism, and politics (see *THN*, xv–xvi). He only got as far as morals. Having completed books 1 and 2, he tells us, he considered that he had "finished what regards logic, and [had] laid the foundation of the other parts in his account of the passions" (*Abs.*, 646). Clearly, book 1 was his "logic," which, together with his theory of the passions in book 2, allowed him to proceed in his "morals" in book 3. This book likewise would lay the foundation of his "criticism" and "politics." But by the time Hume could turn to aesthetics and political science he had abandoned the form of the treatise by installment. These topics, at least in part, are to be found instead in his essays. In criticizing the form of the *Treatise*, we should in fairness remember that we have only an incomplete

---

[48] "Hume, David," *A Dictionary of Philosophy*, ed. Antony Flew et al. (London, 1979). But Hume had much more in common with Copernicus than he did not. He did not place man at the center of the cosmos in the sense of claiming that the cosmos exists for man's benefit: he was just saying that all knowledge of the cosmos is shaped by human nature. Human nature is ultimately a part of general nature, which is just another name for the cosmos. The cosmos is not limited to man's capacity to know it (see Wright, *Sceptical Realism*, 125 and *passim*). The thrust of Hume's scepticism is that there are more things in heaven and earth than can possibly be dreamt of in philosophy.

work from which to judge, perhaps only half of what Hume had projected.

It might be that no grand architecture would reveal itself if we could view the work in its completed state. Still, a logical order is discernible even in its unfinished state, an order implied in Hume's statement about laying foundations for the installments to come. In his advertisement to book 3 he did claim some independence for that book from books 1 and 2, but his ulterior purpose there plainly was to disengage the two installments in the public's mind so that the earlier would not put off readers from the later. ("Of the Understanding" and "Of the Passions" comprise one installment, having been issued together in January 1739. The second installment, "Of Morals," followed in October 1740.) Each book in fact depends upon its predecessor, so it is to be surmised that this dependence would have extended to those books that never materialized. As has been said, epistemology, or "logic," precedes everything else, establishing the terms in which other sciences could proceed. Then comes the "passions." Curiously, Hume did not mention the passions in his list of subjects to cover. Why he neglected to do so we may never know, but why it belongs where he placed it is not mysterious. Its purpose, with the "logic," was to lay the foundation for the other subjects. Its place in the foundation appears when we remember how Hume's psychology of action denies reason the rule of man's behavior—moral, critical, political, or otherwise. Only passions motivate action, though reason can have a salutary effect on the passions. The importance in human nature of passion relative to reason being one of Hume's major themes, reason and passion would deserve equal weight in his foundation. Since behavior is indirectly affected by reason and directly incited by passion, the first step toward a scientific study of moral, aesthetic, and political behavior would have to be the author's own systems of epistemology and psychology. Books 1 and 2 are a coordinated unit and *"make a compleat chain of reasoning by themselves"* (advt. to 1 and 2, *THN*, xii). And then since Hume wished to show that morality was "more properly felt than judg'd of" (3. 1. 2 [470]), morals would follow the passions in the order of discussion. It is evidence of Hume's having carefully decided upon this sequence that he took steps to return to it in the 1758 edition of *Essays and Treatises on Several Subjects*. Clearly he gave some thought to the disposition of his works in this collection, changing the title of the *Philosophical Essays* to *An Enquiry concerning Human Understanding* to make it correspond to *An Enquiry concerning the Principles of Morals*. Between these two he placed "Of the Passions," taken from the *Four Dissertations* published the year before. Though the *Treatise* itself is not included in this collection, its ordering of subjects into logic, passions, and morals is duplicated.

It is not easy to speculate why the last three subjects should have followed their assigned order since we can only guess from the essays what the contents of the criticism and politics would have been. Morals would have to precede politics since Hume's account in book 3 of justice as an "artificial virtue" would serve as his initial step toward reducing politics to a science. But why should criticism precede politics? Perhaps Hume wished criticism to follow morals so as to underscore his claim that morality and beauty are aspects of the same psychological phenomenon, both stemming from feeling rather than abstract fitnesses of things. Morality, Hume urged against rationalists, could no more be deduced logically than the success of a work of art: however calculation might allow us to refine upon morality and beauty, ultimately that calculation can only succeed when directed toward appealing to men's feelings. So closely are morality and aesthetics related for Hume, Mackie points out, we are justified in using his critical essays to throw light on his moral theory.[49]

Although in its entirety the *Treatise* can be defended as being a "mighty maze! but not without a plan," this leaves plenty of room within each book for the bewildering disorder complained of. The public bewilderment, at any rate, is an undeniable historical fact. If the parts and sections of the *Treatise* are structured with too much subtlety for ordinary capacities,

<hr>

[49] Mackie, *Hume's Moral Theory*, 65.

then it must be allowed that this structure did not well serve its author, whose first priority, after all, was to be perspicuous. Some such structure, however, is to be found there, and Adam Smith provides a critical model that roughly describes it. In his twenty-fourth lecture on rhetoric and belles-lettres Smith contrasted two methods of exposition. First, "in Natural Philosophy, or any other science of that sort, we may . . . , like Aristotle, go over the different branches in the order they happen to [be] cast up to us, giving a principle, commonly a new one, for every phenomenon." This sounds like the method, or lack of one, that Burton thought Hume followed, in which the writer supposedly took up his subjects in whatever order they suggested themselves. The second method that Smith described follows a model more attractive to Enlightenment tastes:

> [O]r, in the manner of Sir Isaac Newton, we may lay down certain principles, primary or proved, in the beginning, from whence we account for the several phenomena, connecting all together by the same chain. This latter, which we may call the Newtonian method, is undoubtedly the most philosophical, and in every science, whether of Morals or Natural Philosophy, etc., is vastly more ingenious, and for that reason more engaging, than the other. It gives us a pleasure to see the phenomena which we reckoned the most unaccountable, all deduced from some principle (commonly, a well-known one) and all united in one chain, far superior to what we feel from the unconnected method, where everything is accounted for by itself, without any reference to the others.[50]

Undoubtedly Smith was thinking of how Newton had explained the movements of the tides and the celestial bodies

[50] 24 Jan. 1763, *Lectures on Rhetoric and Belles Lettres*, ed. John M. Lothian (Edinburgh, 1963), 139–40; hereinafter cited as *Lect*. This method could be Cartesian if the principles employed are arrived at rationalistically. Smith prefers empiricism. See R. H. Campbell and A. S. Skinner, eds., *An Inquiry into the Nature and Cause of the Wealth of Nations*, 2 vols., Glasgow Ed. 2 (Oxford, 1976), 1: 3; D. D. Raphael and A. L. Macfie, eds., *Theory*, 22.

with his law of gravitational attraction. It is a measure of the impression that Newton made upon the Scottish Enlightenment that Smith describes the principle of gravitation as pleasing: Newton's influence had penetrated even into aesthetics. Equally struck with the beauty of Newton's principle, Hutcheson made it an example of his own aesthetic principle of uniformity amidst variety.[51] Such a method of exposition as Smith called Newtonian would recommend itself equally to Hume as a way to present abstruse material attractively. The scholastic practice of contriving new principles for every phenomenon he considered jejune. Such a practice merely generates new jargon that explains nothing, empty words divorced from clear and distinct ideas:

> To invent without scruple a new principle to every new phaenomenon, instead of adapting it to the old; to overload our hypotheses with a variety of this kind; are certain proofs, that none of these principles is the just one, and that we only desire, by a number of falsehoods, to cover our ignorance of the truth.
> 
> (*THN* 2. 1. 3 [282])

Instead, philosophers should "endeavor to render all [their] principles as universal as possible, by tracing up [their] experiments to the utmost, and explaining all effects from the simplest and fewest causes" (*THN*, xvii). In the *Abstract* he repeated this statement of his procedure: "If, in examining several phaenomena, we find they resolve themselves into one common principle, and can trace this principle into another, we shall at last arrive at those few simple principles, on which all the rest depend" (p. 646). But it hardly needs substantiation here that Hume was following a program inspired by Newton's example. This thesis has long been generally accepted in Humean studies, and even commentators' qualifications of it attribute Hume's ideal of simplicity to Newton's influence.[52]

---

[51] *Inquiry*, 30–38.

[52] See Noxon, *Hume's Philosophical Development*, 71, 81–82; Wright, *Sceptical Realism*, 194–98.

The "Newtonian method" was to explain diverse phenomena with a small number of principles. Hume explains all of human activity with three general "maxims," which he sets in italics for our convenience. The first, the "copy principle" as Noxon calls it, is *"That all our simple ideas in their first appearance are deriv'd from simple impressions, which are correspondent to them, and which they exactly represent"* (1. 1. 1 [4]). This is Hume's refinement on Locke's theory of ideas and is the basis for Hume's own meaning-empiricism, with which he hoped to banish school jargon and befuddlement from the republic of letters.

The second principle is that *"of the liberty of the imagination to transpose and change its ideas"* (§ 3 [10]). This liberty is what allows for imaginative fabrications such as centaurs, in which the ideas of man and horse are transposed. It is also one of the natural processes that allow us to misconceive things rather than simply collect in our minds perfect idea-copies of the objective reality impressed upon us through our senses. The possibility of misconceptions proves that the fanciful transpositions the imagination creates are made of logically discrete ideas, and that therefore logic cannot detect their falseness. Only experience can. For example, the idea of a centaur is not illogical; it is chimerical. It is just false to the facts. If it were illogical it could not be conceived, in the same way that it cannot be conceived that twice two is five or that some husbands do not have wives. A centaur can be conceived, or rather misconceived, because its component ideas are matched or mismatched in a way to which logic is inapplicable. The way we detect its falseness is entirely through experience.

The third maxim, a refinement on the old concept of the association of ideas, is *"that when any impression becomes present to us, it not only transports the mind to such ideas as are related to it, but likewise communicates to them a share of its force and vivacity"* (1. 3. 8 [98]). This means that an immediate impression will share some of its impressiveness with the associated ideas that the mind automatically calls up, fortunately for us since otherwise we could not act. For example, when a man takes a step he expects the ground to support him. The basis for this belief is not reason because no one could ever walk if he had to calculate anew at each step the probability that the earth would remain solid. People do trust the future to resemble the past and do walk, so the belief must come from an instinctive reaction resulting from habituation, which works as follows according to the third law. The man's impression of the ground beneath him is fairly lively since it is a sensory perception. Associated memories of past steps come forth unbidden, and these ideas partake of the vivacity of the present sensory perception of the ground. Thus he is forcibly impressed with the ground's good record of resistance to the push of his feet and is assured that his experience will be repeated. Such causal expectations are implicit in all human activity.

The transferability of vivacity and its two companion principles set out the terms by which man can know things and act upon that knowledge. It is hard to imagine laws of human nature more universal. In the rest of the *Treatise* Hume employs these principles, and others draw from them, to explain a wide variety of human behavior. That readers missed this underlying "Newtonian" structure for so long is not surprising because, in regarding Hume as a sceptic only, they generally had paid disproportionate attention to the meaning-empirical principle with which he disposed of commonly held misconceptions. But the principle is only one of three that together allow him to construct a positive system.[53] Hume is blameless for this confusion except insofar as he inadvertently made scepticism seem the most prominent aspect of the *Treatise*.

As well as this overt Newtonian structure, there are generic structures integrated into or embedded within the *Treatise*. Rosalie Colie has shown how new forms are created by the combination of old genres, many of which might be considered extraliterary.[54] Often it is only the new composite genre

---

[53] For a fuller discussion of these maxims, see Nicholas Capaldi, *David Hume: The Newtonian Philosopher* (Boston, 1975), esp. chaps. 3–4.

[54] See *The Resources of Kind: Genre-Theory in the Renaissance*, ed. Barbara K. Lewalski (Berkeley, 1973). For an application of the mixed-genre ap-

that lives on in literary history while the component genres, readily recognizable to contemporary readers, die and are forgotten. This being the case with the *Treatise*, one would not expect it necessarily to exemplify one genre through and through, as though the author had constructed it according to generic specifications. Instead one would expect to find several genres to be applicable in part, at the same time allowing the *Treatise* in its totality its full individuality. Oversanguinely perhaps, Hume would have expected his readers to recognize such genres and to adjust their responses accordingly. To his disappointment, they generally failed at one or both of these interpretive stages. The interpretive process is still more difficult for modern readers, whose recognition of such genres will depend upon scholarship to recover lost knowledge.

One such genre is the anatomy. It has already been noted that Hume was fond of calling his investigations an anatomy, either of mind or of human nature. How seriously he took this metaphor is shown in his response to Hutcheson's criticisms that book 3 lacked "Warmth in the Cause of Virtue." His answer was that he had deliberately chosen not to be emotional or exhortatory because this would be out of place in a work of anatomy.[55] Warmth in the cause of virtue is a fine thing, but it is not a part of the conventions of the genre in which he was working as he conceived it. In deference to Hutcheson, or in anticipation of similar reactions from the public, Hume added to the end of book 3 another of his caveats, explaining that rhapsodies on morality would not have befitted the "genius" of the work: "The anatomist ought never to emulate the

---

proach to eighteenth-century writings, see Ralph Cohen, "On the Interrelations of Eighteenth-Century Literary Forms," *New Approaches to Eighteenth-Century Literature: Selected Papers from the English Institute*, ed. Phillip Harth (New York, 1974), 33–78.

[55] 17 Sept. 1739, *LDH* 1: 32. Actually, in the seventeenth century the genre that Barbara Lewalski calls the "anatomy in the complaint mode" called for warmth for virtue (or rather against vice); but plainly Hume is thinking of what she calls "analytic" anatomy rather than of a satirical version. See her *Donne's "Anniversaries" and the Poetry of Praise: The Creation of a Symbolic Mode* (Princeton, 1973), 225–63.

painter: nor in his accurate dissections and portraitures of the smaller parts of the human body, pretend to give his figures any graceful and engaging attitude or expression" (3, § 6 [620–21]). How would Hume reconcile the tension between his anatomical and belletristic propensities? Later he tried to effect a compromise between the two, but when he wrote the *Treatise* he evidently felt that anatomy had its own kind of unprepossessing elegance that would only be vitiated by painterly intrusions:

> Any warm Sentiment of Morals, I am afraid, wou'd have the Air of Declamation amidst abstract Reasonings, & wou'd be esteem'd contrary to good Taste. And tho' I am much more ambitious of being esteem'd a Friend to Virtue, than a Writer of Taste; yet I must always carry the latter in my Eye, otherwise I must despair of ever being servicable to Virtue.[56]

Hume made his choice with an eye to generic proprieties. Characteristically, even when he seems to be drawing a line between science and art, he thinks of what is in good taste.

It is reasonable therefore to ask to what extent the *Treatise* shares properties with the semiliterary genre, the anatomy. This literary kind had always been associated with natural philosophy through its connection with medical science, and such an association would appeal to Hume. In the passages just cited Hume publicly claimed one property of the genre and hoped his readers would countenance it: the freedom from exhortatory obligations. Another such property to be found in the *Treatise* is *divisio*, or the systematic division and treatment of subjects. *Divisio* is most noticeable in book 2, which begins with a section entitled, straightforwardly, "Division of the Subject." Here the author reviews some distinctions drawn earlier, then proceeds to further divisions, and finally arrives at the division between the indirect and direct passions, around which he arranges the whole book, assigning discussion of the former to the first two parts and the latter to the third part.

[56] 17 Sept. 1739, *LDH* 1: 33.

*Divisio* is intended as an aid to comprehension of a large subject, but, as Adam Smith pointed out, beyond a certain point of complexity it has the opposite effect.[57] Undoubtedly this effect contributed to the perception that the *Treatise* was unfathomable. In choosing the anatomical treatise as his genre Hume was almost asking for trouble, for by 1739 the old Renaissance genre was decidedly out of fashion. This attitude was reflected in and shaped by *A Tale of a Tub*, which comprises in itself a satire on treatises. Swift's persona, the hack writer, is a one-man factory for the production of treatises. Among the ludicrous treatises advertised in the book's preliminaries is one entitled *Lectures upon a Dissection of Human Nature*. In a digression within a digression, the hack writer puffs this treatise, saying,

> I have some Time since, with a World of Pains and Art, dissected the Carcass of *Humane Nature*, and read many useful Lectures upon the several Parts, both *Containing* and *Contained*; till at last it *smelt* so strong, I could preserve it no longer. Upon which, I have been at a great Expence to fit up all the Bones with exact Contexture, and in due Symmetry; so that I am ready to shew a very compleat Anatomy thereof to all curious *Gentlemen and others*.[58]

Swift here likens the pleasures of anatomy to the kind of morbid impulse that makes pedestrians crowd the scene of an automobile accident in hopes of glimpsing the victims. The treatise as a literary kind he viewed as the likely repository for all manner of intellectual abuse. Had Hume been sufficiently sensitive to literary fashions when he wrote his first work, he might have taken this influential satire as a warning against adopting the anatomical treatise.

Another genre that deserves consideration in connection with the *Treatise* is the essay as it evolved in the hands of Montaigne, Bacon, and Locke. From these practitioners the essay would have acquired associations of scepticism and em-

---

[57] 24 Jan. 1763, *Lect.*, 136–41.
[58] *Tale*, 2, 123.

piricism that would have appealed to Hume. Colie has described how Locke used the conventional intimacy and tentativeness of the form to serve his rhetorical purposes.[59] Certainly Locke's *Essay* was the exemplar of popularly successful philosophy, and therefore seems a likely model for the *Treatise*. The generic names "essay" and "treatise" might seem to us to represent inconsonant things, but they did not necessarily to Locke or Hume. Indeed, Locke described the second of his *Two Treatises of Government* as "An Essay Concerning The True Original, Extent, and End of Civil-Government." It was an early trait of the genre that its titles took the form of *essai de* or *essay of*, signifying that the contents were a test or a probing *of* some subject; so it is not trivial to note that Hume's treatise was a treatise *of* rather than *on* human nature.[60] Most of the section titles in the *Treatise*, like those in Hume's various essays so-called, are in the *essai* formula, and such titles as "Of Vice and Virtue" and "Of the Love of Fame" could fit inconspicuously into the table of contents of Montaigne's or Bacon's essays. It is true that Hume entitled his collected works *Essays and Treatises*, indicating that he thought of essays and treatises as different genres; but this does not mean that the *Treatise of Human Nature* could not be a hybrid of the two, as the title suggests.[61]

One property of the essay that the *Treatise* shares is a sense of intimacy between reader and author. Conveyance of an impression of the author's personality has always been a distinguishing virtue of the genre. Often the essay has been made almost entirely into a vehicle for this personality rather than

[59] "The Essayist in His Essay," *John Locke: Problems and Perspectives, a Collection of New Essays*, ed. John W. Yolton (London, 1969), 234–61.

[60] Fac. title page, *Two Treatises*, 153. For the early form of essay titles, see A. M. Boase, "The Early History of the *Essai* Title in France and Britain," *Studies in French Literature Presented to H. W. Lawton . . .* , ed. J. C. Ireson et al. (Manchester, 1968), 67–73. Sir Francis Palgrave ridiculed Hume for using the preposition "of" instead of "on" in the title of the *Treatise* (art. 7, *Quarterly Review* 73 [1843–44]: 550).

[61] Hume could be careless with the distinction. In the advertisement to the 1758 quarto *Essays and Treatises* he referred to all the contents, essays included, as "Treatises" (*LDH* 1: 251 n.).

for the transmission of useful and agreeable information. Colie argues that Locke's shows of modesty in his *Essay* successfully engaged his readers and deflected captious reactions to his tenets. This self-depreciation, however, is not to be confused with self-effacement; it actually serves to convey a stronger sense of Locke's presence in his book. That a strong sense of Hume's personality was conveyed to contemporary readers of the *Treatise* is shown by the reviewers' unanimous disapproval of what they saw as his cockiness. If Hume was thinking in terms of the conventions of the essay when he composed the *Treatise*, he may well have regarded his own appearance in the work as chaste enough in a genre in which some authorial character is to be expected. Next to Montaigne, who avowedly made himself the center of his musings and whose *essais* were virtually assays at self-acquaintance, Hume could have supposed his own speaking voice to be rather subdued. But he miscalculated if he expected from his readers the indulgence usually allowed to the essayist's eccentricities of character. No indulgence was shown, and there is no indication that anyone made allowances for the generic tradition to which Hume was attaching the *Treatise*.

It is tempting to exaggerate the extent to which the *Treatise* partakes of the conventional tentativeness of the essay genre. Many philosophical negligences and contradictions with which the work has been faulted could then be explained away as instances of Hume's adhering to the tradition of vividly depicting particular moments in rumination. Montaigne fairly disclaimed any truth value in his essays other than the accurate depiction of his fancies of the moment. Anyone, he warned, who quarreled with the validity of his statements was simply misunderstanding his intentions.[62] An essayist promises no complete system; he merely submits his own ruminations as a self-examination, perhaps more ambitiously as heuristics or, at most, as hypotheses for testing. Arguing that Hume was working within this tradition, we could turn every vice of Hume the philosopher into a virtue of Hume the es-

[62] See e.g., "Des livres."

sayist. But probably Hume does not need this defense since the tendency of Humean scholarship for some time has been to clear him of charge after charge of inconsistency. With more accurate readings, Hume appears more and more systematic; and in fact throughout the *Treatise* he repeatedly calls its contents a system. To be sure, there are points in it where he seems to have reached a dead end, which is to be expected, though, in an inquiry expressly devoted to finding the limits beyond which human nature will not let knowledge pass. Hume cannot be said to have claimed the prerogative of the essayist to be philosophically half-baked.

Of course Hume submitted his maxims and their related laws as hypotheses open to falsification, just as Locke had his, but hypotheses of this sort can be submitted with a very low level of tentativeness. Hume submitted his maxims with the same proportions of tentativeness and confidence as Newton had submitted the laws of gravitation. Far from being stabs in the dark, such hypotheses were formulated to account for a body of corroborating phenomena. Like Newton, Hume would have relinquished his maxims were they falsified through the "experimental method," but this would not keep both empiricists from being fairly convinced that they had hit their marks and that no confuting evidence would be likely to appear. It was the confidence born of this conviction that annoyed the reviewers of the *Treatise*.

Generally speaking, then, the reader's strong sense of Hume's personality in the *Treatise* has the opposite effect of Montaigne's personality in his *Essais*: whereas we do not expect a conclusive position from Montaigne on any topic, we get a feeling from Hume that he is trying hard to get his tenets as conclusively right as human limitations allow. Still, the depiction of the author's fancies of the moment does appear in one place in the *Treatise*, the famous conclusion to book 1. Burton thought that Hume had taken up his subjects for discussion just as they occurred to him, that is, according to the principle of association. We have seen that this was not so, but then, interestingly, Noxon says something similar, recording his impression that in places Hume was thinking through his problems while he wrote instead of delivering a premeditated set of tenets. From Noxon's citations, one surmises that the passages giving him this impression are primarily in part 4, section 7 of book 1.[63] Now the *Treatise* is too full of cross-references for Hume to have written it without a great deal of premeditation and revision. But, as Colie says, a particular trait of the essay was the portrayal of the author in the act of thinking, with an emphasis on process, development, growth, and change of thought rather than on a finished intellectual position.[64] In the hands of a skilled essayist, this appearance of artless self-revelation is actually the result of great artistry. There are not a few instances in the *Treatise* in which Hume depicts himself in the act of thinking, of deferring problems so as to approach them obliquely (1. 3. 2. [77–78], § 6 [87–88]), of examining his ideas in what he quaintly calls "experiments" (§ 8 [101–3]), and so on. But only in part 4, section 7, the most blatantly literary portion of the *Treatise*, is he less interested in expounding his system than in self-portrayal. There he portrays the momentary effects on him of the sceptical aspects of his system, most of which he had set forth in the preceding sections of part 4.

In part 4 of book 1, Hume's probing of our ideational limits brings him to the sceptical conclusion that we know much less than we think we do about matter, spirit, and our selves. The upshot will be that no certainty is possible in such topics (Pyrrhonism wins) but that no such certainty is needed in life because instinctive, "moral" knowledge fills the gap (Pyrrhonism loses). Noxon guesses that here Hume is only feeling his way toward the compromise of "mitigated" scepticism that he later expounded fully in the *Philosophical Essays*. He thinks that Hume's mitigated scepticism is inchoate in the *Treatise*, despite the fact that there Hume specifically identified "true" philosophy as "moderate scepticism" (1. 4. 2 [224]). Having not yet fully reached an equilibrium between his constructive empirical program and his sceptical program to expose occult

[63] Noxon, *Hume's Philosophical Development*, 9, 14.
[64] "Essayist in His Essay," 237.

qualities as illusory, Hume supposedly finds himself in a quandary. Pyrrhonism can gain the upper hand in any argument, and, to Hume's dismay, undermines his empiricism. Resulting from this quandary are the notorious histrionics of section 7.

Perhaps Noxon has noticed something that is really there but, understandably, has not recognized it for what it is, the dramatic aspect of the essay genre as fully exploited within section 7. Hume does sometimes appear to be thinking through the implications of Pyrrhonism at the moment of composition, but there is reason to believe that this appearance was a deliberate creation and that Hume expected readers to recognize it as a literary device. First it is necessary to show that Hume was not genuinely vacillating between scepticism and empiricism. To attempt to do so only by examining his arguments probably would be inconclusive, but fortunately it is possible to bypass the arguments and exegetical controversies altogether and show that, whether or not his arguments do commit him to Pyrrhonism, Hume did not think that they do. Perhaps it will then be claimed that Hume was a true sceptic and of Pyrrho's party without knowing it, but this rejoinder would be beside the point in our discussion of his authorial intentions. That Hume thought he was not a Pyrrhonist can be established because he said so without a hint of irony or equivocation in *A Letter from a Gentleman to His Friend in Edinburgh*. Writing anonymously, he defended himself against the charge of scepticism in the *Treatise*. The accuser had specifically cited the apparent vacillations in section 7; therefore Hume's response also refers to that crucial segment:

> *1st*, As to the *Scepticism* with which the Author is charged, I must observe, that the Doctrine of the *Pyrrhonians* or *Scepticks* have been regarded in all Ages as Principles of mere Curiosity, or a Kind of *Jeux d'esprit*, without any Influence on a Man's steady Principles or Conduct in Life. In Reality, a Philosopher who affects to doubt of the Maxims of *common Reason*, and even of his *Senses*, declares sufficiently that he is not in earnest, and

that he intends not to advance an Opinion which he would recommend as Standards of Judgment and Action.

If in his sceptical arguments he was not recommending standards of judgment and action, what was he doing? He goes on
to say,

'Tis evident, that so extravagant a Doubt as that which Scepticism may seem to recommend, by destroying *every Thing*, really affects *nothing*, and was never intended to be understood
*seriously*, but was meant as a *mere* Philosophical Amusement,
or Trial of *Wit* and *Subtilty*.                    (*LGent.*, 19, 20)[65]

It need hardly be pointed out that one of the old meanings of
"essay," which gave the genre its original character, was
"trial." Hume had intended his scepticism to be recognized as
part of a *jeu d'esprit* in which he portrayed himself as vacillating between Pyrrhonism and the science of man, but had un-
derestimated his own skill in playing the Pyrrhonist role.
Probably no one ever played the role better before or since.
The accuser and many others through the years have taken
Hume for an unmitigated sceptic, and such has in fact been
the majority opinion until recently. It was a mistake for Hume
to depend as much as he did on what he took to be the self-
evident untenability of Pyrrhonism to signal to his readers
that in section 7 he was not revealing his true, Pyrrhonian
self.

I have said that readers have generally been so struck by
Hume's scepticism that they are led to ignore the empirical
system propounded in the *Treatise*. Consequently its "Newtonian" structure is not as apparent as it should be. Readers
have tended to project the scepticism of book 1, part 4 onto
the rest of the *Treatise*, and have found no system because
they were predisposed to see only doubts. Hume made this

---

[65] One might question Hume's ingenuousness in the *LGent.*, but he made
a like disavowal in *THN* 1. 4. 1 (183). Cf. also *EHU* xii. 2 (131), in which he
says that when the Pyrrhonist "awakes from his dream, he will be the first to
join in the laugh against himself, and to confess, that all his objections are
mere amusement."

misinterpretation possible by not making it plain what he was doing in part 4. His explanation that his scepticism was merely a *jeu d'esprit* is misleading, too, in its exaggeration, for while philosophical amusement was evidently one of his aims in part 4, he clearly also deemed the sceptical arguments valid. A discussion of the role of scepticism in Hume's system appears later, but before treating part 4 as a literary artifact I should at least state my view briefly. From his belief in the validity of certain sceptical arguments Hume might have drawn irrationalist conclusions, or he might have concluded that the fact of our being stumped by scepticism supports his contention that there are limits to human understanding beyond which we cannot go successfully. The interpretation of Hume as an irrationalist runs counter to his system, while the second interpretation fits in with his system and his program of philosophical reform. The places in which Hume entertains irrationalist conclusions are only two, in section 7, where he gives vent, as he says, to "the sentiments of [his] spleen and indolence" (p. 270), and briefly in two paragraphs foreshadowing this effusion. In this last instance he undercuts his remarks by presenting them merely as the feelings of the moment:

> I begun this subject with premising, that we ought to have an implicit faith in our senses, and that this wou'd be the conclusion, I shou'd draw from the whole of my reasoning. But to be ingenuous, I feel myself *at present* of a quite contrary sentiment, and am more inclin'd to repose no faith at all in my senses. . . .                                    (1. 4. 2 [217])

Likewise the irrationalist conclusions entertained in section 7 should be interpreted as a dramatic representation of a momentary loss of confidence rather than as a statement of the purport of Hume's philosophy.

The effusions of section 7 are a reaction to the sceptical arguments in the six previous sections and should be seen in that context. In these sections he surveys, in light of the sceptical implications of meaning-empiricism, a number of topics (demonstrative reason, the reliability of our senses, the external and internal worlds) and finds faulty the accounts of them in other systems. Upon completing this survey he says,

> Thus we have finish'd our examination of the several systems of philosophy, both of the intellectual and natural world; and in our miscellaneous way of reasoning have been led into several topics; which will either illustrate and confirm some preceding part of this discourse, or prepare the way for our following opinions. 'Tis now time to return to a more close examination of our subject, and to proceed in the accurate anatomy of human nature, having fully explain'd the nature of our judgment and understanding. (§ 6 [263])

He is now poised, he says, to resume his accurate anatomy of human nature, having interrupted it with miscellaneous reasonings. Then, as the reader commences section 7 he finds Hume changing his mind and pausing to assess his progress:

> But before I launch out into those immense depths of philosophy, which lie before me, I find myself inclin'd to stop a moment in my present situation, and to ponder that voyage, which I have undertaken, and which undoubtedly requires the utmost art and industry to be brought to a happy conclusion. (p. 263)

Of course Hume did not actually change his mind while he was writing, but was simply depicting himself as acting on impulse. Ensuing is a philosophical and emotional extravaganza, running from scepticism to common sense, from doubt to despair to cheerfulness (but skipping heroic resolve). But it should be remembered that in section 7 Hume is still engaging in something other than his "close examination," the regular course of his investigations.

For students of the *Characteristics* Hume's expression "miscellaneous way" will be reminiscent of Shaftesbury's "way of miscellany or common essay, in which the most confused head, if fraught with a little invention and provided with commonplace book learning, might exert itself to as much advantage as the most orderly and well-settled judgment." The way of miscellany is an admittedly low genre but has accompanying liberties. Miscellanarians are not constrained to be orderly or to exposit the findings of a well-settled judgment. The miscellaneous essay is the outlet for the "capricious and odd,"[66] a genre in which a writer may put on an antic disposition and not fear censure. If Hume had Shaftesbury's miscellaneous essays in the back of his mind when he composed part 4, it does not mean that we should imagine him in that part as wearing cap and bells: liberties may be exercised with variable degrees of self-restraint. But it would mean that Hume did not identify the sceptical extravagances of part 4 with the finished system he would care to defend when challenged.

We know that Hume acquired his copy of the *Characteristics*, the third edition, when he was at the impressionable age of fifteen.[67] Like Locke's *Essay*, it would have been an example to Hume of abstruse philosophy that had achieved popular success, so that in following Shaftesbury's example he would have had reason to hope to repeat that success. Part 4 is no mere imitation of the way of miscellany, though, and few people other than students writing doctoral theses on Shaftesbury would disagree that Hume's version is by far the more interesting and important. One is justified in wondering whether Hume had had Shaftesbury's miscellaneous essays in mind because, like Shaftesbury, he used his miscellaneous reasonings to bring to a suitable close a protracted session of demanding ratiocination. Hume was illustrating and confirming things he had said earlier, while suggesting the things to come in book 2; Shaftesbury used his essays to review and comment informally upon his preceding material, while making "excursions" into new material. Shaftesbury's purpose was to introduce into his work "more of the fashionable air and manner of the world." His essays were to counterpoise the abstruse deliberations immediately preceding, for "these being of the more regular and formal kind may easily be oppressive to the airy reader, and may therefore with the same assurance as

---

[66] "Miscellaneous Reflections on the Preceding Treatises," *Characteristics* 2: 158–59, 160.

[67] See Mossner, *Life*, 31 n.

tragedy claim the necessary relief of [a] little piece or farce."[68] After some heavy going, a philosophical amusement provides some relief. Too much should not be made of Shaftesbury's way of miscellany as an index of Hume's activities in part 4 since Hume engages in dramatics only in the last section. But it is clear that Hume regarded himself in part 4 as having temporarily put aside his regular and formal investigations. He had put aside the anatomy of human nature, his primary undertaking, for a diversion into scepticism.

He begins in section 1 with the more certain of the two types of possible knowledge, that of the logical relations of ideas, or demonstrative knowledge. Even demonstrations such as mathematical computations cannot withstand a sustained intention to doubt. In sections 2–4 Hume turns a doubting eye on the other prong of his fork: no knowledge of matters of fact can be rationally justified when no such justification can survive for the most fundamental of beliefs, our assurance in the continued existence of the material world independent of the perceiving mind. System after system, modern and ancient, fails to provide a rational justification that is immune to doubt. Scepticism seems to lead us to solipsism, but, as if this were not bad enough, we learn in sections 5 and 6 that it will not even leave the self untouched. The continued existence of the mind, identical with itself through time, is dubious. All we know are connected but fleeting perceptions, and to infer back from interrupted perceptions to an uninterrupted, perceiving self is not an unassailable logical step. There now seems to be no reason to believe in mind or matter. Apparently brought up short on the brink of an abyss, Hume gazes in section 7 into a void emptier even than Chaos (for Chaos, though formless, at least included matter).

Contrary to what might be expected, this prospect does not bother Hume overmuch, for, where ratiocination fails, nature steps in to compel beliefs that are indispensable to life. If one sets out to explore the natural boundaries of ratiocination, one should not be upset over success in finding the place where it

---

[68] *Characteristics* 2: 161.

fails. A rational justification for belief in the continued, self-identical existences of mind and body is impossible but obviously superfluous to life since man has always gotten along without it. As he portrays himself, Hume is bothered rather by two things: (1) feelings of inadequacy to the task of prosecuting the science of man, especially in the face of ostracism resulting from the advancement of tenets that outrage common opinion; and (2) the apparent radical instability of reason due to its dependence upon instinctual mental propensities. From these follow the profound ditherings of section 7, which in their self-dramatized storm and stress are unlike anything else that Hume wrote. He confesses:

> When I look abroad, I foresee on every side, dispute, contradiction, anger, calumny and detraction. When I turn my eye inward, I find nothing but doubt and ignorance. All the world conspires to oppose and contradict me; tho' such is my weakness, that I feel all my opinions loosen and fall of themselves, when unsupported by the approbation of others. Every step I take is with hesitation, and every new reflection makes me dread an error and absurdity in my reasoning.                    (pp. 264–65)

If Hume intended the foregoing confession to disarm the reader, it failed with the reviewer for *The History of the Works of the Learned*, whose response to this passage was "What Heart now would not almost bleed? what Breast can forbear to sympathize with this brave Adventurer? For my part, I cannot, without the utmost Emotion and Solicitude, take even a transient Prospect of the Dangers and terrible Catastrophe to which he is exposed."[69] The reviewer saw the confession only as more evidence of the author's self-absorption.

John Passmore has reacted similarly to Hume's distress over the dubious status of reason, objecting to what he calls Hume's lapse into a stagey, melodramatic tone.[70] Such reactions reflect personal tastes and therefore are not subject to

---

[69] *History of the Works of the Learned*, 402.
[70] *Hume's Intentions*, 3d ed. (London, 1980), 133.

refutation or confirmation. It can be shown, however, that a more charitable response is possible. Indeed, Raymond Williams thinks that section 7 deserves classical status.[71] If one does not allow an author the generic premises on which he operates, his writing will look contrived and ridiculous. Hence soliloquies and arias seem ludicrous to people unsympathetic to the conventions of theater and opera. If Hume is given his premise, that in keeping with his genre he is portraying the moment by moment act of philosophizing, much or all of the annoying self-absorption and melodrama takes on a new aspect. Consonant with his hope to give readers the experience of philosophizing, Hume offers a glimpse into the feelings of a thinker wrestling with the consequences of his own tenets. Rather than being melodramatic, Hume seems to me to show considerable distance from his own emotions. At some removes from himself, he examines his own personal responses to the predicament in which he finds himself. It also seems to me that his ironically detached attitude toward his ditherings is not without humor.[72] Furthermore, concluding his miscellaneous reasonings with his own struggles with scepticism is artistically fitting, completing a pattern in which scepticism discomfits one system after another until there is only the sceptic himself left to be discomfited. Whereas in section 1 Hume had shown how scepticism devours itself, in section 7 he enacts the cycle in his own person.

The personal drama of ideas unfolds as follows. Unmitigated scepticism is itself the culmination and decadence of reason. It is the stage at which critical scrutiny critically scrutinizes itself, finding that for each belief, even for supposedly

---

[71] "David Hume: Reasoning and Experience," *The English Mind: Studies in the English Moralists* . . . , ed. Hugh Sykes Davis and George Watson (Cambridge, 1964), 124.

[72] I find that my impression is shared by Donald T. Siebert (" 'Ardor of Youth': The Manner of Hume's *Treatise*," *The Philosopher as Writer: The Eighteenth Century*, ed. Robert Ginsberg [Selinsgrove, 1987], 181–83). A. D. Nuttall, however, thinks that Hume was here succumbing to "a kind of schizophrenia" (*A Common Sky: Philosophy and Literary Imagination* [Berkeley, 1974], 105–6).

certain deductive truths, a thorough sceptic must calculate
the possibility of error, and that, however favorable that calculation may be, its fallibility must be calculated in turn, and
so on *in infinitum*: "Let our first belief be never so strong, it
must infallibly perish by passing thro' so many new examina-
tions, of which each diminishes somewhat of its force and vig-
our" (1. 4. 1 [182–83]). Were it possible to be thoroughly
sceptical, it would be paralyzing. It is not possible, however,
because the mind is so constituted as instinctively to believe
and act despite sceptical reason; but then instinct has been
known to be fallible. The question becomes whether to follow
unstable reason or surrender to instinct. Neither alternative
is satisfactory. In its sceptical phase reason "entirely subverts
itself, and leaves not the lowest degree of evidence in any
proposition, either in philosophy or common life" (§ 7 [267–
68]). Instinct, rendered unreliable by its liberty to transpose
and change ideas, is hardly an acceptable guide in most issues. "We have," Hume laments, "no choice left but betwixt
a false reason and none at all" (p. 268). But this is an over-
statement prompted by the intensity with which the problem
presents itself at the moment. There is another choice, and
now Hume begins to feel his way toward it. A practical compromise restores him to his usual calm. It emerges that philosophy as well as instinct is natural to man. Neither can be
renounced; neither can be chosen to the exclusion of the
other. The most that we can do is somehow to use them to
check and balance each other: "Where reason is lively, and
mixes itself with some propensity, it ought to be assented to.
Where it does not, it never can have any title to operate upon
us" (p. 270). Reason, for example, cannot overcome our natural propensity to believe in body, and in that instance can be
discounted. Superstition, on the other hand, can and should
be overcome.

Not many people have found this accommodation between
reason and instinct satisfactory, but there is no indication that
Hume himself is not satisfied with it when he proffers it to us
at the end of section 7. And if we look at the mind naturalis-
tically, as Hume did, it does not seem so bizarre to conclude

that the mind has limits inherent in the natural processes by which it functions, that reason cannot verify its own presuppositions indefinitely, that the point at which verification must stop is the veil of perception, and that belief in indispensable but unverifiable presuppositions is instinctive. If all this is the case, then it should be expected that eventually the mind will run into insoluble difficulties.

If accurate, this plot summary should make it clear that Hume's mitigated scepticism is at least implicit in the last paragraphs of section 7. Hume was not discovering the power of scepticism for the first time as he wrote part 4, but rather was trying to impart a sense of discovery. At the same time, the dramatic qualities of section 7 should not lead us to discount Humean Pyrrhonism as an empty posture. Hume did not make a show of scepticism in the same way that Johnson, from joy in the exercise of his eristic powers, would sometimes take the side opposite to his true opinion of an issue. Plainly the question of Pyrrhonism was very real to Hume, just as the question of suicide was very real to Hamlet; but a man's final pronouncement of an issue cannot safely be educed from a soliloquy. Part 4 should be recognized as a set of seven episodes in a philosophical amusement ending with an internal debate rather than taken as a set of formal arguments in support of a Pyrrhonian thesis. The point of the depiction was to convey what it is like to butt one's head against the boundaries of human knowledge. Hume's guiding purpose all along had been to establish these boundaries, and the only way to do so is to push experience sceptically until it can go no further. One cannot know where the boundary is until one tries to pass it and fails. We see Hume in section 7 trying and failing, but this failure is, in the larger view, what he was after. Having failed to pass the boundary, he had succeeded thereby in finding it. In this respect, frustrated probing of the veil of perception is a genuine trial of wit. So if Hume is at his wit's end here, he is deliberately so.[73]

---

[73] Philosophers might suspect that a student of literature will be prone to imagine a nonexistent narrative strain in Hume's text. Fortunately a philoso-

Recognizing part 4 as a diversion from Hume's proper order of business, we can correct the traditional interpretation of the *Treatise* in two ways. First, Hume's scepticism is placed in perspective. The picture of Hume as sceptically destroying reason gives way to that of him as a naturalist, adducing the foundation of reason in instinct as confirmation of his thesis that the mind follows and is constrained by certain identifiable causal laws of its nature. It should be noted here that to confirm the naturalist thesis the sceptical arguments must be valid; otherwise Hume could not suppose that he had found the limits of understanding. The question is not their validity, but whether Hume wishes us to conclude from them that reason and philosophy are impossibilities or that they can only progress within their natural limits.

Second, the vanity allegedly betrayed by the self-preoccupation shown in section 7 becomes a part of Hume's attempt to provide a philosophical amusement. An inoffensive, even appealing, vanity was something that was supposed to go along with an essayist's strong personal presence in his essays. This generic tradition lives to this day in the informal essay, as E. B. White acknowledged when he wrote, "Only a person who is congenitally self-centered has the effrontery and the stamina to write essays."[74] That Hume thought of the genre in this way is indicated by his literary appraisal of Sir William Temple. Although he does not identify which particular writings he has in mind, the context makes it probable that he is thinking preponderantly of the belletristic ones, Temple's highly popular essays, issued in three parts entitled *Miscellanea* (1680, 1690, 1701). Hume writes,

> That mixture of vanity which appears in his works, is rather a recommendation to them. By means of it, we enter into acquaintance with the character of the author, full of honour and

---

pher, Donald Livingston, has also found a narrative strain, and has made much more of it than I do here. See *Hume's Philosophy of Common Life* (Chicago, 1984), 9–59.

[74] *Essays of E. B. White* (New York, 1977), vii.

humanity; and fancy that we are engaged, not in the perusal of a book, but in conversation with a companion.[75]

Such was the atmosphere of conversational intimacy that Hume had wished to create. Doubtless he had hoped that the familiarity allowed to the essayist would serve to endear him to his readers.

Hume's later unreasonable dislike for the *Treatise* now becomes understandable. To be publicly rebuked by reviewers for writing too personally must have been a humiliation much the same as one suffers in being rebuffed for behaving too familiarly with an unreceptive acquaintance. Browning suffered a similar humiliation in the reception of his first publication, *Pauline*, and the experience was unpleasant enough to drive him from confessional poetry to the dramatic monologue. His and Hume's only protection was their anonymity. Such a painful experience might easily sour an author's feelings toward the work that occasioned it. Never again would Hume expose himself in confessional writing.

The above interpretation of part 4 does little to extenuate the many instances in other places in the *Treatise* of what could be called vanity. Repeatedly Hume adopts peremptory or adversarial tones that would be quite inoffensive among intimates accustomed to the amicable sparring of private debate. But any reader unwilling to put himself into such an imaginative framework would not see Hume's peremptoriness as bluff camaraderie. As mentioned earlier, Hume excused his occasional peremptoriness by explaining that it was the heat of the moment that pushed him into uncharacteristic behavior. But this is to claim the prerogative of the essayist to be impetuous, and there is no indication that Hume was in these places engaged in philosophical amusements. The *jeux d'esprits* are confined to part 4. Still, if Hume was not on his best behavior in places where he should have been, it should be remembered that the work was, after all, given to the public anonymously. We have seen that anonymity was often

[75] *Hist.* 6: 544 (A.D. 1689).

thought to afford a measure of authorial license. Johnson's self-defense in *Rambler* 208 illustrates this point:

> The seeming vanity with which I have sometimes spoken of myself, would perhaps require an apology, were it not extenuated by the example of those who have published essays before me, and by the privilege which every nameless writer has been hitherto allowed. "A mask," says Castiglione, "confers a right of acting and speaking with less restraint, even when the wearer happens to be known." He that is discovered without his own consent, may claim some indulgence, and cannot be rigorously called to justify those sallies or frolicks which his disguise must prove him desirous to conceal.[76]

Here vanity is doubly extenuated, by the generic tradition of the essay and by the claim of anonymity to indulgence. That Johnson felt constrained to remind his readers that certain responses were due to an anonymous essayist indicates that such responses were not always and dependably forthcoming from the public. If they were not to be depended upon for what were unmistakably essays, they were commensurately less to be depended upon for the amphibious *Treatise*. The combination of the essay and the formal treatise that had worked for Locke had not for Hume.

[76] *Rambler*, ed. W. J. Bate and Albrecht B. Strauss, vols. 3–5 of the Yale Edition of the Works of Samuel Johnson, 14 vols. to date (New Haven, 1958–), 5: 317–18.

# Chapter III

## THE *ESSAYS, MORAL AND POLITICAL*

> I am highly indebted to you for Hume. I like his
> essays better than any thing I have read these many
> days. . . . [T]he highest & most difficult effect of art—
> the appearance of its absence—appears throughout.
> —Thomas Carlyle, 24 May 1815, *Collected Letters*

### HUME AS PERIODICAL ESSAYIST

With his next publication, the *Essays, Moral and Political*,
Hume made a modest start in an unspectacular but steady as-
cent to literary fame. The work was received favorably
enough, he tells us, to make him forget his disappointment at
the stillbirth of the *Treatise*.[1] Today these essays are not the
subject of intense study; still less are they the pleasure reading of many people's leisure hours (whereas the *Treatise* is
one of the most closely scrutinized works in our language).
But our comparative neglect of these essays is no great indict-
ment of the obtuseness of the times, for this measure of
ephemerality inevitably follows from their essentially journalistic character. T. S. Eliot observed that, were it not for the
achievement of *Gulliver's Travels* and the biographical interest of its author, the *Drapier's Letters* could not sustain an
audience beyond occasional students of Anglo-Irish history:
though quite good literature, the letters could not have sur-
vived on their own merits because journalism can only outlive
its own epoch with extraneous help.[2] Similarly, Hume's essays probably would not now be available in inexpensive pa-
perbacks were it not for the interest that Hume arouses as the

[1] "My Own Life," *LDH* 1: 2.
[2] "Charles Whibley," *Selected Essays*, 3d ed. (London, 1951), 493–94.

author of the *Treatise*. But the essays are not without intrinsic interest quite apart from their value for the study of Hume's thought or of Georgian Britain; and in the study of Hume's literary development they take on a particular importance.

The journalistic character of the *Essays* is obscured for the modern reader somewhat by Hume's successive revisions, and more so by the absorption of the book into collections with nonjournalistic essays (from the supplementary *Three Essays, Moral and Political* [London, 1748], the *Political Discourses* [Edinburgh, 1752], and the *Four Dissertations* [London, 1757]. With some omissions, the Library of Liberal Arts collections divide the essays into two books according to whether their subjects are political or miscellaneous. The World's Classics edition, the Green and Grose edition (*Wks.*, vols. 3–4), and the Liberty*Classics* edition (*EMPLit.*) all follow the arrangement of Hume's personally superintended collection, *Essays and Treatises*, appending the essays that Hume had jettisoned or suppressed. But it is precisely the jettisoned essays, now displaced from their original settings in the table of contents, that best show Hume's initial conception for his second book.[3]

Hume and his editors were not interested in preserving the original character of the *Essays* when they assembled their collections. We, however, are not concerned with the author's final intentions for the state and arrangement of his works, but rather with his intentions at the time of composition and how far they were realized. The present object is not to appraise the degree of perfection that the works eventually reached through Hume's many emendations; it is to elucidate his development as a writer, one phase at a time. Because it introduces a distinct new phase of his career, the *Essays* is more important for present purposes than if we were interested primarily in his thought.

---

[3] *Of the Standard of Taste, and Other Essays*, ed. John M. Lenz (Indianapolis, 1965); *David Hume's Political Essays*, ed. Charles W. Hendel (New York, 1953); *Essays Moral, Political, and Literary* (World's Classics, 1903; repr. Oxford, 1963). The table of contents of the *Essays* as first published may be found in Miller's foreword to *EMPLit.*, xii–xiii, nn. 5–6.

Just as it was important to remember that the *Treatise* as we have it is an abandoned project, it is necessary to bear in mind that the *Essays* is a salvage of an abandoned project. In a mildly self-depreciatory advertisement Hume explained to readers that the *Essays* had begun as a periodical and ended up a miscellany. Prospective readers, he implied, should adjust their expectations accordingly.

> Most of these Essays were wrote with a View of being publish'd as Weekly-Papers, and were intended to comprehend the Designs both of the Spectators and Craftsmen. But having dropt that Undertaking, partly from Laziness, partly from Want of Leisure, and being willing to make Trial of my Talents for Writing, before I ventur'd upon any more serious Compositions, I was induced to commit these Trifles to the Judgment of the Public.[4]

So the reader should not be dismayed when in one essay Hume raises the question of the relative strength of vicious and virtuous motives in man, only to drop it, saying, "I may, perhaps, treat more fully of this Subject in some future Essay" ("DMHNat.," 620). No such essay is to be found in the collection. In a periodical this deferral would have been sound procedure, at once husbanding topics and advertising a future paper. The reader's full appreciation of the book depends, therefore, upon his understanding from the beginning just what it is, a collection of papers written mostly to be published periodically and intended to appeal to the public's interests of the day. Furthermore, the pieces are to be understood to be miscellaneous essays. Hume is unusually explicit about this, as if he wished to avoid the generic vagaries of the *Treatise*:

> The Reader must not look for any Connexion among these Essays, but must consider each of them as a Work apart. This is an Indulgence that is given to all Essay-Writers, and is an equal

---

[4] *Essays, Moral and Political* (Edinburgh, "MDCCXLI"), iii–iv.

Ease both to Writer and Reader, by freeing them from any tire-
some Stretch of Attention or Application.[5]

Here Hume seems consciously to be moving to an opposite
extreme from the rigors of attention and application that the
*Treatise* required of readers.

Even while preparing book 3 of the *Treatise* for publication
Hume was turning out these "Trifles" and sending them to
Kames for criticism.[6] One is reminded here of Samuel Johnson's relieving himself from the severer labors of lexicography
with turning out the numbers of the *Rambler*. Hume would
have been laboring on the *Treatise* under the cloud of its, by
then, evident public rejection. After the intellectual rigors of
the last few years, the writing of a weekly piece might easily
have seemed, in the contemplation, a diverting and potentially remunerative project. Certainly any supplement to his
modest patrimonial annuity would have been welcome. Perhaps finding the necessary pace of production unsustainable,
he put what he had before the Edinburgh and London publics
in two anonymous volumes dated 1741 and 1742,[7] and in this
form they were well received. On 13 June 1742 Hume wrote
to Kames that

[t]he Essays are all sold in London; as I am inform'd by two
Letters from English Gentlemen of my Acquaintaince. There is
a Demand for them; & as one of them tells me, Innys the great
Bookseller in Paul's Church Yard wonders there is not a new
Edition, for that he cannot find Copies for his Customers. I am
also told that Dr Butler has every where recommended them.
So that I hope they will have some Success. They may prove
like Dung with Marle, & bring forward the rest of my Philoso-

[5] Ibid., v.
[6] See 4 June and 1 July 1739, *NLDH*, 5–7.
[7] There is some question as to whether "1741" was Old Style. See T. E.
Jessop, *A Bibliography of David Hume and of Scottish Philosophy from Francis Hutcheson to Lord Balfour* (London, 1938), 15–16; W. B. Todd, "David
Hume: A Preliminary Bibliography," *Hume and the Enlightenment: Essays
Presented to Ernest Campbell Mossner*, ed. W. B. Todd (Austin, 1974), 191–
92.

phy, which is of a more durable, tho of a harder & more stubborn Nature. You see, I can talk to you in your own Style.[8]

This success with what was essentially a *pis aller* suggests not only the excellence of Hume's writing, but also the prudence of giving readers more or less what they expect and want. Too much should not be made of the simile quoted above, since Hume was teasing Kames more than he was unbosoming himself, but it does suggest something of Hume's attitude toward the *Essays*: the book was not going to be his claim to the attention of posterity, and would serve its purpose if it created an audience for his deeper thoughts, whether as presented in the *Treatise* or some other vehicle. Here he was not writing for the ages. Of course not everything should be written for the ages. Journalism has its own valid purposes. To discover what the purposes of the *Essays* were, other than to win Hume a reputation that he could turn to the advantage of more important things, we must consider precisely what sort of periodical Hume originally had projected.

The periodical was intended, he explains, to "comprehend the Designs both of the Spectators and Craftsmen," a double program reflected in the corresponding titular adjectives, "Moral and Political." Its audience was to be Scottish, principally the urbanites of Edinburgh and the gentry, like Boswell, who made Edinburgh the center of their cultural lives. So much can be gathered from hints in essays omitted from later editions. When Hume rallies "our SCOTTISH ladies," it is a piece of camaraderie among male Scots, with the ladies overhearing. Evidently he does not have it in mind that the English might be listening ("LM," 559). Elsewhere he contrasts party allegiances in "this *kingdom*" with those in England ("PGen.," 616). When he refers to "a famous miser in this city" ("A," 570), what city this is he expects to be understood, and it would only be understood if the periodical was a local publication, strongly identified by readers with its community. Since the *Essays* was printed and first published in Edinburgh, and since at that time Edinburgh was Hume's home

[8] *NLDH*, 10.

away from Ninewells, that city may safely be assumed to be the community in question.

More hints can be had from "Of Essay Writing," which, as T. H. Grose pointed out,[9] Hume obviously intended to initiate the periodical. It has two parts: a statement of purpose and a solicitation of women readers. Hume begins the first part by dividing the "elegant" of mankind into two types who should complement each other but in recent memory had fallen out: the learned, whose talents are cultivated in solitude, and the conversable, whose talents are exercised in society. When he writes, "The Separation of the Learned from the conversible World seem[s] to have been the great Defect of the last Age, and must have had a very bad Influence both on Books and Company" (*EMPLit.*, 534), he plainly is thinking of Shaftesbury's and Hutcheson's lamentations over the retreat of philosophy into the "schools." If the antagonism between learning and society was no longer so acute, it was because these writers and others like them had initiated a process of reconciliation, a process that Hume now undertakes to carry on. His declaration of purpose deserves quotation in full:

'Tis with great Pleasure I observe, That Men of Letters, in this Age, have lost, in a great Measure, that Shyness and Bashfulness of Temper, which kept them at a Distance from Mankind; and, at the same Time, That Men of the World are proud of borrowing from Books their most agreeable Topics of Conversation. 'Tis to be hop'd, that this League betwixt the learned and conversible Worlds, which is so happily begun, will be still farther improv'd, to their mutual Advantage; and to that End, I know nothing more advantageous than such *Essays* as these with which I endeavour to entertain the Public. In this View, I cannot but consider myself as a Kind of Resident or Ambassador from the Dominions of Learning to those of Conversation; and shall think it my constant Duty to promote a good Correspondence betwixt these two States, which have so great a Dependence on each other. I shall give Intelligence to the Learned of whatever passes in Company, and shall endeavour to import

[9] "History of the Editions," *Wks.* 3: 43.

into Company whatever Commodities I find in my native Country proper for their Use and Entertainment. The Balance of Trade we need not be jealous of, nor will there be any Difficulty to preserve it on both Sides. The Materials of this Commerce must chiefly be furnish'd by Conversation and common Life: The manufacturing of them alone belongs to Learning. (p. 535)

When he says that he will give intelligence of what passes in company, Hume might just mean that the learned who consult his papers will find out what the fashionable topics of conversation are, but he might also mean literally that he would give intelligence of events in society. After all, most conversations *are* about what befell between whom. In the *Spectator* such intelligence took the form of discussions of clothing fashions, clubs, and diversions like the theater and Italian opera; in the *Craftsman*, of notices of political events.

The only specimen from which we can judge of what such intelligence would have been like in Hume's papers is the letter reproduced in "Of Moral Prejudices" (*EMPLit.*, 542–44). This letter, sent from Paris by an unnamed friend, recounts how a feminist of independent means acted on her resolution to enjoy motherhood without the encumbrance of marriage. Her story, and the pending custodial suit, were "the common Topic of Conversation" in Paris in 1737 when the letter was written. This is gossip, but Hume was uninterested in it merely as such. It was already old gossip, and Hume did not even bother to relate the outcome of the suit. His interest in it was as a counterexample to the preceding story of Eugenius, whose moderate philosophy did not forbid him the indulgence of conventional familial sentiments. The letter illustrates Hume's point, that philosophy goes awry when followed without a respectful deference to our incorrigibly passional human nature and the received maxims of conduct that channel our passions into acceptable forms of behavior. Refusal to recognize this fact is philosophical enthusiasm. [10]

[10] For more on philosophical enthusiasm, see "Dialogue," *EPM*, last four paragraphs. In view of these paragraphs, we must conclude that Hume exaggerates when in *EHU* xi (121) he says, "There is no enthusiasm among phi-

To judge from this sample, then, we may suppose that the intelligence Hume had planned to give of what passed in company would not have been included merely for its entertainment value, but would have illustrated a point and been well integrated into the literary structure of the paper. Perhaps he hoped to supply this feature by means of other letters, solicited from Kames, Hutcheson, and friends in England and France. Printing letters was, of course, a standard practice of the *Spectator, Craftsman,* and other papers. It recommended itself in two ways, easing the author's burden of composing for the periodical press and, more importantly, involving readers in the paper by giving them the hope of seeing their own writing in print. Readers enjoyed guessing the authorship of particular numbers and letters. Thus the *Spectator* was closely involved with the community of London, and thus Hume's paper would have been involved with the community of Edinburgh. But Hume must have dropped this intended feature fairly quickly, since no other examples of social intelligence, through letters or other means, appear in the *Essays.* The difficulties of sustaining such a feature would have been great in Edinburgh, as it was then without a theatrical or musical scene to report on, bereft of the Scottish Parliament, and with a society so small and intimate that the personal adventures of individuals could not be related without identities being discovered in short order. The proceedings of the Philosophical and Select Societies and the Poker Club might have made good copy, but none of these organizations existed yet.

Were it not an incontrovertible fact that Hume wrote the *Essays,* those who have worked their way through the profundities of the *Treatise* might find it difficult to accept that the same man had written both books, so radically different are they. But, looking closely at internal evidence alone, one can see between them a continuity of attitudes and prejudices.

---

losophers." His considered opinion, I believe, was that philosophical enthusiasm is so uncommon and uncontagious to a populace that it need not be much feared as a threat to society. Religious enthusiasm, however, is quite common and contagious: "Generally speaking, the errors in religion are dangerous; those in philosophy only ridiculous" (*THN* 1. 4. 7 [272]).

For instance, the mercantile figure with which Hume concluded his declaration of purpose is revealing. It is not just that the vehicle conforms with Hume's liberal views on trade; the tenor agrees with his program for cultural reform. Underlying the witticism is the presupposition that learning is conducted empirically, in which case it and common life are truly interdependent.[11] "The Materials of this Commerce," Hume wrote, "must chiefly be furnish'd by Conversation and common Life: The manufacturing of them alone belongs to Learning." Life is at best inane without the knowledge provided by learning; learning, at least among the humanities, is chimerical or irrelevant without close reference to actual life. Scientific methodology requires that the life observed be common rather than unusual, for empirical generalizations cannot be drawn from particular, possibly exceptional, cases. The raw materials of empirical learning are the common experiences of men, prominent among which are their social activities, and the manufacture from these materials of knowledge for society's use is the contribution of the learned. Any disruption of trade between the providers of raw materials and the producers of commodities impoverishes both. Hume's object here, as in the *Treatise* and the *Philosophical Essays*, is to bring polite society and the empirical sciences into an alliance. The difference is that here Hume is not speaking solely of abstruse philosophy, but of all empiricist learning, and hence does not single out adulterate philosophy as the common foe. Instead he speaks vaguely of the common foe as the "Enemies of Reason and Beauty, People of dull Heads and cold Hearts" (p. 536).

At this point Hume entangles himself in his own figurative language (his literary strengths lay elsewhere). He declares, "Let no Quarter be given, but to those of sound Understandings and delicate Affections." But no quarter should have to be given to those of sound understandings and delicate affec-

---

[11] The empirical presuppositions of this essay have been recognized by James Moore in "The Social Background of Hume's Science of Human Nature," *McGill Hume Studies*, ed. David Fate Norton et al., vol. 1, *Studies in Hume and Scottish Philosophy* (San Diego, 1979), 34.

tions, for such people, by definition, do not have dull heads and cold hearts; such people are supposed to be his allies. Only such Philistines should be spared as are not Philistines, he seems to say. It would be interesting, had Hume not deleted this essay in later editions, to see whether and how he would have revised this passage.

The model of harmony between learning and society that would suggest itself to Hume, as to any cosmopolitan Occidental of the time, would be France. While French culture might not be foremost in every art and science, Hume wrote, it excelled all others except the ancient Greek in distinguishing itself in all fields. Further, and relatedly, it had "in a great measure, perfected that art, the most useful and agreeable of any, *l'Art de Vivre*, the art of society and conversation" ("CL," 91). The preeminent theater for this art was the matriarchal salon, and it is this French institution that Hume invokes when soliciting the patronage of women readers:

> In a neighbouring Nation, equally famous for good Taste, and for Gallantry, the Ladies are, in a Manner, the Sovereigns of the *learned* World, as well as of the *conversible*; and no polite Writer pretends to venture upon the Public, without the Approbation of some celebrated Judges of that Sex.          ("EW," 536)[12]

If the ladies would put aside books of romance and mystic devotion and read the works mentioned in his papers, Hume engages to lead them to a state of sophistication as would qualify them to extend their rule beyond the conversable to the learned world.

It follows that an important feature of the essays is as much erudition as could be carried lightly through topics of interest to "the fair Sex." An example is Hume's importation into "Of Love and Marriage" of Plato's allegory of sexual relations from the *Symposium* (189 d-91). Conversely, in essays preponderantly of erudition he manages to include something calculated to hold or retrieve the attentions of the ladies, as when in "Of

---

[12] Cf. "RPASci.," 626, and "PDiv.," 628, for the value of free commerce with the fair sex.

the Rise and Progress of the Arts and Sciences" he digresses to discuss gallantry and dueling. "Of the Study of History" is an overt attempt to direct the ladies' reading away from romances and mystic devotion to something more solid. History, he argues, is particularly suited "to those who are debarred the severer studies, by the tenderness of their complexion, and the weakness of their education" (*EMPLit.*, 565).

At such times as Hume attempts to charm the ladies he is, to modern sensibilities, at his least attractive (unless it is when he is reprehending priestcraft). This fault cannot be explained away entirely as a misguided imitation of Addison's manner. Hume's banter of the ladies may owe something to Addison's way of "fair-sexing" it, as Swift called it; but if so it was so deeply assimilated as to be second nature to Hume. It is true that the essays in which he is most priggish and patronizing are those that he withdrew in subsequent editions, but we do not know that he withdrew them out of repentance for male chauvinism. It is possible to sustain our objection to his condescension and yet refrain from quite condemning him for not being in advance of his epoch in the treatment of women. As it was generally thought proper to protect ladies from the harsher sides of life, even in their reading, it was necessary for the periodicals to make special overtures assuring readers that ladies would be confronted with nothing offensive. This was no more true for the *Spectator* than for the *Craftsman*, in which "Caleb D'Anvers" claimed to "have always paid the utmost Regard to the *fair Sex*," and resolved "to let slip no Opportunities of entertaining them, in the most agreeable Manner, consistent with that good Breeding, which is due to them."[13]

Hume was hardly unusual in imitating the *Spectator* and the *Craftsman* when creating his periodical paper. They were the respective standards in Britain of social and political jour-

---

[13] No. 45, *Craftsman*, 14 vols. (London, 1731, 1737 [1736]) 2: 5. For the publication of the *Craftsman* in volume form, the numbers and dates were altered from those of the original pamphlets. For a restoration, see Herbert Davis, "Reprinting *The Craftsman*," *Book Collector* 2 (1953): 279–82.

nalism by which other periodicals were judged. The writers of the *Craftsman* had in some ways imitated its "immortal Predecessor, the Spectator."[14] Both were associated in the public mind with the best writers of their time, the *Spectator* with Addison's coterie and the *Craftsman* with the Scriblerians. (Whether or not Pope or Swift did contribute to the latter, the public were inclined to think so.[15]) But both were very much London papers. We may suppose that Hume's plan was to transplant their combined best qualities to Edinburgh. Had the plan been realized, we could expect to find included Persian tales, parables, dream visions, fables—any of the various literary genres employed in those papers. As it is, we find only some allegories and one letter to the editor. Both of Hume's models featured elaborately conceived (if fitfully maintained) personae, the reticent Mr. Spectator and the retired Caleb D'Anvers, who observed and commented upon the World from an objective station outside of it. While Hume does not seem to have intended to create a character through whom to speak, he too presented himself as one step removed from the World, a self-appointed ambassador from the realm of solitary study to the *beau monde*.

Precisely to what extent and to what ways did Hume comprehend the designs of both his models? For the details of Hume's debt to the *Spectator* the reader can consult Norah Smith, who identifies the numbers from which he took particular topics, devices, and attitudes.[16] A parallel study of the borrowings from the *Craftsman* would yield much less of interest. Hume could make much less use of the *Craftsman* because it was polemical, exactly what he wished not to be. To comprehend perfectly the designs of both the *Spectator* and the *Craftsman* was impossible because they were incompatible. In the first number Mr. Spectator publicly "resolved to observe an exact Neutrality between the Whigs and Tories"

---

[14] No. 26, *Craftsman* 1: 150.

[15] See Simon Varey, ed., *Lord Bolingbroke: Contributions to the "Craftsman"* (Oxford, 1982), xix–xxii.

[16] "Hume's 'Rejected' Essays," *Forum for Modern Language Studies* 8 (1972): 354–71.

unless forced from it "by the Hostilities of either side."[17] He would leave politics alone if politics left him alone. Addison and Steele were not averse elsewhere to vying with the Tories, but they designed the *Spectator* to be an island of calm amidst the broils of the day; and although the *Spectator* is not perfectly devoid of political content, that content was not overt or polemical. In contrast, the *Craftsman* was vehemently partisan. Hume's way of combining these incompatible designs precluded following the example of the *Craftsman* very closely. He resolved this incompatibility by remaining neutral, like Mr. Spectator, while also confronting political controversies, like Caleb D'Anvers, and maintained his neutrality by treating political topics as subjects for scientific study. Today we are accustomed to think of political scientists as operating, as scientists, above the contentions of political parties. In Hume's day such objectivity was something of an innovation. Political science was only then being created, by luminaries such as Montesquieu, Adam Smith, and Hume himself. This scientific neutrality meant that in his "political" essays Hume could not be nearly so beholden to the *Craftsman* as he was in his "moral" essays to the *Spectator*. We shall take up both categories of essay in turn.

## The Moral Essays

[Y]our thought hath all the charm of Novelty, altho it is
so extremely apposite and obvious: but in this lies the
Superiority of you Sons of true Genius, that every one
wonders the same did not occur to themselves, even
where you are least capable of being rival'd.
—Thomas Percy, 12 Mar. 1760, *Corr. with Shenstone*

A discussion of the moral essays must begin with the essays that Hume withdrew from publication at different times over the years, not one of which, significantly, was political. When planning the 1748 edition Hume struck out "Of Essay Writing," "Of Moral Prejudices," and "Of the Middle Station in

---

[17] *Spectator* 1: 5. Addison reiterated this policy in no. 445.

Life," describing them as "frivolous & finical." He also intended at that time to strike out "Of Love and Marriage" and "Of the Study of History" as being "too frivolous for the rest, and not very agreeable neither even in that trifling manner," but was dissuaded by Millar, who, Hume wrote, "made such Protestations against it, & told me how much he had heard them praisd by the best Judges; that the Bowels of a Parent melted, & I preserv'd them alive." Nevertheless, they disappeared after the 1760 edition of *Essays and Treatises*. This leaves unmentioned only "Of Impudence and Modesty" and "Of Avarice" among the essays withdrawn, but these are plainly cast from the same mold as the others and may be presumed to have been withdrawn for the same reasons. In 1772, speaking of some or all of these withdrawn essays, Hume wrote that "they coud neither give Pleasure nor Instruction: They were indeed bad Imitations of the agreeable *Triffling* of Addison."[18] The reason the withdrawn essays are all of the moral category, one suspects, is that Hume had imitated the *Spectator* much more closely than he had the *Craftsman*. After finding his own voice, he naturally would look back with some dissatisfaction on the pieces that most showed an apprenticeship to Addison.

Though she is careful not to overstate Hume's indebtedness to Addison, Norah Smith has shown that the rejected essays have a distinctly Addisonian character. One may reasonably conjecture that Hume composed these essays first, consciously imitating the *Spectator*, and then learned to adopt only what he found congenial in Addison. Hence there are two distinct classes among the moral essays, the imitations and those he deemed fit to retain in his collected works.

What strikes the reader as most remarkable in the essays of apprenticeship, because so out of Hume's character, is their utter emptiness of new or even rigorous thought. This superficiality was clearly deliberate. Hume was consciously writing in the "trifling manner" of Addison, who now has the reputation of being one of the most uninteresting minds to have

---

[18] 13 Feb. 1748, 24 Sept. 1752, 7 Feb. 1772, *LDH* 1: 112, 168; 2: 257.

written works of classic status. (Matthew Arnold thought his ideas commonplace and trite.[19]) Imitating Addison's style was, of course, a common practice among aspiring writers, especially among those unsure of their grasp of idiomatic usage. Voltaire, Benjamin Franklin, Boswell, and even Gibbon, at Mallet's advice, are some of the notable figures who in cultivating a supple, "correct" style gave their days and nights to the volumes of Addison.[20] But of these pupils only Hume, and perhaps Boswell in his *Hypochondriack* papers, felt the necessity of imitating the master's banality. The explanation is that Hume was imitating Addison's genre, the moral periodical essay, as much as his style. It is sometimes observed of Addison that although it may be doubted whether he could have written otherwise, the trifles he produced were admirably suited to his journalistic purposes, which were pedagogical and homiletic.[21] Johnson, whose understanding of Addison's achievements was sympathetic and profound, explains the aptness of the periodical to such purposes. In order to

survey the track of daily conversation and free it from thorns and prickles, which teaze the passer, though they do not wound him[,] . . . nothing is so proper as the frequent publication of short papers, which we read not as study but amusement. If the subject be slight, the treatise likewise is short. The busy may find time, and the idle may find patience.[22]

To the question, Why would a man of Hume's intellect imitate Addison's triviality as well as his tone? the answer is that, at least initially, Hume's genre and purposes were the same as Addison's.

---

[19] "The Literary Influence of Academies," *Lectures and Essays in Criticism,* in *The Complete Prose Works of Matthew Arnold,* ed. R. H. Super, 11 vols. (Ann Arbor, 1960–77), 3: 247–48.

[20] See Bond, *Spectator* 1: lxxxvi–lxxxvii, xcviii–cii; Pottle, *Boswell's London Journal,* 3; *Edward Gibbon: Memoirs of My Life,* ed. Georges Bonnard (New York, 1966), 98.

[21] E.g. James Sutherland, "Some Aspects of Eighteenth-Century Prose," *Essays on the Eighteenth Century, Presented to David Nichol Smith . . . ,* ed. J. R. Sutherland and F. P. Wilson (Oxford, 1945), 95.

[22] "Addison," *Poets* 2: 93.

Insofar as his purposes were pedagogical, Hume too had to adjust his material to the needs and capacities of his audience. The audience for his projected paper was, as for the *Spectator*, a rough-and-tumble urban populace. Johnson's defense of Addison's superficiality is largely applicable to Hume's imitations:

> [H]is instructions were such as the characters of his readers made proper. That general knowledge which now circulates in common talk [that is, c. 1780] was in his time rarely to be found [the 1710s]. Men not professing learning were not ashamed of ignorance; and in the female world any acquaintance with books was distinguished only to be censured. His purpose was to infuse literary curiosity by gentle and unsuspected conveyance into the gay, the idle, and the wealthy; he therefore presented knowledge in the most alluring form, not lofty and austere, but accessible and familiar.[23]

Hume's disadvantage was that he did not have in appreciable number a gay, idle, and wealthy audience, for in Edinburgh this class of person was much smaller than in London, and less distinct in taste and manners from the general populace. A depressed economy rendered Scotland socially backward in comparison with the south of England. Divested of the Scottish Parliament at the Union of 1707, Edinburgh had been demoted to a mere provincial capitol, and the gay, idle, and wealthy turned their attentions to London. Social life in the city was left subject to the untender mercies of a censorious Presbyterian Church. In addition, the confining geography of Edinburgh kept the upper class from segregating itself from the other classes, forcing at least some levelling of manners among the strata of society. The "elegant," those who, in Hume's words, "are not immers'd in the animal Life" ("EW," 533), did not in the 1740s have the refuge of the New Town, to which Hume was among the earliest to move when in his late years it was being developed. The rich and the poor, the professionals and the laborers, the "polite" and the "vulgar"

23 "Addison," 146.

lived crowded together in the wynds, closes, and lands of the tenements.[24] If Hume did not have at hand a large, distinct class of elegant readers to appeal to, he had to assist in the creation of such an audience.

Insofar as Hume imitated Addison's homiletic methods, he would deliberately avoid moral theory or casuistic reasoning, concentrating on well-known moral truths. Old moral truths, because they are old, inevitably grow trivial; or to be more precise, they grow trivial in the sense of growing humdrum, not in the sense of growing unimportant. It is of capital importance, for example, that promises should be kept, however trite the precept of good faith may have become. But assent to a moral truism and living according to its dictates are different things. It is precisely this triviality that lulls men into relaxing their practice of old moral truths. "[M]en more frequently require to be reminded than informed," wrote Mr. Rambler.[25] In his role as Edina's own Mr. Spectator, Hume would not have aimed so much at advancing new theories or insights as at softening manners, arousing literary interest, and reminding men of moral truisms they tend to forget. Elsewhere in the *Essays*, where he is not walking so closely in Mr. Spectator's steps, Hume can be found advancing new theories and insights, but not in the apprentice pieces, where instead he propounds the following trivial theses: that learning is a desirable conversational trait, that philosophical enthusiasm is to be eschewed, that members of the middle class should be content with their station, that impudence is to be distinguished from decent self-confidence, that marriages would be happier if spouses did not seek dominance, that it would be good for women to read books of history, and that avarice is a ridiculous vice. These are in sharp contrast to the penetrating theses and insights of the political and the retained moral essays. But in the apprentice pieces Hume

---

[24] See Henry Grey Graham, *Social Life of Scotland in the Eighteenth Century* (London, 1906), 81–126. For the effects of this social life on literature, see David Craig, *Scottish Literature and the Scottish People, 1680–1830* (London, 1961), 19–71.

[25] No. 2, *Rambler*, Yale Ed. 3: 14.

wished to be edifying rather than stimulating. His object was fundamentally conservative, to reinforce rather than reform standards of behavior. So intent was he on this conservative object that he here did something rather out of his character: he appealed to his readers' piety. He quotes Agur's prayer from Proverbs 30: 7–9, as had Addison in *Spectator* 464; and, entirely without irony, he twice refers to a wise and beneficent providence.[26] Bishop Butler must have approved.

Addison's concentration on moral truisms was a time-honored homiletic practice, with its roots, one suspects, in the Anglican tradition of sermonic literature. From Queen Elizabeth's day, doctrinal subtleties were deemphasized in favor of what the Church considered the essentials for right living. The libertarian ethos of the modern age usually keeps writers from trying to influence their readers' conduct in the minor affairs of daily life, but readers in Hume's time actively sought such guidance. They placed great importance on the "common occurrences of life; the right enjoyment of which," Hume wrote, "forms the chief part of our happiness" ("DTP," 4). Private life, wrote Mr. Rambler, "derives its comforts and its wretchedness from the right or wrong management of things which nothing but their frequency makes considerable."[27] Religious works dominated the presses and bookshops; and the popularity of the *Tatler* and the *Spectator* is partly attributable to their satisfying the general desire for instruction.[28] Johnson wrote that the "task of an author is, either to teach what is not known, or to recommend known truths, by his manner of adorning them."[29] We have seen in chapter 1 that Hume fully recognized this literary dichotomy, dividing philosophical writing into the "accurate and abstruse," which exposits newly discovered truths, and the "easy and obvious," which "purposes only to represent the common sense of man-

---

[26] "MSL," 546, 548; "IM," 552.

[27] No. 60, *Rambler*, Yale Ed. 3: 319.

[28] See Ian Watt, § 2 of chap. 2, "The Reading Public and the Rise of the Novel," *The Rise of the Novel: Studies in Defoe, Richardson and Fielding* (London, 1957).

[29] No. 3, *Rambler*, Yale Ed. 3: 14–15.

kind in more beautiful and more engaging colours." The dialogue, Hume felt, is one vehicle that is well suited to deliver any "point of doctrine, which is so *obvious*, that it scarcely admits of dispute, but at the same time so *important*, that it cannot be too often inculcated" (*DNR*, par. 1 [127]). There is no question that he regarded the Addisonian essay also as a vehicle for the easy and obvious philosophy since he specifically offered Addison as an example of an easy and obvious philosopher, contrasting him with Locke (*EHU* i [5]). The superficiality of the seven apprentice pieces turns out to be neither a lapse in Hume's genius nor a prostitution of his talents for the applause of the multitude, but simply a result of his attempt to write easy and obvious philosophy. These essays, then, are in design and purpose the exact reverse of the *Treatise*. With these essays he briefly joined those philosophers who

> select the most striking observations and instances from common life; place opposite characters in a proper contrast; and alluring us into the paths of virtue by the views of glory and happiness, direct our steps in these paths by the soundest precepts and most illustrious examples. (*EHU* i [3])

The retained moral essays are less purely easy and obvious, much to the enhancement of their interest for modern readers. Whether he consciously forsook agreeable trifling or simply failed to suppress his inquiring nature, Hume began to introduce into his social essays interesting and original reflections. In pieces like "Of the Delicacy of Taste and Passion" and "Of Superstition and Enthusiasm" he entered into a way of writing that belongs wholly to neither category of the literary dichotomy, that might be described as agreeably acute or easy and accurate. He continued to discuss topics such as could have or actually had appeared in the *Spectator*, but treated them with his characteristic analytic acuity.

Comparing essays with similar or overlapping topics, one from the apprentice pieces with one from the other moral essays, we can illustrate the difference between these two groups. Both "Of Love and Marriage" and "Of Polygamy and

Divorces" are concerned with the best possible arrangement of conjugal relations and are directed largely to women readers. The former consists of about half banter and half allegorical fable. Into his banter of the ladies Hume incorporates a story of the Scythian women who, sacrificing love for dominion, rendered their men dependent by blinding them. Thus he manages to show his readers how learning can enliven discussion of the most mundane topics while, at the same time, making the point that marital dominion is only won at a cost higher than the value of the prize. He then admits that this point applies equally to husbands as to wives and concludes that "pretensions to authority on either side" are undesirable (*EMPLit.*, 560). The two fables—the allegory of love from the *Symposium* and Hume's sequel to it—are supposed to induce us to embrace sexual equality, but if they do so it is only by means of illustration and not by argument. They could not convert someone who does not believe in sexual equality, though they could reinforce egalitarian practices in someone who does. Hume's sequel to Plato's allegory formulates the ingredients of conjugal happiness: only those couples able to combine the pleasures of love with the prudence of marriage will successfully unite; unmarried lovers and unloving spouses alike will form discordant unions. This is merely conventional morality, of course, but new truths were not Hume's object here. The principle of sexual equality certainly is an important and insufficiently observed moral truth, but not at all a new or daring one as Hume thought of it (for although he talks of "perfect equality" in marriage, it would be anachronistic to assume he means anything so radical as equal-employment opportunities).

In "Of Polygamy and Divorces," on the other hand, the pattern of easy and obvious philosophy is violated by the intrusion of an unconventional idea. This essay, too, features a good deal of banter with the ladies (which, because largely excised from later publications, can be found in the variant readings given in *EMPLit.*), together with a plentiful erudition that draws illustrations from diverse cultures and ages. But here the banter and erudition are integrated into argumentation, which pervades the essay. The presence or absence of argumentation is significant but not in itself a sufficient point of distinction between the two groups of moral essays. Among the seven withdrawn essays only "Of the Study of History" and "Of the Middle Station of Life" contain any considerable argumentation. But the crucial point of distinction is whether the reasoning extends beyond old moral verities. In "Of Polygamy and Divorces" the reasoning consists of three parts: preliminaries, argument over the comparative merits of polygamy and monogamy, and argument over whether it would be good to allow divorce. Hume's thesis—that indissoluble, monogamous marriages are best—is perfectly conventional, as are its supporting arguments; but in the preliminaries he strays somewhat from easy, obvious philosophy.

He begins with an assertion: "As marriage is an engagement entered into by mutual consent, and has for its end the propagation of the species, it is evident, that it must be susceptible of all the variety of conditions, which consent establishes, provided they be not contrary to this end" (*EMPLit.*, 181). Though the notion would not go unchallenged today, few in Hume's contemporary audience would have questioned that at least one of the primary ends of marriage is procreation. (The author of *The Whole Duty of Man* [London, 1682], a book Hume knew well, follows the Anglican marriage service in designating the ends of marriage as being the begetting of children and the avoidance of fornication [Sunday 7].) This idea qualifies as common wisdom, then, and even, to the unsuspecting Christian reader, would have suggested the teleological assumptions of theism. The theist would not have asked whose end procreation is; he would have assumed that it is God's end, shared by people insofar as they are right-minded. Yet it is incompatible with the sanctioned Christian form of marriage to assert, as Hume proceeds to do, that all established varieties of conjugal relations are legitimate that do not hinder the propagation of the species. This heterodoxy becomes plain when in the second paragraph he calls it "mere superstition to imagine, that marriage can be entirely uniform, and will admit only of one mode or form" (pp. 181–82). It is superstitious to think that one conjugal arrangement is holy and all others unholy, or that, employing Clarke's phraseology, only one is the morally "necessary result of the unalterable reason and nature of Things."[30] The lack of a supernatural prescription of one arrangement does not release us from moral constraints, however. As well as natural moral sentiment, there remains civil morality to be observed. There being no higher authority, no form of marriage furthering procreation and sanctioned by civil morality can be illegitimate:

> Municipal laws are a supply to the wisdom of each individual; and, at the same time, by restraining the natural liberty of men, make private interest submit to the interest of the public. All regulations, therefore, on this head are equally lawful, and equally conformable to the principles of nature; though they are not all equally convenient, or equally useful to society. (p. 183)

In the preliminaries Hume has been fixing the terms of the ensuing deliberation concerning the various forms of marriage. The deliberation over polygamy and divorce is to be carried out in terms of the principle of utility, without appeal to supernatural sanctions and prohibitions. He does not discount the supernatural in order to weaken the case for monogamy without divorce, but to strengthen it by basing it on observable realities.[31] Philosophically this is all of a piece with the political philosophy of book 3, part 2 in the *Treatise*. The

[30] *Discourse concerning the Unchangeable Obligations of Natural Religion* (London, 1706), 143–44.

[31] It should be noted that Hume intended his utilitarian argument to be understood only as an academic exercise not to be applied to a program of reform. He would not, for example, incite the Turks to civil disobedience against the laws establishing polygamy. Such a revolutionary project would probably cost more in subverting the moral order than it could yield in improved marital felicity. Similarly, Hume could argue that in theory his own constitutional design would produce the most perfect conceivable commonwealth and yet not propose his design for enactment because, in politics, "[t]o tamper . . . or try experiments merely upon the credit of supposed argument and philosophy, can never be the part of a wise magistrate, who will bear a reverence to what carries the marks of age" ("IPComm.," 512).

prose of the relevant passages contrasts with that of the rest of the essay in being almost legalistic. Although "Of Polygamy and Divorces" cannot be called accurate and abstruse, it is only impurely easy and obvious. Hume is mixing his literary kinds once again.

If we compare "Of Essay Writing," from the apprentice pieces, with "Of the Delicacy of Taste and Passion," from the retained essays, we can illustrate further the distinction that we are drawing between the two groups of moral essays, as well as sharpen our understanding of what benefit Hume thought could accrue from reading his writings. Both are employed as introductions to their respective volumes of the *Essays* and are intended to recommend cultivation. In "Of Essay Writing," as we have already observed, Hume offers himself as a liaison between learning and society. Through his offices the works of the former can gain polish and the conversation of the latter, substance. We have seen in chapter 1 that the idea of an unhealthy antagonism between learning and society was neither new nor unusual, and Hume develops it here with assertion and banter rather than argument. He is trying to charm rather than convince his readers. In "Of the Delicacy of Taste and Passion," however, the banter is gone, and he attempts to entice readers by intimating that they will gain in delicacy of taste, for the value of which he spends most of the essay arguing. There is much in the argument of interest even to *aficionados* of accurate and abstruse philosophy.

Hume begins by comparing the delicacies of passion and taste. They are, he suspects, closely connected in "the original frame of the mind" and are alike in serving to enlarge "the sphere both of our happiness and misery, and [make] us sensible to pains as well as pleasures, which escape the rest of mankind" (*EMPLit.*, 603, 5). They are different, he argues, in that delicacy of passion tends to make men unhappy whereas that of taste tends to the opposite. Unfortunately, "[g]reat pleasures are much less frequent than great pains," so that in the course of life, generally speaking, the sum of the passionate person's pain will far exceed that of his pleasure (p. 4). The pain and pleasure are too disproportionate even to cancel each other out. By and large, the man of sensibility will be miserable. For a cure to excessive sensibility Hume prescribed the cultivation of delicacy of taste. A "fine taste" for the sciences and liberal arts helps in two ways: in the collateral cultivation of judgment and good sense, which will place mishaps and reverses in proper perspective, and in channelling the passions from "rougher and more boisterous emotions" toward the "tender and agreeable" (p. 6). Years later, when Rousseau's "extreme Sensibility of Temper" began to poison their friendship, Hume wrote a diagnosis of Rousseau's malady that illustrates this thesis well:

> He has read very little during the Course of his Life, and has now totally renounc'd all Reading: He has seen very little, and has no manner of Curiosity to see or remark: He has reflected, properly speaking, and study'd very little; and has not indeed much Knowledge: He has only felt, during the whole Course of his Life; and in this Respect, his Sensibility rises to a Pitch beyond what I have seen any Example of: But it still gives him a more acute Feeling of Pain than of Pleasure. He is like a Man who were stript not only of his Cloaths but of his Skin, and turn'd out in that Situation to combat with the rude and boisterous Elements, such as perpetually disturb this lower World.[32]

Extreme sensibility, without judgment and diversions from outside of itself, dwells morbidly on its own sensations. If this psychological insight does not seem new or particularly astute, it is because we have the advantage, as Hume had not, of a great body of criticism on Romanticism.

But why does delicacy of taste not, as one would expect, yield the same unhappy disproportion of misery and pleasure as delicacy of passion? Surely the natural course of life does not expose us to a higher number of things in good taste than in bad? Even someone so fortunate as to be admitted to study at Oxford University, where amidst architectural beauty he will spend his days pondering the best that has been thought

[32] 25 Mar. 1766, *LDH* 2: 30, 29.

and said, will be subjected to the deficiencies of institutional cooking; to the occasional incivilities of scouts, porters, and administrative secretaries; to the din of city traffic; to the unreliability of the civic orchestra's French horns; and many other thorns and prickles that tease though do not wound a person of normal tastes. A fastidious person will be wounded, though, and must be wounded proportionately as he is fastidious; and fastidiousness is of course an adjustable attitude, so that a fastidious person can and will raise his standards of taste even if his environment is improved. As Hume says elsewhere, a "great inferiority of beauty gives pain to a person conversant in the highest excellence of the kind" ("ST," 238).

The same reservations apply to Hume's discussion of the salutary effect of delicacy of taste on friendship, to which he devotes his concluding paragraph. He approves of the tendency of delicate taste to confine our circle of friendship to a select few because the affections, thus focused, will be more intense and solid than if dispersed indiscriminately among a larger number of acquaintances. But why would it follow that the happiness arising from friendship would be greater for the discriminating than for the undiscriminating? The discriminating's affections might be more intense and solid, but the undiscriminating have many more friendships to compensate for the tepidity of their affection. It might be argued that the affection generated by many tepid friendships and by a few intense ones cannot be quantified and equated, that they are qualitatively different. But on the other hand the undiscriminating, feeling less intensely, do not suffer as much as the discriminating from souring friendships and separations. If the undiscriminating's affections are not so intense, neither are their disaffections and bereavements.

Is delicacy of taste not more vulnerable to the distasteful than indelicacy, and is not the comparative happiness yielded by delicacy and indelicacy thereby at least brought into a rough equilibrium? Hume says not, because in matters of taste, he thinks, we have a measure of control over our environment:

> The good or ill accidents of life are very little at our disposal;
> but we are pretty much masters what books we shall read, what
> diversions we shall partake of, and what company we shall keep.
> Philosophers have endeavored to render happiness entirely in-
> dependent of every thing external. That degree of perfection is
> impossible to be *attained*: But every wise man will endeavour
> to place his happiness on such objects chiefly as depend upon
> himself: and *that* is not to be *attained* so much by any other
> means as by this delicacy of sentiment. When a man is pos-
> sessed of that talent, he is more happy by what pleases his taste,
> than by what gratifies his appetites, and receives more enjoy-
> ment from a poem or a piece of reasoning than the most expen-
> sive luxury can afford.                                           (p. 5)

A taste for poetry or good conversation is less expensive and
generally less vulnerable to vicissitude than a passion for elaborate equipage or high station. Perhaps because he wished
not to lose his readers in detail, Hume does not consider cases
in which good taste and expense coincide, as with a taste for
opera or Sèvres porcelain, but according to his argument the
principle of control must prevail in such cases: though delicate, these are strategically undesirable tastes on which to
base one's happiness.

It is important to remember that Hume is not positing an
intrinsically greater beauty and worth of the liberal arts and
sciences over vulgar pleasures. He is not arguing along Platonic lines that the life of mind yields a higher, spiritual happiness by putting us more closely in touch with ideal beauty
and goodness. Hume subscribed to a mitigated scepticism according to which "beauty and worth are merely of a relative
nature" ("Sceptic," 163)—relative, that is, to the eye of the
beholder. All valuations, aesthetic or moral, reside in each individual's feelings rather than in the objects valued, just as
odor and color are aspects of sense perception rather than of
things in themselves:

> Objects have absolutely no worth or value in themselves. They
> derive their worth merely from the passion. If that be strong,
> and steady, and successful, the person is happy. It cannot rea-

sonably be doubted, but a little miss, dressed in a new gown for a dancing-school ball, receives as compleat enjoyment as the greatest orator, who triumphs in the splendour of his eloquence, while he governs the passions and resolutions of a numerous assembly [assuming that the two are of roughly the same delicacy of passion].                    (p. 166, and see n. 3)[33]

The greater pleasure to be had from poetry over riches is not due to the inherent superiority of poetry, but rather to two circumstances. First, collaterally to good poetic taste one (theoretically) cultivates good judgment and sense, which will prevent delicate taste from degenerating into fastidiousness. A sensible person, however refined, will not make himself miserable over thorns and prickles that should only tease him. Second, the pleasures of the life of the mind, being largely internal, are more within our control than those of the life of affairs:

> [T]he passions, which pursue external objects, contribute not so much to happiness, as those which rest in ourselves; since we are neither so certain of attaining such objects, nor so secure in possessing them. A passion for learning is preferable, with regard to happiness, to one for riches.          (p. 168; cf. p. 179 n.)

Without these two circumstances, delicacy of taste has nothing to recommend itself over indelicacy. But a supervenient superiority is no less real than an inherent one provided that the supervening circumstances do obtain, and it is against the circumstantial case that a Gradgrind would have to argue in order to refute Hume.

Doubtless had Hume been writing unadulteratedly accu-

[33] I am assuming with Boswell and Peter Jones that the views expressed by "The Sceptic" in his monologue at least closely approximate Hume's own views. See Feb. 1766, *Life of Johnson* 2: 9; and " 'Art' and 'Moderation' in Hume's Essays," *McGill Hume Studies*, ed. cit. 172–79. I have added the proviso in brackets to prevent readers from mistakenly concluding with Boswell that Hume means here "that all who are happy are equally happy." In "Of the Delicacy of Taste and Passion" Hume explicitly states the contrary, that there are people of greater than normal sensibility who will generally be happier or unhappier than others.

rate and abstruse philosophy he would have stated his case more cogently. But such an uncontroversial thesis as the worth of cultivation would hardly call for accurate and abstruse treatment. It was much more suitable for easy and obvious handling. There was no widespread disagreement or intellectual error that needed to be dispelled concerning the worth of cultivation; there was only a commonly held but weakly prosecuted desire for cultivation. On this point Hume's readers did not need convincing so much as encouragement. Yet Hume's method of encouragement has an argumentative richness that Addison, had he been capable of concocting it, would have avoided in a periodical essay.

Even above his role in the establishment of a new genre, Addison has always been noted for his style. In our own day, when the reverence in which his contemporaries held him seems a curious historical fact needing explanation, so eminent a critic as F. W. Bateson has judged, remarkably, that "Addison's prose style is probably the best, considered simply as style, in the whole range of English literature.[34] To what extent, then, was Hume Addison's pupil in style as well as genre? To answer this question we should first distinguish between lessons that Hume probably had learned as a youngster from Addison, studying English almost as an alien dialect, and those he may be seen to have learned in writing the *Essays*. If we count Addison's probable contribution to Hume's competence in the fundamentals of idiom, syntax, and diction, his influence will be estimated as much greater than if we narrow the question to his particular influence on the *Essays*. But the former kind of influence Addison had over many, perhaps the majority, of prose stylists of the time. The answer to the narrower question is that for the *Essays* Hume particularly studied Addison so as to be "polite," not simply in the old sense of literary polish, but also in the modern sense, only then gaining currency, of courtesy and congeniality. A lesson to be

[34] "Addison, Steele and the Periodical Essay," *Dryden to Johnson*, ed. Roget Lonsdale, vol. 4 of *History of Literature in the English Language* (repr. London, 1971), 146.

learned from the critical response to the *Treatise* was that a less aggressive, more equable style was called for, and a style so highly regarded as Addison's for its "modesty" would be the obvious model to follow.[35]

Yet even in politeness Addison's influence is only general and rather amorphous. Hume visibly strives to charm in the apprentice pieces, but relaxes his efforts somewhat in the other moral essays (perhaps with the effect actually of enhancing their charm), and fairly drops the effort in the political essays in favor of just being pleasant and evenhanded. Since the apprentice pieces contain his only published attempts at levity outside of satirical political pamphlets, we may suppose that Hume was emulating Addison's celebrated humor, which Johnson called "singular and matchless."[36] On the other hand, humor came quite naturally to Hume, as is evident in many of his letters. The testimony of his friends indicates that innocent humor was a particular distinction of his character. Smith's eulogy of Hume, for instance, contains the following characterization:

> His constant pleasantry was the genuine effusion of good-nature and good-humour, tempered with delicacy and modesty, and without even the slightest tincture of malignity, so frequently the disagreeable source of what is called wit in other men. It never was the meaning of his raillery to mortify; and therefore, far from offending, it seldom failed to please and delight, even those who were the objects of it. To his friends, who were frequently the objects of it, there was not perhaps any one of all his great and amiable qualities, which contributed more to endear his conversation.
>
> (Letter from Adam Smith to William Strahan, in *DNR*, 247)

Alexander Carlyle wrote of Hume that "For Innocent Mirth and Agreable Raillery, I never knew his Match," and provided a critical account of Hume's humor when he remarked

---

[35] For Addison's modesty of style, see Blair, no. 19, *Rhet.* 1: 395; Smith, 13 Dec. 1762, *Lect.*, 48–49.

[36] "Addison," 109.

that Hume shared with John Jardine "the Peculiar Talent of Rallying their Companions on their Good Qualities."[37] Naturally Hume exercised his flattering raillery more often in conversation and in letters than in published works. An example of this is his way of congratulating William Robertson upon the success of the *History of Scotland*: "A plague take you! Here I sat near the historical summit of Parnassus, immediately under Dr Smollett; and you have the impudence to squeeze yourself by me, and place yourself directly under his feet."[38] To appreciate fully this raillery, one must know, as Robertson undoubtedly did, that Hume did not think very highly of Smollett's *History*, and catch the allusion to the *Battle of the Books*, in which the duncical Moderns attempt to dislodge the Ancients from their rightful place at the summit of Parnassus.[39] Hume ironically reverses Swift's allegory, assigning the summit to a negligible writer and performance while depicting Robertson and himself, the worthies, in an unseemly scramble for second place. Thus he makes fun of the misconception circulating then that he and Robertson were rivals as historians and, further, suggests to Robertson that his merit puts him above concern for uninformed, fickle popular applause.

While in his published writings Hume did not have much occasion to praise individuals, his characteristic mode of raillery does appear in altered form in the *Essays* when he wishes to recommend modesty:

> Many a man, being sensible that modesty is extremely prejudicial to him in making his fortune, has resolved to be impudent, and to put a bold face upon the matter; But, it is observable, that such people have seldom succeeded in the attempt, but

[37] *Anecdotes and Characters of the Times*, ed. James Kinsley (London, 1973), 141, 133–34.

[38] 12 Mar. 1759, *LDH* 1: 302. Cf. 4 Feb. 1773, *LDH* 2: 271, and Price's discussion of it in *The Ironic Hume*, 121–22. For a different kind of flattering raillery, which might be called congratulation-by-commiseration, see 12 Apr. 1759, *NLDH*, 51–55.

[39] On Smollett, see 6 Apr. 1758, *LDH* 1: 273–74. For the allusion, cf. *Battle of the Books*, 219–22.

have been obliged to relapse into their primitive modesty.
Nothing carries a man through the world like a true genuine
natural impudence. Its counterfeit is good for nothing, nor can
ever support itself. In any other attempt, whatever faults a man
commits and is sensible of, he is so much the nearer his end.
But when he endeavours at impudence, if he ever failed in the
attempt, the remembrance of that failure will make him blush,
and will infallibly disconcert him: After which every blush is a
cause for new blushes, till he be found out to be an arrant cheat,
and a vain pretender to impudence.

                    ("IM," 553–54; cf. no. 231, *Spectator* 3: 400)

Here Hume outreaches Addison himself in agreeable raillery.
Its truth to life is painfully recognizable to anyone who has
had much to do with adolescents and observed them experi-
menting with impudence to see how it carries them through
the world. Its humor derives from an ironic situation: we are
accustomed to think of people's aspiring to a virtue and resolving to acquire it, but not of their aspiring to, and resolving
to acquire, a vice. Hume's diction develops the irony through
an artful clash of connotations, wherein the positive adjectives
"true genuine natural" are surprisingly applied to "impudence" while the hopelessly modest person is denounced as
an "arrant cheat, and a vain pretender." To be blamed for af-
fecting impudence is not praise, but neither is it simply
blame: blame is deflected, even transmuted, when it is remembered that the cheat is, after all, exposed as being incorrigibly modest. This sort of dexterity with diction and connotation is, according to Bateson, one of the distinguishing
excellences of Addison's style.[40] Hume did not exercise it frequently and therefore might be thought in these instances to
be writing with Addison's style in mind. But the general
ironic procedure, the wit without sting, is true, genuine, natural Hume. Addison's contributions here were only in having
shown Hume's generation what, according to Johnson, had
been forgotten in the age of Wycherly and Rochester, that

[40] Bateson, "Addison, Steele and the Periodical Essay," 148–49.

inoffensive wit is possible; and in connecting it in the public mind with the periodical essay.

Beyond his humor and his proficiency in the stylistic fundamentals mentioned above, Hume's politeness resists examination. The greater part of politeness was restraint, and restraint is difficult to demonstrate by quotation. To write politely, one had to be lively without making a spectacle of oneself, to be penetrating without being clever "in the dyslogistic sense of the word," as John Passmore finds Hume to have been in the *Treatise*.[41] In literature as in company, restraint makes the difference between pleasing others and merely displaying oneself; and herein resides the interconnectedness of politeness in manners and in writing.

In his system Hume places good manners among the artificial rather than the natural virtues, that is, among the "human contrivances for the interest of society" (*THN* 3. 3. 1 [577]) rather than among the instinctual traits like benevolence, the natural counterpart to politeness. Self-regard is equally as natural as benevolence, and quite as strong; so societies develop conventional rules of courtesy so as to compensate for the narrowness of our benevolence and "to curb and conceal that presumption and arrogance, so natural to the human mind" ("RPASci.," 126). This is what Johnson meant when he commended politeness as "fictitious benevolence."[42] Far from being a fraud, fictitious benevolence is a delicate aesthetic ceremony in which we willingly suspend our disbelief in each other's shows of deference. "These Ceremonies," Hume wrote,

> ought to be so contriv'd, as that, tho they do not deceive, nor pass for sincere, yet still they please by their Appearance, & lead the Mind by its own Consent & Knowledge, into an agreeable Delusion. One may err by running into either of the two Extremes, that of making them too like Truth or too remote from it. . . .

[41] *Hume's Intentions*, 152.

[42] 21 Aug. 1773, *Journal of a Tour to the Hebrides*, in *Life of Johnson* 5: 82.

The correct note must be struck. To be too truthful makes it difficult for others to suspend their disbelief in our self-regard. To be too artificial has the same effect by drawing attention to the fictitiousness of our benevolence, "just as it is a Transgression of Rules in a Dramatic Poet to mix any Improbabilities with his Fable; tho' tis certain that in the representation, the Scenes, Lights, Company & a thousand other Circumstances, make it impossible he can ever deceive."[43] A modern taste, for example, will probably find Hume's overtures to the fair sex overly ceremonious ("I approach them with Reverence" ["EW," 535]), though whether contemporary taste did may be doubted.

Hume preferred English manners (though not temperament) to French because French civilities were too artificial and "glaring."

> An English fine Gentleman distinguishes himself from the rest of the World, by the whole Tenour of his Conversation, more than by any particular part of it; so that tho' you are sensible he excells, you are at a loss to tell in what, & have no remarkable Civilities & Complements to pitch on as a proof of his Politeness. These he so smooths over that they pass for the common Actions of Life, & never put you to trouble of returning thanks for them. The English Politeness is alwise greatest, where it appears least.[44]

The old idea of *sprezzatura* had evolved into a code of behavior more genuinely calculated to please than to impress. Now brashness was not only to be tempered, but suppressed. One had not just to make one's accomplishments seem effortless, but to efface them so as not to reduce one's auditors to an audience. And if in conversation one's auditors are not to be treated as an audience, just so in polite letters one's audience is not to be treated as followers or misguided opponents. In

[43] 12 Sept. 1734, *LDH* 1: 20. Cf. *EPM* iv (200): "Too much or too little ceremony are both blamed, and every thing, which promotes ease, without an indecent familiarity, is useful and laudable."

[44] *LDH* 1: 20. Cf. Goldsmith, letter 4, *Citizen of the World* (London, 1760), last par.

politeness Hume had Mr. Spectator's and Mr. Tatler's examples to improve upon. Doubtless he had read Steele's character of "a Gentleman, or man of conversation":

> [H]is conversation is a continual feast, at which he helps some, and is helped by others, in such a manner, that the equality of society is perfectly kept up, and every man obliges as much as he is obliged; for it is the greatest and justest skill in a man of superior understanding, to know how to be on a level with his companions.[45]

He should not talk for fame or from ostentation, as Johnson myopically complained of Goldsmith and Burke.[46] If in writing an author cannot solicit the opinions of others as he can in conversation, he can conduct himself as one who regards his opinions as fallible and of no extraordinary authority. His discourse can be conducted "without vehemence, . . . without eagerness for victory, and without any airs of superiority" (*EPM* viii [239]), faults for which reviewers had blamed the anonymous author of the *Treatise*. Hume had explained in the *Treatise* that his occasional peremptoriness was extorted from him by the excitement of the moment and that he was not really dogmatic or conceited. But this is an admission that he had not always minded his manners. When he kept possession of himself, he was "*le bon David*," the most charming of men. For his conduct in society one can only trust to contemporary reports, such as John Home's, that "[t]ho' all men saw, no one ever felt his superiority."[47] For Hume's literary politeness one can adduce the style of the *Essays*. But to demonstrate a negative virtue like restraint we will have to show what is absent from the *Essays* that is present in the *Treatise*.

An example of restraint is Hume's suppression of his habit, evinced throughout the *Treatise*, of assuming a posture of de-

[45] No. 21, *Tatler*, ed. George A. Aitken, 4 vols. (London, 1898–99) 1: 175, 176.

[46] 7 Apr. 1778, *Life of Johnson* 3: 247.

[47] *A Sketch of the Character of Mr. Hume and Diary of a Journey from Morpeth to Bath, 23 April–1 May 1776*, ed. David Fate Norton (Edinburgh, 1976), 11.

bate with the reader, a practice that unnecessarily forces the reader to see himself as Hume's opponent. The one exception to this suppression, in which Hume forces his reader into the role of a Mandevillean cynic, is a passage added later for the *Essays and Treatises* of 1753 ("DMHNat.," 84–86), by which time Hume could revert to old habits, forgetting the spirit in which he had originally written. This exception underscores the generalization, that in the late 1730s and early 1740s Hume was suppressing his natural debater's instincts.

Another stylistic restraint in the *Essays* is against anything that would have been considered "false wit." Restraint in style meant charm and wit that was even and inconspicuous, a style that avoided eccentricities and egotisms. As Adam Smith observed approvingly of Addison, Swift, and Temple,

> [T]here is a certain uniformity in their manner: there are no passages that remarkably distinguish themselves; their admirers don't seem particularly fond of any one more than the rest; there are none which they get by heart and repeat with admiration, as they would a piece of poetry.[48]

Against such a standard, in a capsule literary survey appended to the *History*, Hume judged all writings from the classics to the Renaissance, faulting the writing of the latter period as being more Asiatic than Attic. Following Addison's criticism of false wit, he also called ostentatious wit "Gothic" (see, for example, *Spectator* 62). What he regarded as Asiatic, or Gothic, can be described in some detail. In English he disliked latinate inversions. He deprecated the "glaring figures of discourse, the pointed antithesis, the unnatural conceit, the jingle of words," "[u]ncommon expressions, strong flashes of wit, pointed similes, and epigrammatic turns." The effect of these tricks is that "the mind, in perusing a work overstocked with wit, is fatigued and disgusted with the constant endeavour to shine and surprize." Such, it will be remembered, was

---

[48] 15 Dec. 1762, *Lect.*, 52. Cf. Burke's "Character of a Fine Gentleman": "There is no part of his discourse you prefer to another; and he is never the man whose bons mots are retailed in every company" (*A Notebook of Edmund Burke*, ed. H. V. F. Somerset [London, 1957], 105).

the effect of *Tristram Shandy*. Rather than for the vulgar effect of surprise, the polite author tries for an "easy, unforced strain of sentiment," a "natural turn of thought and composition." The best critical formulation of stylistic politeness, Hume thought, was given in *Spectator* 345: "Fine writing, according to Mr. Addison, consists of sentiments, which are natural, without being obvious. There cannot be a juster, and more concise definition of fine writing."[49] Thus Hume embraced the critical criterion of natural novelty. This is an austere, some would say ascetic, ideal, one that might appear to involve the complete defoliation of literature. Hume's critical taste is an extreme example of what used to be called neoclassical, or Augustan, and which Romantic- and Victorian-age critics tried to debunk. (Perhaps it would more accurately be called neo-Attic.) Even Henry James, the least contentious of critics, regretted the "stupidity of a taste which had ended by becoming an aggregation of negatives."[50]

This is, of course, an unfair description of the neo-Attic ideal. Such an ideal would not necessarily reduce all writing to the blandness of the *Spectator*, as Hume's example, for one, shows. Adherents to it certainly had their likes and dislikes and held them ardently, but not more so than Romantics in their campaign against their predecessors and Modernists in theirs against Romanticism. After all its proscriptions, Hume's Attic ideal still leaves a good deal for an artist to work with.

Of the features listed above as false wit, Hume can be accused of perpetrating in the *Treatise* only strong flashes of wit and epigrammatic turns. The passages most often quoted by commentators are those that serve to startle, to shine and surprise. Such statements as

"Any thing may produce any thing" (1. 3. 15 [173])
"We have . . . no choice left but betwixt a false reason and none
    at all" (1. 4. 7 [268])
"Reason is, and ought only to be the slave of the passions, and

---

[49] *Hist.* 5: 149–50 (app. to the Reign of James I, s.v. "Learning and Arts") and "SRW," 191–93.
[50] *A Little Tour of France* (London, 1900), 29.

can never pretend to any other office than to serve and obey
them" (2. 3. 3 [415])

" 'Tis not contrary to reason to prefer the destruction of the
whole world to the scratching of my finger" (2. 3. 3 [416])

"Morality . . . is more properly felt than judg'd of" (3. 1. 2
[470]), and

"Carelessness and in-attention alone can afford us any remedy"
(1. 4. 2 [218]),

are memorable because, at first glance, they seem to reverse
the normal views of their subjects. But none of them means
what it seems to mean. Isolated from their contexts, they
seem to espouse irrationalism, when actually they are just an-
tirationalist and proempiricist. They are condensations of
lengthy and difficult arguments into hyperbolical, epigrammatic conclusions. They are also in contravention of the rule
of politeness that sentiments be natural. A mild paradox, such
as the humorous discussion of impudence and modesty
quoted above, can pass as natural, but not such violent paradoxes as these. Consequently no such unnatural turn of
thought and no such epigrammatic turn of expression are allowed in the *Essays*.

The *Treatise* and the *Essays* are not only different, then,
because the one is accurate and abstruse while the other is
easy and obvious. They are also different because they partake
of different, even opposed traditions of the essay genre. The
earlier book evinces the eccentricity and vitality of the essay
as established by Montaigne, while the later evinces the polite restraint of the essay as developed by Addison. The *Spectator* and *Tatler* papers are themselves not all in the Addisonian manner, written as they were by divers hands; and Steele,
perhaps, with his reliance on his own bluff personality to carry
his numbers, wrote in the tradition of Montaigne. But Addison's contributions were always the more influential. That his
distinction was found in his gentlemanly manners is shown in
Johnson's often-quoted description of the "middle-style" perfected by Addison, which was "always equable, and always
easy, without glowing words or pointed sentences. Addison

never deviates from his track to snatch a grace; he seeks no ambitious ornaments, and tries no hazardous innovations. His page is always luminous, but never blazes in unexpected splendour."[51] Modern critics, too, have generally described Addison's stylistic excellence in terms of restraint. Applying one of Eliot's criteria of a classic, that the writing give the feeling that the genius of the language is being realized rather than that a man of genius is using the language, Bateson finds Addison's prose a "plausible representative of the English classic moment."[52] The artist is not to be admired at the expense of the artifact. This criterion helps draw the contrast between the *Treatise* and the *Essays*. Readers have always responded to the earlier book as though they encountered in it a man of genius using the language. It is evident that in the later book, whether or not he succeeded, Hume wished rather to realize the genius of the language, to provide an immitable model of elegance for readers wanting to acquire polish. If it is not a style of exquisite subtlety or sensibility, it is one of eminent sensibleness. It is not well suited for the highest flights of feeling, but it is for the transactions of society.

## THE POLITICAL ESSAYS

The continuity of the *Treatise* and the political essays resides in their sharing Hume's humanist-inspired empiricist program. In chapter 1 we considered Hume's works as being shaped by the humanist notion, as currently expressed in Scriblerian and other writings, that no good could come of idle disputation, and that therefore it was important for the peace of society to direct men's inquisitiveness away from questions that offer no hope of settlement. The empiricist movement can be seen as having been motivated in part by the need to distinguish between questions that could and could not in their natures allow of progress. Individual empiricists may not in all instances have been rigorously empirical,

---

[51] "Addison," 149.
[52] Bateson, "Addison, Steele and the Periodical Essay," 150.

but by and large they judged the questions that could be taken up profitably to be such as could be referred to experience and observation rather than to reasoning a priori. Unaided reason has shown itself quite unable to adjudicate speculative disputes. As a standard against which to judge opposing views it was entirely too impeachable, one man's right reason being another's sophistry, heresy, or treason. Experience seemed to offer a more stable, authoritative standard and a hope at least to temper speculative disputes, which, history had taught, all too easily spill over into factional divisions and social unrest. Viewed from this perspective, Scriblerian and empiricist writings were different creases of the same humanist cloth: the thrust of Scriblerian satire was largely negative, toward deterring men from intellectual abuse, while conversely the thrust of empiricist philosophy was largely positive, toward enjoining men to follow the slow but surer way of experience rather than that of errant reason. With his attacks on adulterate philosophy Hume had sought to harness to the empiricist cause the antimetaphysical sentiment of the reading public. Accordingly he emphasized the constraints within which philosophy must be made to operate: demonstrative knowledge he strictly confined to purely conceptual issues, and knowledge of contingent fact he submitted to the limitations of what the mind is capable in its nature of experiencing. In chapter 2 we saw that with the *Treatise* he failed to enlist the public into an alliance against "school" philosophy.

Hume's empirical science of man was in its ultimate intent ironic in that idle disputation was to be replaced with constructive debate that could be settled by experimentation and observation. But to establish peace the scholastic disputants, those who love argument for its own sake, had to be disposed of first, and consequently the *Treatise* was no eirenicon. Not concealing his disapprobation, Hume brusquely dispatched the schoolmen, their modern counterparts, and their controversies. Making no attempt to show disputants that they had enough in common to compose their differences, he dispelled their issues, showing them that, literally, they had no idea of what they argued about. Just so, he exposed both sides of the dispute over the materiality or immateriality of the soul's substance as having been exercised over unintelligibilities (*THN* 1. 4. 5). Hume could hardly have expected such disputants to bless him as a peacemaker. But he did expect the reading public to distinguish between him and the disputants. Instead he was generally regarded, by those whose regard he gained, as just another clamorous, pugnacious metaphysician.

In the *Essays* he was at pains to deport himself in a manner better suited to an irenic purpose. Here the resolutions to be reached were not between scholastic disputants, but between parties exercised over issues of more immediate practical consequence, between Whig and Tory, Court and Country. Instead of exposing opposed arguments as being equally unintelligible, he sought to clarify issues, separating genuine differences from unresolvable, abstract disputes. These genuine issues could not simply be dispelled, being derived from real differences of interests and values, but if formulated properly they might be susceptible of compromise. Even-handedness and equability were now required. No longer was he out to silence the cavils of sophisters. But he was still trying to divert men's attention from arguments that in their natures could not be resolved.

The change in stance from the first work to the next is indicated by their mottoes. On the title page to the first two volumes of the *Treatise* Hume quotes from Tacitus: "*Rara temporum felicitas, ubi sentire, quae velis; & quae sentias, dicere licet.*" Mossner translates this as "Seldom are men blessed with times in which they may think what they like, and say what they think."[53] Anticipating opposition to his ideas, Hume invokes beforehand freedom of thought and expression. He is ready for a fight. On the title page and advertisements for the *Essays* he put "*Tros Rutulusve fuat, nullo discrimine habebo,*" which in the Loeb edition of the *Aeneid* is translated as "be he Trojan or be he Rutulian, no distinction

[53] Mossner, ed., *Treatise* (Baltimore, 1969), 32 (from Tacitus, *Histories* 1. 1).

shall I make." Dryden is more succinct: "*Rutulians, Trojans,
are the same to me.*"[54] Hume hereby declares himself disinterested in the party contentions that had everyone then,
even the contenders, worried about the stability of the state.
In case the motto had not made its point, Hume states it explicitly in the advertisement:

> [T]he Reader may condemn my Abilities, but must approve of
> my Moderation and Impartiality in my Method of handling Political Subjects: And as long as my Moral Character is in Safety,
> I can, with less Anxiety, abandon my Learning and Capacity to
> the most severe Censure and Examination. Public Spirit, methinks, shou'd engage us to love the Public, and to bear an equal
> Affection to all our Country-Men; not to hate one Half of them,
> under Pretext of loving the Whole. This Party-Rage I have endeavour'd to repress, as far as possible; and I hope this Design
> will be acceptable to the moderate of both Parties; at the same
> Time, that, perhaps, it may displease the Bigots of both.[55]

All public-spirited readers will approve of an attempt to repress party rage. As for the rest, Hume can live with the displeasure of those who can endure nothing that does not follow
their own party lines. He manages to be ingratiating and defensive at the same time. But, despite his defensiveness, he
refuses to fight, for to do so would impair his ability to mediate between the parties. It would make him just another
clamorous, pugnacious political scribbler. Such had been the
case with the *Craftsman*, in which one of Caleb D'Anvers's
major themes was "that it is Time to cast off the Delusions of
*Party*, and to be no longer satisfied with Names instead of
Things."[56] Yet at the same time that he trumpeted this theme
he was zealously partisan in opposition to the Walpole ministry. Opposition to the court party was the very raison d'être

[54] Trans. H. Rushton Fairclough, *Aeneid*, rev. ed., 2 vols. (London, 1934),
2: 177, 179 (10. 108); *Poems of John Dryden*, ed. James Kinsley, 4 vols. (Oxford, 1958), 3: 1324 (10. 167).

[55] *Essays* ("MDCCXLI"), iv–v.

[56] No. 17, *Craftsman* 1: 101. The reader will recognize the Lockean phrasing of this passage. Cf. no. 40, 1: 248–53.

of the periodical. Hume's performance would be different in that his commitment to correct the delusions of party was genuine.

Hume only proposes to repress party rage "as far as possible," and is not perfectly clear about what the possibilities are. He says in "Of the Coalition of Parties" that it may not be possible or even desirable to "abolish all distinctions of party" (*EMPLit.*, 493), but in that same paragraph he declares himself ready to try. Perhaps he thought the effort salutary whether it succeeded or not. In "Of Parties in General," explaining factions as a natural if baleful phenomenon, he is equivocal about the possibility of eliminating those formed out of opposed interests: "It requires great skill in a legislator to prevent such parties; and many philosophers are of opinion, that this secret, like the *grand elixir*, or *perpetual motion*, may amuse men in theory, but can never possibly be reduced to practice" (*EMPLit.*, 59). He does not want to undersell the possible contributions to government of the as yet unfledged science of man, but, on the other hand, the superior promise of the science of man lies in its pledge to operate within the limits of man's nature. Man's nature, we learn in the *Treatise*, is to be confined in his generosity, to be only self-referentially altruistic, as Mackie says.[57] Arising from the limits of man's benevolence, competition and opposed interests are facts that an empiricist simply must face up to. Factions are inevitable unless governments can change man's nature, and about that possibility Hume had no illusions: "All plans of government, which suppose great reformation in the manners of mankind, are plainly imaginary" ("IPComm.," 514).

What government can do, and what the science of man can help it to do better, is to control competition so that life will not be solitary, poor, nasty, brutish, and short. Scientific government controls competition by accommodating opposed interests when possible and maintaining a factional balance of power that keeps the peace:

[57] *Hume's Moral Theory*, 83–84.

When there offers . . . to our censure and examination, any plan of government, real or imaginary, where the power is distributed among several courts, and several orders of men, we should always consider the separate interest of each court, and each order; and, if we find that, by the skilful division of power, this interest must necessarily, in its operation, concur with public, we may pronounce that government to be wise and happy. If, on the contrary, separate interest be not checked, and be not directed to the public, we ought to look for nothing but faction, disorder, and tyranny from such a government.     ("IParl.," 43)

Hume's attempts in these essays to reduce politics to a science do not themselves offer detailed guidance in how to divide power so that factional interests concur with the public interest. They purport only to be essays toward the beginning of a science capable of such guidance. Empirical science progresses slowly, incrementally, "by timorous and sure steps" (*EHU* xii. 1 [123]).

In the meantime Hume could help in a small way to temper party rage by dealing piecemeal with individual issues. He could show members of the contending parties where the heat of argument pushed them into positions more extreme than they would normally take. A disinterested, scientific view of the issues, showing things in their full complexity, can counter doctrinaire simplifications. A good example of this procedure is "Of the Independency of Parliament," in which Hume tries to sober up the country party with regard to the issue of court influence in the House of Commons. In responding to Bolingbroke's Dissertation on Parties, Hume represents the country party as showing

vehemence and satyre, . . . too rigid an inflexibility, and too great a jealousy of making concessions to their adversaries. Their reasonings lose their force by being carried too far; and the popularity of their opinions has seduced them to neglect in some measure their justness and solidity.     ("IParl.," 609)

Hume wants to be seen here by the country party not as contradicting them, but as helping them to formulate their case better. But later he reveals that he is adjusting their case so that it is capable of compromise with that of the court party.

The Dissertation on Parties, of course, originally appeared in the *Craftsman*. In number 395 Bolingbroke asserts, in purple prose, that the independence of Parliament from the court is vital to the constitution. If the Parliament is corrupted, that

> noble Fabrick, the Pride of *Britain*, the Envy of her Neighbours, raised by the Labour of so many Centuries, repair'd at the Expence of so many Millions, and cemented by such a Profusion of Blood; that noble Fabrick, I say, which was able to resist the united Efforts of so many Races of Gyants, may be demolish'd by a Race of Pygmies, [sic] The Integrity of *Parliament* is a Kind of *Palladium*, a tutelary Goddess, who protects our State. When She is once removed, We may become the Prey of any Enemies. No *Agememnon*, no *Achilles* will be wanted to take our City. *Thersites* himself will be sufficient for such a Conquest.[58]

Hume's view is that, to the contrary, some court influence in Parliament is vital to the constitution. Without it the monarchy would be subjugated by the legislature and the mixed government would collapse. (It was just this danger of legislative encroachment on the executive that concerned the framers of the American Constitution.) Hume points out that there are no formal constraints on the power of the Commons, which "must necessarily have as much power as it demands, and can only be confined by itself" ("IParl.," 44). Informally, however, the monarch commands the allegiance of sufficient numbers in the legislature to hold his own in particular contests. This allegiance he commands through his disposal of remunerative offices among members of Parliament:

> We may, therefore, give to this influence what name we please; we may call it by the invidious appellations of *corruption* and *dependence*; but some degree and some kind of it are insepara-

[58] No. 395, *Craftsman* 12: 108.

ble from the very nature of the constitution, and necessary to
the preservation of our mixed government.

Instead then of asserting absolutely, that the dependence of
parliament, in every degree, is an infringement of BRITISH liberty, the country-party should have made some concessions to
their adversaries, and have only examined what was the proper
degree of this dependence, beyond which it became dangerous
to liberty.                                                    (p. 45)

This essay counterbalances "Of the Liberty of the Press," in
which Hume argues a moderated country-party position, that
a press in great degree free and independent is integral to the
constitution. Some degree of parliamentary dependence on
the court, he now argues, is no less integral to the constitution. He goes on to explain the difficulties involved in settling
such a question of degree. But though such an accommodation is difficult, and must be continually readjusted according
to the power of each succeeding monarch and minister, it is
the kind of debate into which statesmen should and must enter. And it is not the kind of debate that is likely to inflame
factious zeal.

"That Politics May Be Reduced to a Science" is interesting
because it shows Hume countering a rival plan to reduce
party rage. The danger of conducting political debates on the
level of principle, as the science of politics involves, is that
people are prone to think of their own principles as absolute,
in which case it becomes a vice to compromise. They are not
sceptical enough of principles, mistakenly supposing them to
be part of a moral structure inherent in the universe. Hume
shows himself well aware of this danger when he makes such
remarks as "when a faction is formed upon a point of right or
principle, there is no occasion, where men discover a greater
obstinacy" ("FPGov.," 33), and

A man, who esteems the true right of government to lie in one
man, or one family, cannot easily agree with his fellow-citizen,
who thinks that another man or family is possessed of this right.

> Each naturally wishes that right may take place, according to his
> own notions of it.                                    ("PGen.," 60)

In reaction to this difficulty a notion had gained currency that
political principle was not really significant after all, that attention should be focused instead on the character of the gov-
ernor(s):

> It is a question with several, whether there be any essential dif-
> ference between one form of government and another? and,
> whether every form may not become good or bad, according as
> it is well or ill administered? Were it once admitted, that all
> governments are alike, and that the only difference consists in
> the character and conduct of the governors, most political dis-
> putes would be at an end, and all *Zeal* for one constitution above
> another, must be esteemed mere bigotry and folly.
>                                               ("PSci.," 14–15)

To illustrate this notion Hume quotes a famous couplet from
the *Essay on Man*:

> For Forms of Government let fools contest;
> Whate'er is best administer'd is best. . . .
>                                               (iii. 303–4)[59]

If it were true that forms of government are inconsequential
to the public welfare, and that therefore it is pointless to advocate on principle one form against others, political science
would be impossible, presupposing as it does that man's institutional behavior follows laws that can be discovered by observation. Hume refutes the personal-character theory of government at some length by citing cases throughout classical
and modern history in which the forms of government had
profound effects on the public welfare. He maintains that
"[s]o great is the force of laws, and of particular forms of government, and so little dependence have they on the humours
and tempers of men, that consequences almost as general and

---

[59] Pope recorded that he had not meant that forms of government are inconsequential; but Hume was not alone in so construing this couplet. See
*Poems*, 534–35 n. to lines 303–4.

certain may sometimes be deduced from them, as any which the mathematical sciences afford us" ("PSci.," 16). Hume confines himself to the question of whether it is true that forms of government are inconsequential, probably because he was primarily concerned to show that political science is possible, but as he wrote he must also have had in mind the practical effects of such a thesis on the conduct of political disputes. In the background of this essay are the vituperative wars of the *Craftsman* against Walpole and of the ministry papers like the *Gazetteer* against Bolingbroke and other figures in the opposition. The conduct of these papers showed that the effect of centering disputes on the character of politicians would not be to lessen partisan zeal, but to make debates personal and acrimonious. Personal animosities are as serious an impediment to compromise as differences of principle. Furthermore, the science of man, once disseminated, could help prevent men from holding their principles dogmatically. The only medicine for political superstition, as for any superstition, is true philosophy.

The above descriptions of the contents of the political essays should indicate how little these essays resemble the numbers of the *Craftsman*. The moral essays show a development from the imitations of Addison toward impurely easy and obvious writing. Continuing this progression, the political essays might be described as impurely accurate and abstruse. This strain of accuracy and abstruseness, as has been said, makes them much less the recognizable scions of the *Craftsman* than the moral essays are of the *Spectator*. The *Craftsman* has little to teach us about the literary form of Hume's political essays, however valuable it is as a work of reference that explains the controversies of the day. Gerhard Streminger has said that it is now usual in the English-speaking world to commence philosophical discussion with a look at Hume's thoughts on the matter at hand.[60] Hume seems to have used the *Craftsman* as philosophers now use his works, as a point of departure. It was good for this purpose because among the

---

[60] "Hume's Theory of the Imagination," *Hume Studies* 6 (1980): 91.

politically minded it was widely recognized as a standard work. But the *Craftsman* was satirical and controversial, while the essays merely touch on contemporary issues as they relate, sometimes only tangentially, to an objective, anatomical approach to political phenomena. The emphasis is on the science of man.

In categorizing Hume's writings as more or less easy and obvious or accurate and abstruse, we should remember that this dichotomy is not equivalent to that conventionally drawn today between first- and second-order investigations. Accuracy, abstruseness, easiness, and obviousness refer simply to degrees of intricacy, stringency, graspability, and newness of the material. Where the abstruse ends and the obvious begins is not precisely determinable, whereas the modern dichotomy is between more discrete kinds of investigations.[61] A first-order factual problem concerns the discovery of the truth in a particular case. (Is it true, for example, that republican principles were integral to the ancient English constitution and that the Stuarts had violated the genius of the nation?) An ethical first-order problem of this level of particularity concerns whether in given circumstances a certain course of action or inaction is right or wrong. (Ought one's allegiance to go to the house of Stuart or of Hanover?) At a level of greater generality, first-order problems are normative. For example, what methodology can help determine questions of fact, such as the historical nature of the constitution? (Hume was concerned with the rules for weighing the credibility of historical sources. He was also concerned with the rules for judging of cause and effect.) A question of normative ethics is one concerning what standard we should adopt to tell right from wrong. (Should we judge of morality by following our own consciences, church doctrine, civil law, the mores of society, or some principle like utility? A pressing normative question then was how to tell when the citizenry were entitled to re-

---

[61] See Jonathan Harrison, "First-order / Second-order," chap. 1, *Our Knowledge of Right and Wrong* (London, 1971), 13–19; Mackie, *Ethics: Inventing Right and Wrong* (Harmondsworth, 1977), 9–10; David Miller, *Philosophy and Ideology in Hume's Political Thought* (Oxford, 1981), 10–11; P. F. Strawson, *Introduction to Logical Theory* (London, 1952), 15.

place their sovereign.) These are first-order problems of varying levels of generality. Second-order problems, in contrast, deal with the status—analytical, logical, linguistic, or psychological—of first-order problems. They are meta-problems, problems *about* first-order problems. One *meta*physical question concerns the relation of human knowledge to objective reality. (When we descry causal relations, do we apprehend a necessary connection between events, or does the regularity of events just condition us to feel a connection?) A meta-ethical problem concerns the status of moral judgments. (Do we apprehend the fitness or unfitness of actions to the scheme of things, or do we just experience reactive feelings of pleasure or displeasure?)

The examples given above show that even the *Treatise* and the *Philosophical Essays* do not remain always at the second-order level of inquiry, but descend to the normative level of first-order investigation. Methodology, a first-order subject, is obviously of primary importance in books intended to initiate the new science of man. The object in one of the most famous philosophical essays is to establish the criterion by which to judge the reliability of testimony concerning miracles, a question of historical methodology. Yet this essay appears in the book that Hume introduced with the warning (discussed above in chapter 1) that therein the reader would encounter accurate and abstruse philosophy, albeit sweetened with an elegant presentation. Hume regarded these normative first-order discussions as abstruse. The problems dealt with in the political essays are all first-order questions of fact. (Does the British government, for example, incline more to absolute monarchy or to a republic? What are the first principles of government?) But they are also at least somewhat abstruse and accurate. In the first of the *Political Discourses*, which book Hume called "the second Part of my Essays,"[62] he prepares the reader for the abstruseness ahead:

> All people of *shallow* thought are apt to decry even those of *solid* understanding, as *abstruse* thinkers, and metaphysicians, and refiners; and never will allow any thing to be just which is

[62] "My Own Life," in *LDH* 1: 3.

beyond their own weak conceptions. . . . They cannot enlarge their view to those universal propositions, which comprehend under them an infinite number of individuals, and include a whole science in a single theorem. Their eye is confounded with such an extensive prospect; and the conclusions, derived from it, even though clearly expressed, seem intricate and obscure. But however intricate they may seem, it is certain, that general principles, if just and sound, must always prevail in the general course of things, though they may fail in particular cases; and it is the chief business of philosophers to regard the general course of things.

Hume goes on to warn that he will put forth some new propositions: "If false, let them be rejected: But no one ought to entertain a prejudice against them, merely because they are out of common road" ("Comm.," 253–54, 255).

Despite its abstruseness, the political branch of the science of man is potentially of high practical value to society. It is true, admittedly, that the social benefits of philosophy arise only indirectly. But to be indirectly rather than directly beneficial is not necessarily to be less beneficial; it is only to be, to the less discerning, less obviously beneficial. If it is the chief business of philosophers to regard the general course of things, "it is also the chief business of politicians" (p. 254). In politics as in anything else, "it is of consequence to know the principle whence any phenomenon arises, and to distinguish between a cause and a concomitant effect. Besides that the speculation is curious, it may frequently be of use in the conduct of public affairs" ("Int.," 304). It can be of use in that politicians with a philosophical regard for the general course of things "will acquire greater foresight and subtility, in the subdividing and balancing of power" (*EHU* i [7]), rendering society less factious and more stable. This is preventative medicine, helping to prevent instability rather than to cure it once the state is endangered. Insofar as philosophers can help politicians to understand the current state of affairs by revealing its place in the general course of things, they are public benefactors: "Those who employ their pens on political subjects, free from party-rage, and party-prejudices, cultivate a science, which, of all others, contributes most to public utility" ("CL," 87).

One surprising limitation of political science as Hume conceived it should be noted. Its utility does not extend beyond domestic affairs since only they, Hume thought, were susceptible of being reduced to underlying principles. "Effects will always correspond to causes; and wise regulations in any commonwealth are the most valuable legacy that can be left to future ages" ("PSci.," 24). Potentially philosophers can help politicians formulate regulations so as to have the effects desired in domestic affairs. There might be considerable practical impediments to constitutional reform, but at least there is nothing in the nature of the topic to prevent the discovery of what a wisely constituted commonwealth would be like. Then politicians could know in what direction to move insofar as circumstances permit. This is possible because the causal relations of domestic politics can be discovered. But those of international politics are less penetrable. The general course of things is penetrable only "in the domestic government of the state, where the public good . . . depends on the concurrence of a multitude of causes; not, as in foreign politics, on accidents and chances, and the caprices of a few persons" ("Comm.," 254–55). Of course when Hume speaks of chance and accident he is deferring to ordinary language. He was a determinist and believed "that what the vulgar call chance is nothing but a secret and conceal'd cause" (*THN* 1. 3. 12 [130]; cf. *EHU* vi [par. 1]). But when causes are impenetrable he is willing to call it chance and go along with the vulgar: he needs a word to designate unknown causes and "chance" will do. So the problem with international politics is not that causal regularity is somehow suspended between nations; it is that the causal relations cannot be observed. They are the kind of relations that operate in the particular psychologies of individual men. And, as has been said, empirical generalizations cannot be drawn safely from particular, possibly exceptional, cases. Hume thought that events in international politics are largely caused by individual monarchs, ministers, and military commanders, whose capacities and peculiarities of character are largely unknown factors. Even when they are known, one cannot safely draw conclusions from their behavior that would apply to other monarchs, ministers, and commanders; humankind is uniform, but individuals are various. In contrast, events in domestic politics are caused mostly by forces much larger and more discernible. Therefore,

> the domestic and the gradual revolutions of a state must be a more proper subject of reasoning and observation, than the foreign and the violent, which are commonly produced by single persons, and are more influenced by whim, folly, or caprice, than by general passions and interests.          ("RPASci.," 112)

It is much easier, for example, to predict how the British populace would react to the abrogation of the liberty of their press than to predict whether Walpole would go to war over Jenkins's ear. The science of man, therefore, can help to achieve a stabilizing balance of power between factions in a body politic, but not, unfortunately, between the nations of the world.

It could not even help domestically if it were not disseminated and developed. It narrowly missed being disseminated first, in its political branch, in the form of the humble periodical paper. The *Political Discourses*, the next installment in Hume's political science, was not originally conceived as essays for the periodical press and is unencumbered with the attending characteristics of that genre. But the exercise of writing in that genre had had lasting benefits for Hume's style. The overt irenic purpose of that writing made the pyrotechnics of the *Treatise* inappropriate. This time Hume cultivated the middle style, the dominant effect of which on the reader, instead of surprise, is of a gentle and insistent pressure toward sanity.

# Chapter IV

## THE *ENQUIRIES*

The style of *The Treatise of Human Nature* is so
obscure and uninteresting, that if the author had not in
his [*Philosophical*] *Essays* republished the capital
doctrines of that work in a more elegant and sprightly
manner, a confutation of them would have been
altogether unnecessary.
—James Beattie, *An Essay on the Nature and
Immutability of Truth*, pt. 3, chap. 3.

In [1751] was published at London my Enquiry
concerning the Principles of Morals, which, in my own
opinion (who ought not to judge on that subject) is of
all my writings, historical, philosophical, or literary,
incomparably the best.
—"My Own Life"

IN THE two *Enquiries* Hume's literary development reached
what he felt to be a kind of culmination. It was not that they
dwarfed his other writings in the importance of their contents.
The culmination lay in his having solved to his satisfaction
some literary problems to which his experience with the *Treatise* had made him sensitive. Certainly he did not not see this
culmination as philosophical.[1]

It is generally agreed that the *Enquiries*, together with the
dissertation "Of the Passions," constitute a new presentation
of substantially the same philosophy as Hume expounded in
the *Treatise*. Argumentative details and some entire topics
are omitted, some change is made in emphasis, and some dis-

[1] In order to avoid confusion, I shall call the *EHU* after its original title,
*Philosophical Essays*. I shall call the *EPM* "the second *Enquiry*."

cussions of religion are added; but all is at least broadly in alignment with what had been said before.[2] It might be more accurately said that some discussions of religion are *restored*: the argument concerning testimony as to the occurrence of miracles we know to have been old material that Hume had deleted from the *Treatise* before its publication;[3] the same may easily have been the case with the refutation of the "argument from design" (see *EHU* x–xi). There is no striking progression in or revision of Hume's thinking between the *Treatise* and the *Enquiries*. Yet Hume regarded the latter as significant improvements, enough so that in the advertisement to the *Essays and Treatises* he renounced the *Treatise* and referred the public to the new versions.

In stating that his dissatisfaction with the *Treatise* had derived "more from the manner than the matter," Hume implied that the *Philosophical Essays*, into which he had recast most of book 1, was superior more for its literary than philosophical merits. Elsewhere he wrote that the *Philosophical Essays* contained "the same Doctrines, better illustrated & exprest."[4] His surprising final appraisal of the second *Enquiry*, given above among the epigraphs to this chapter, was no mere freak of his dotage. He had held this opinion at least since 3 May 1753, when he wrote, "I must confess, that I have a Partiality for that Work, & esteem it the most tolerable of anything I have composd." Later, in comparing the suitability of the two *Enquiries* for translation into French, he wrote, "My Enquiry concerning the Principles of Morals wou'd prob-

[2] *THN* 1. 2. 1–6, it seems likely, Hume reworked into the lost dissertation, "Considerations Previous to Geometry and Natural Philosophy." See 12 June 1755 and 25 Jan. 1772, *LDH* 1: 223, 2: 253; and Mossner, "Hume's *Four Dissertations*: An Essay in Biography and Bibliography," *Modern Philology* 48 (1950): 37–57.

In chap. 4 of *Hume's Philosophical Development* Noxon argues that in the *Enquiries* Hume played down psychology in favor of logical analysis, but, if true, this would be a shift in emphasis rather than a substantial revision of his tenets, as Noxon shows himself aware when he speaks of Hume's "stability of conviction" during forty years of philosophical thinking (p. 153).

[3] See 2 Dec. 1737, *NLDH*, 2.

[4] "My Own Life" and [Feb. 1754,] *LDH* 1: 3, 187.

ably be more popular; and indeed, it is my favorite Performance, tho' the other has made more Noise."[5]

These are remarkable judgments, the reasons for which are not readily apparent to posterity. The explanation proposed here will be that Hume was satisfied with the *Enquiries* because in them he had found a form and a voice that he could hope would serve both philosophical and literary purposes, that could please and instruct with accurate and abstruse materials. To reconcile pleasure and instruction is difficult enough, retaining the old didactic meaning given then to "instruction"; but to reconcile them both moreover with abstruse philosophy will to literary and philosophical purists alike seem a misguided endeavor. The error is compounded, they might add, in that Hume's evident purpose in simultaneously attempting divergent aims was popularization. We moderns have grown so accustomed to the notion that great minds are inevitably alienated from their societies that we are suspicious of any writer not following solely the dictates of his own genius in scorn of popular tastes. Hume would have thought this alienation a species of enthusiasm. In his letters, as he ages, we do find him increasingly impatient with the public, but there is no indication that he ever wrote according to some ideal excluding the intent to please and instruct. On the other hand, that he did not write philosophy for philosophy's sake does not mean that he was unwilling to challenge the public. A writer may choose to be uncompromising when popular tastes and his genius do not happen to coincide, or he may as legitimately seek a balance between conflicting demands. In the *Enquiries* Hume thought that he had found such a balance. His career was a series of attempts to disseminate the science of man, and dissemination required that he be widely read. Consequently we find him after the *Treatise* feeling his way through imperfectly modulated oscillations between the poles of accurate abstruseness and easy obviousness. Whether

[5] *LDH* 1: 175 and 5 Nov. 1755, *LDH* 1: 227. It might be that when Hume made these statements he was not considering the *DNR*, which was only published posthumously.

the compromise adopted in the *Enquiries* was successful, and whether the second *Enquiry* was the best of Hume's works, every reader had best judge for himself; but he will be better able to do so with an understanding of the nature of that compromise. Such an understanding is the object of this chapter.

## THE CONCISE STYLE

In chapter 1 we saw Hume declaring his intention in the *Philosophical Essays* to attempt a compromise between easy obviousness and accurate abstruseness, combining as far as possible the merits of the two species of philosophical writing. Hume would achieve this compromise "by care and art, and the avoiding of all unnecessary detail" (i [12]). If successful, the book would be easy despite its accuracy. It would be minimally abstruse, and not at all obvious since his purpose was to teach new truths rather than to represent the common sense of mankind in more engaging colors. The second *Enquiry* shows every sign of having been intended to comprise the same elements (with the significant difference, discussed, in the last section of this chapter, that Hume was there able to evade having to choose between presenting either new or obvious truths). There Hume endeavors "to take objects, according to their most simple views and appearances" because "[t]hese sciences are but too apt to appear abstract to common readers, even with all the precautions which we can take to clear them from superfluous speculations, and bring them down to every capacity" (app. 4 [283 n. 1]). Hume's solicitude for the reader's ease approaches courtly ostentation, as when he prepares us for a discussion of free will and determinism. The issue is so vexed and has been so mishandled, he concedes, that a sensible person may justifiably

> indulge his ease so far as to turn a deaf ear to the proposal of such a question, from which he can expect neither instruction nor entertainment. But the state of the argument here proposed may, perhaps, serve to renew his attention; as it has more nov-

elty, promises at least some decision of the controversy, and will not much disturb his ease by any intricate or obscure reasoning.

(*EHU* viii. 1 [66])

This is, of course, too good to be quite true. Hume offers what he hopes is an original and definitive resolution to an ancient dispute, a resolution that is, moreover, easily enough understood *pour distraire les honnêtes hommes*, who normally recoil from such topics with disgust. Hume is ambitious and confident; but a large part of his attitude is ambition for the science of man as well as for himself, a confidence in its capacity to solve those problems definitively that can be solved and dispose of those that cannot. The reader does not take offense at this bravado, for it is offset by Hume's solicitude. The same solicitude caused him in the second *Enquiry* to relegate to an appendix his discussion of the relative functions of reason and sentiment in moral judgment, "lest it should . . . involve us in intricate speculations, which are unfit for moral discourses" (app. 1 [258]).

This new easiness seems to take place more at the level of ordonnance than of the construction of individual sentences, at which Hume had been fairly skillful before.[6] It is an organizational reform. What are now appendices 2 and 4 of the second *Enquiry* were originally portions of sections 2 and 6, respectively. Presumably because of their abstruseness, Hume moved these portions to their present locations, the former

---

[6] I record my impressions of Hume's sentence construction with a due sense of their fallibility. The specialist study of style has advanced far enough to have shown that such impressions are prone to be drastically wrong. It is interesting to note in this connection that a statistical comparison of the sentences of forty-one authors, as sampled from forty-two books, shows the *EHU* as having an average of thirty-three words per sentence, the fifth highest, exceeding Locke's *Letter concerning Toleration* and Carlyle's *French Revolution* but not Berkeley's *Principles*. In average word length, reckoned by number of syllables, the *EHU* exceeds all the competition. See Wilhelm Fucks, "Possibilities of Exact Style Analysis," *Patterns of Literary Style*, ed. Joseph Strelka, vol. 3 of *Yearbook of Comparative Criticism* (University Park, Pa., 1971), 54. Regrettably for our purposes, Fucks does not compare the *EHU* with the *Treatise*.

for the *Essays and Treatises* of 1777, the latter for the edition
of 1764. These movements are an extension of the policy that
Hume had adopted from the beginning of employing appendices to render his most egregiously intricate reasonings less
obtrusive. He did not do this in the *Philosophical Essays*, perhaps because his original conception of it as a collection of
essays deterred him from that expedient. There, rather than
attach appendices to a work to which their formality might
seem generically inappropriate, he simply posts a warning
that abstruse reasonings are coming up and then segregates
them into a section division of their own. For example, the
principle of the transferability of the vivacity of ideas he recommends only to the attention of

> such as love the abstract sciences, and can be entertained with
> speculations, which, however accurate, may still retain a degree
> of doubt and uncertainty. As to readers of a different taste; the
> remaining part of this section is not calculated for them, and the
> following enquiries may well be understood, though it be ne-
> glected.                                                    (v. 1 [40])

If we had encountered these words in a modern book we
would have taken them for sarcasm. But Hume acknowledges
that sensible people do not want to lose their time in endless
investigations, and here he can only offer progress rather than
a conclusive decision.

Even within these semiquarantined pockets of abstruseness
Hume limits the argument to essentials. Illustrative elabora-
tions are kept to a minimum and are better calculated for popular tastes, as in section 3 of the *Philosophical Essays* in which
Hume barely states his three principles of the association of
ideas (resemblance, contiguity, and causation). (In the *Treatise* [1. 1. 4–6] he had gone on to extrapolate from them the
three types of complex ideas [relations, modes, and sub-
stances].) The question naturally arises whether, as Hume
claims, the three principles of association are exhaustive. But
the only way to substantiate, if not prove, this claim is to consider as many instances of cognitive relations as possible, reducing each to one or some combination of the three, a pro-

cedure that Hume declines to pursue because it "would lead into many useless subtilties" (*EHU* iii [19, n. 1]). In the *Treatise* Hume produces one such instance, showing that, appearances to the contrary, the relation between words and their meanings is just causal association (1. 3. 6 [92–93]). In the *Philosophical Essays* he serves up instead a discussion much more likely to be of interest to a gentleman, the neoclassical critical doctrine of the unities as it exemplifies the association of ideas. This discussion gives us an indication of what Hume's "criticism" would have been like if he had finished the *Treatise*. Unfortunately he decided not to develop the topic fully in the *Philosophical Essays* so as not to "lead us into reasonings too profound and too copious for this enquiry" (p. 23 n.). Even this illustration is dropped from the 1777 edition of *Essays and Treatises*, reducing section 3 to only three paragraphs. It might be that Hume had come to disagree with something in it, but it is as likely that in editing that section he found the unities to be tangential and expendable.

We might doubt that this increased expository conciseness actually yields greater clarity in sum than had the expansiveness of the *Treatise*. It exchanges one kind of clarity for another, and something is lost as well as gained. Locke had opted for the clarity of expatiation on the excellent grounds that " '*tis not one simple view*" of an unfamiliar and peculiar idea "*that will gain it admittance into every Understanding.*" "*There are few,*" he explains,

> who have not observed in themselves or others, That what in one way of proposing was very obscure, another way of expressing it, had made very clear and intelligible: Though afterward the Mind found little difference in the Phrases, and wondered why one failed to be understood more than the other.[7]

Voltaire, the greatest philosophical popularizer since Cicero, defended Locke's lack of concision on the same grounds: "I admit that he is a bit diffuse, but he was speaking to prejudiced and ignorant minds, to whom it is necessary to present

[7] *Essay*, 8.

reason in all her aspects and all her forms."[8] Bishop Butler also agreed "that of two different expressions of the same thing, though equally clear to some persons, yet to others one of them is sometimes very obscure, though the other be perfectly intelligible."[9] It is because the *Treatise* partakes of this clarity of expatiation that it remains indispensable to the student of Hume, notwithstanding the author's own injunctions against reading it.

Following Blair's nomenclature, we may say that Hume exchanged the Diffuse Style for the Concise. There is nothing pejorative in the epithet "Diffuse" as used in this connection. "Each of these manners has its peculiar advantages," says Blair.[10] They are not to be confused with the *styles périodique* and *coupé*, having little to do with sentence length or construction. They have to do instead with "an author's spreading out his thoughts more or less," with the pace at which material is covered. Blair favors the Diffuse Style "when you are to inform the understanding, which moves more slowly" than the fancy.

Plainly Hume subscribed to some such view when he wrote the *Treatise*. About the argument concerning miracles, in the version excised from the *Treatise*, he asked Kames whether the style was "too diffuse," explaining that "as that was a popular Argument I have spread it out much more than the other Parts of the Work." The adjective "popular" as used here should be read as meaning "intended for ordinary people, who need to have things spelled out for them"; as it should also in the following remark on a manuscript submitted to Hume: "If this Sermon were not a popular Discourse, I shoud also think it might be made more concise."[11] Hume's policy seems to have been to counterpoise abstruseness with diffuse-

---

[8] My translation from 3 Oct. 1758, *Voltaire's Correspondence*, ed. Theodore Besterman, 107 vols. (Geneva, 1953–65), 34: 135.

[9] "Correspondence between Dr. Butler and Dr. Clarke," 4 Nov. 1713, *Works* 1: 340.

[10] Blair's discussion of the two styles may be found in no. 18, *Rhet.* 1: 371–75, from which pages all quotations from him on this topic will be taken.

[11] 2 Dec. 1737; 30 June [1743], *NLDH*, 2, 12.

ness in proportion as he hoped for a popular audience for particular arguments in the *Treatise*. "A diffuse writer," Blair explains, "unfolds his thought fully. He places it in a variety of lights, and gives the reader every possible assistance for understanding it completely." In apparent accordance with this notion of clarity, Hume proposes in the *Treatise* to "turn [a] subject on every side, in order to find some new points of view, from which we may illustrate and confirm" certain principles (1. 3. 9 [106–7]). Later, he writes that because a particular argument "may seem abstruse and intricate to the generality of readers, I hope to be excus'd, if I endeavour to render it more obvious by some variation of the expression" (1. 4. 4 [229]).

By the time that Hume came to recast his philosophy he no longer subscribed to the superior clarity of diffuseness. In the *Philosophical Essays* we find him plumping consciously for the clarity of concision. The concise writer, according to Blair, "never gives you the same thought twice. He places it in the light which appears to him the most striking; but if you do not apprehend it well in that light, you need not expect to find it in any other." In apparent accordance with this notion, after expounding his subjectivist thesis of causal necessity, Hume writes

> I know not, whether the reader will readily apprehend this reasoning. I am afraid, that, should I multiply words about it, or throw it into a greater variety of lights, it would only become more obscure and intricate. In all abstract reasonings, there is one point of view, which, if we can happily hit, we shall go farther towards illustrating the subject, than by all the eloquence and copious expression in the world.     (*EHU* vii. 2 [65])

Having had a bad experience with the Diffuse Style, Hume is reacting against it.

Precedents and parallels to this critical preference are to be found in the realm of belles-lettres rather than of philosophy. Perhaps the passage just quoted shows the influence of La Bruyère, who asserted that

Amongst all the various expressions which can render our thoughts, there is but one which is correct. We are not always so fortunate as to hit upon it in writing or speaking, but, nevertheless, such a one undoubtedly exists, and all others are weak, and do not satisfy a man of culture who wishes to make himself understood.[12]

But this notion seems to have become a part of the common currency of critical ideas. Boswell agreed with "what has been often said, . . . that there is for every thought a certain nice adaptation of words which none other could equal, and which, when a man has been so fortunate as to hit, he has attained, in that particular case, to the perfection of language."[13] Hume's rendition of this idea is more cautious than La Bruyère's and Boswell's, but even so the claim that for every possible conception there is a corresponding best formulation has a rationalistic tone that sounds odd coming from an empiricist.

The passage can be interpreted consistently with Hume's system, however. It does not have to allude to necessary fitnesses and unfitnesses between ideas and words, "founded unchangeably in the nature and reason of things," as Clarke might say.[14] It can be related to Hume's tenets, and with it his new preference for the Concise Style, through the theory of the association of ideas as Hume applied it to aesthetic unity (*EHU* iii [19–23 n.]), in conjunction with his theory of belief (cf. *THN* 1. 3. 13 [144, 153], 1. 4. 2 [186], 3. 1. 1 [455]). Hume does not explicitly discuss the enhanced unity that conciseness gives to philosophy, but we can easily make the adaptation for him: the principles of psychology underlying the

---

[12] *Characters*, trans. Henri Van Laun (London, 1963), 3–4. "*Entre toutes les différentes expressions qui peuvent rendre une seule de nos pensées, il n'y en a qu'une qui soit la bonne. On ne la rencontre pas toujours en parlant ou en écrivant; il est vrai néanmoins qu'elle existe, que tout ce qui ne l'est point et faible, et ne satisfait point un homme d'esprit qui veut se faire entendre*" (no. 17, "Des Ouvrages de l'esprit," *Les Caractères* . . . , ed. Robert Garapon [Paris, 1962], 71).

[13] 7 Aug. 1755, *Life of Johnson* 1: 291.

[14] *Discourse*, 60.

neoclassical doctrine of the unities are not suspended when we write or read abstruse philosophy.

In the passage quoted above, Hume does not posit a single perfect formulation for every possible thought. His point is that there is an inherent disadvantage in diffuseness making it unlikely that one can improve upon a single, simple, accurate, and concise enunciation. The disadvantage is that diffuseness disrupts the unity of a discourse. It is a fact of human nature that we demand of artifacts that they convey a sense of their unity.

> In all compositions of genius, therefore, 'tis requisite that the writer have some plan or object; and tho' he may be hurried from this plan by the vehemence of thought, as in an ode, or drop it carelessly, as in an epistle or essay, there must appear some aim or intention in his first setting out, if not in the composition of the whole work. (*EHU* iii [19 n. 1])

In abstruse writing, in which the unifying aim is more difficult to grasp than in an ode or a familiar essay, it is more difficult for the reader to keep that aim in mind as he proceeds through the work. Consequently the author must work harder to keep the reader in sight of the plan. Philosophical unity lies in the strength of the chain of reasoning produced, and the author "is sensible, that the more unbroken the chain is, which he presents to his readers, the more perfect is his production" (ibid.). Ideally, at any given link the reader should be able to glance back along the chain and recall the central aim. The longer the chain grows, and the more weighted it becomes with appurtenances, however illustrative they may be of their particular links, the more difficult it becomes for the reader to maintain a strong association of the extremity with the central aim.

In composing, the abstruse writer must weigh the illustrative potential of every elaboration against the hindrance it will produce to the unifying process of association. When weighing the advantages and disadvantages, the writer should consider that an illustration might easily fail to clarify the subject, whereas it cannot fail, as a matter of psychological law, to hinder association to some extent. In view of this count against any given illustration, the writer should reject the illustration under consideration if the calculation even turns out neutral or uncertain. Or, to state this conclusion in terms of common sense, "brevity is very good, / When w'are or are not understood," for throwing an obscure point into a greater variety of lights has a good chance of just making matters worse.[15]

This new policy of concision is reflected in the genres into which Hume recast his "logic" and "morals," in the essays that are not quite essays. The thread is not dropped carelessly in them as was frequently the case in the Addisonian apprentice pieces. Near the end of the *Philosophical Essays*, as he had in book 1 of the *Treatise*, Hume places a philosophical amusement, a mock trial of Epicurus within the frame of a dialogue; but even this diversion, he rightly insists, bears a "relation to the chain of reasoning carried on throughout this enquiry" (*EHU* xi [109]). ("A Dialogue," the amusement with which he ends the second *Enquiry*, is also related closely to the chain of reasoning preceding it.) These essays do not exemplify Johnson's first definition of the word "essay," "A loose sally of the mind; an irregular indigested piece," but rather his third definition, "A trial; an experiment."[16] The unifying principle of an irregular, undigested piece is the character of the essayist himself, whose divagations serve to display his interesting peculiarities. Such essays could be experiments of a kind, as in Montaigne's *Essais*, when the interest stems from finding what reactions are produced from the play of an unusual sensibility upon various topics. Hence there is no need for the contents of such essays to be connected argumentatively: miscellaneous essays have their own kind of unity. In contrast, Hume's philosophical essays and inquiries are "experiments" in thought and cognition rather than in character. The two *Enquiries* consist of linked units in which Hume's character is not obtrusively prominent, except under the stress of a con-

---

[15] Samuel Butler, *Hudibras* 1. 1. 663–64.
[16] "Essay," *Dictionary* (London, 1755).

frontation with Christianity. Yet the *Philosophical Essays* are not so closely linked as they would be if they were all marshalled in support of a central thesis. They have a more relaxed linkage in being each an application of empiricist methodology to a particular topic. The sections of the second *Enquiry*, as will be explained in the last section of this chapter, are unified expressly around an empirical procedure that Hume intermittently recalls to our attention.

In condensing whole books of the *Treatise* into collections of linked essays, Hume shortens the chain of reasoning within and between sections, making the interconnections more apparent and helping to prevent the reader from failing to see the forest for the trees. The rationale for publishing the *Abstract* had been that the *"parts* [thus] *lying nearer together can better be compared, and the connexion be more easily traced from the first principles to the last conclusion"* (*Abs.*, 643). That the same rationale lay behind the publishing of the *Philosophical Essays* is evident from Hume's directions to Gilbert Elliot:

> I believe the philosophical Essays contain every thing of Consequence relating to the Understanding, which you woud meet with in the Treatise; & I give you my Advice against reading the latter. By shortening & simplifying the Questions, I really render them much more complete. *Addo dum minuo.* [I add while I diminish.] The philosophical Principles are the same in both: But I was carry'd away by the Heat of Youth & Invention to publish too precipitately. . . . I have repented my Haste a hundred, & a hundred times.[17]

## THE "LOGIC" RECAST: SUPPRESSING POSITIVENESS AND FALSE WIT

> [O]ne would be apt to suspect, that [Rousseau] chooses
> his topics less from persuasion, than from the pleasure

[17] [Mar. or Apr. 1751,] *LDH* 1: 158. The translation is Nidditch's, given in his revision of Selby-Bigge's edition of the *Enquiries concerning Human Understanding and the Principles of Morals*, 3d ed. (Oxford, 1975), 353.

of showing his invention, and surprizing the reader by
his paradoxes.
—*LDH* 1: 373

We know from a letter already quoted that what above all displeased the mature Hume about the *Treatise*, and what we
should expect him to try to avoid in the recastings, was the
"positive Air" of his youth.[18] Although he had, he felt, submitted his system in its entirety with due modesty, he had
allowed himself to "yield to that propensity, which inclines us
to be positive and certain in *particular points*, according to
the light, in which we survey them in any *particular instant*"
(1. 4. 7 [273]). The representation of the particular instant, so
welcome an innovation in the fictions of Defoe and Richardson, was in philosophy perhaps a rhetorical mistake, enliven-
ing the prose but giving an impression of egotism. One should
add that it confused readers too, for the positiveness of the
moments of Pyrrhonian excitement misleadingly overshad-
owed the rest of the book. So that in the recastings there
would be no need to deny being of a "dogmatical spirit" (p.
274), Hume largely abandoned the depiction of particular instants. (One exception is discussed at the end of this chapter.)
Did he succeed thereby in suppressing his propensity to be
positive? Most readers will agree that he generally succeeded in the second *Enquiry* but not in the *Philosophical
Essays*.

The most provoking instance of positiveness in any of
Hume's works has been the introductory remarks to the essay
"Of Miracles": "I flatter myself, that I have discovered an argument . . . which, if just, will, with the wise and learned, be
an everlasting check to all kinds of superstitious delusion, and
consequently, will be useful as long as the world endures"
(*EHU* x. 1 [89]). But this "preliminary trumpet-flourish," as

---

[18] *LDH* 1: 187. Cf. Gibbon's note: "Mr. Hume told me that in correcting
his history, he always laboured to reduce superlatives, and soften positives"
("Materials for a Seventh Volume," *The English Essays of Edward Gibbon*,
ed. Patricia B. Craddock [Oxford, 1972], 338).

Leslie Stephen called it,[19] though delivered with Swiftian tartness, is not so positive as the last paragraph of the *Philosophical Essays* quoted above in chapter 1, in which Hume recommends burning all writings in which the teaching of a priori truths concerning matters of fact is pretended. These instances are quite in the old impishly impudent spirit of the *Treatise*, in which Hume had occasionally indulged in such amiable bullying as the following:

> I think it proper to give warning, that I have just now examin'd one of the most sublime questions in philosophy. . . . Such a warning will naturally rouze up the attention of the reader, and make him desire a more full account of my doctrine, as well as of the arguments, on which it is founded. This request is so reasonable, that I cannot refuse complying with it. . . .
>
> (1. 3. 14 [156])

Jocose officiousness like this would not be out of place in (and probably was imbibed from) *A Tale of a Tub*. But there is a difference between the instances of positiveness in the *Treatise* and those in the *Philosophical Essays*. Those in the latter are too flagrant to have been miscalculations. Rather than the collateral result of the depiction of particular instants, or a jest that falls flat, they are deliberate affronts to what Hume regarded as adulterators of philosophy, to superstition and rationalism. He has turned his peremptoriness from humorous priggishness into an offensive weapon.

Hume's attack on adulterate philosophy is an important feature of the book, important enough to be easily exaggerated. But the book is not predominantly an attack on the forces for the adulteration of philosophy. Foremost it is a recasting of part of an empirical system; and where Hume is not on the attack he can be seen quite evidently suppressing peremptoriness. A comparison of corresponding passages will illustrate this point. In both versions of his "logic" Hume claims that causal prediction is premised upon the continuity of the future with our experience of the past and that we are condi-

---

[19] *History of English Thought* 1: 309.

tioned by the regularity of past events to believe this premise. Ratiocination, he says, does not, indeed cannot, lead us to this premise. "Shou'd any one think to elude this argument," Hume writes in the *Treatise*, "and . . . pretend that all conclusions from causes and effects are built on solid reasoning: I can only desire, that this reasoning may be produc'd, in order to be expos'd to our examination" (1. 3. 6 [90]). This is only one of numerous challenges that he makes to imagined opponents. Such "defiance[s]," he explains, "we are oblig'd frequently to make use of, as being almost the only means of proving a negative in philosophy" (1. 3. 14 [159]). But they did not have to be delivered as defiances. The counterpart to the defiance just quoted, instead of being a demand that an imaginary opponent put up or shut up, is an invitation to the reader: "This question I propose as much for the sake of information, as with an intention of raising difficulties. I cannot find, I cannot imagine any such reasoning. But I keep my mind still open to instruction, if any one will vouchsafe to bestow it on me" (*EHU* iv. 2 [32]). That no such reasoning need enter our heads for us to expect the future to resemble the past Hume proves by adducing the expectations of children and animals, who obviously do not calculate probabilities. Just so, Locke had adduced the ignorance and thoughtlessness of children to disprove the doctrine of innate knowledge. "If I be right," Hume concludes, "I pretend not to have made any mighty discovery. And if I be wrong, I must acknowledge myself to be indeed a very backward scholar; since I cannot now discover an argument, which, it seems, was perfectly familiar to me, long before I was out of my cradle" (pp. 34–35). He makes light of his discovery even as he clinches his argument, deftly disguising his triumph with mock self-depreciation.

Certainly this is more polite, in any sense of the word, than its counterpart. It not only is more deferential, but it fits Addison's description of fine writing, which Hume had elevated into a definition. It consists of a sentiment that is "natural, without being obvious."[20] That is, in Addison's words, the

---

[20] "SRW," 191. In connection with a moral sentimentalist like Hume, it

conclusions "are such as none but a great Genius could have thought of, though, upon the perusal of them, they seem to rise of themselves from the Subject of which he treats."[21] The reader might not follow the niceties of Hume's proof that our expectations cannot be validated before the event, being premised upon the unverifiable uniformity of the future with the past. He might not see, as Hume argues, that formal logic is inapplicable; perhaps he might not even see that it would take experience of the future to verify this uniformity empirically. But in concluding by adducing the expectations of children and animals Hume appeals to common sense. (In the *Treatise* he had waited ten sections before bringing up animals.) To anyone who then examines his own behavior, it will be manifest that for only the slimmest portion of his expectations does he calculate probabilities. This being granted, it is not a drastic step further to suppose these few calculations could be premised upon a belief acquired, as undoubtedly it is in children, through conditioning. It is difficult to imagine quarrelling with this once it has sunk in; yet it is not an obvious truth, or was not until Hume directed attention to it. The appropriate response to this kind of literary effect is expressed colorfully in Huxley's reaction to the theory of evolution: "How extremely stupid not to have thought of that!" By contrast, the effect of false wit is "surprise, surprise, surprise."

Such instances of politeness, though, could not outweigh in the minds of readers the shocking combination of peremptoriness and religious scepticism appearing in the last half of the

---

would be best to forestall possible confusion: the meaning of "sentiment" here must be "the feeling or meaning intended to be conveyed by a passage, as distinguished from the mode of expression" ("Sentiment," 8.b., *Compact Edition of the Oxford English Dictionary* [Oxford, 1971]; hereinafter cited as *OED*).

[21] No. 345, *Spectator* 3: 284. Cf. Johnson's characterization of the "highest Perfection of Writing" as "such Thoughts as are at once new and easy, which, tho' the Reader confesses that they never occurred to him before, he yet imagines must have cost but little Labour." I quote from Hagstrum, *Samuel Johnson's Literary Criticism*, 159. The passage comes from Johnson's annotation to his translation of Crousaz's *Commentary on Mr. Pope's Principles of Morality, or Essay on Man* (London, 1739), 312.

book. There is a marked reversal of tone when Hume touches on religion, and it is the discussions of religion that dominated the public perception of the book. John Leland wrote:

> Mr. *Hume* introduceth his Essay on Miracles in a very pompous manner, as might be expected from one who sets up . . . for teaching men better methods of reasoning, than any Philosopher had done before him. He had taken care at every turn to let his readers know how much they are obliged to him for throwing new light on the most *curious* and *sublime subjects*, with regard to which the most celebrated philosophers had been *extremely defective* in their researches.[22]

Leland is projecting his annoyance at the essay on miracles onto the rest of the book. In the same vein, Johnson's friend William Adams asked rhetorically whether there was anywhere "a more sceptical, disputatious turn of mind, or a more imperious, dogmatical style, than in the writings of this author." To what Adams was reacting specifically is indicated by the title of his book: *An Essay on Mr. Hume's Essay on Miracles* (London, 1752 [1751]).[23]

We have seen that an important part of politeness, and hence of elegance, is personal restraint. Authors are not to be peremptory or exhibitionistic. "[P]roductions, which are merely surprising, without being natural" ("SRW," 192), are in Hume's opinion so far inelegant. Elegance in form and content can be recognized by its effect of natural novelty, by an effect in which the sentiment seems new but fitting. This touchstone of elegance allows us readily to see some grounds for Hume's dissatisfaction with the *Treatise* and for his preference for the second *Enquiry* over the *Philosophical Essays*, in which there are a number of sentiments that readers could not find natural. To make abstruse philosophy conform to

---

[22] *A View of the Principal Deistical Writers*, 2 vols. (London, 1754–55), 2: 48. In the second sentence quoted, Leland is thinking of the last sentence in *EHU* vi.
[23] Pp. 127–29.

what readers will find natural is not always or even often possible, especially when in probing the boundaries of possible knowledge one is obliged to identify the errors into which instinct and common sense lead us. This problem is aggravated when Hume deals with religious error.

Previously I have quoted from the *Treatise* a number of what qualify as more or less violent epigrammatic paradoxes that contravene the literary rule of natural novelty. When, for example, we encounter " 'Tis not contrary to reason to prefer the destruction of the whole world to the scratching of my finger," we must unravel two layers of paradox. First, people of normal sensibilities will find it paradoxical to maintain that such a monstrously selfish preference is not unreasonable. Second, even accepting the selfishness of the preference, there is what we would consider the unreasonableness of preferring a trivial to a momentous good. Even if we enter into the fantastic spirit of hypothetical logic and suppose it possible for the destruction of the world not to include Hume's finger, and the rest of him too, reason tell us that he will be less happy for giving up the world. This preference clearly does not represent a choice of lesser evils. It is equally clear from the context, though, that Hume is amusing himself with an ambiguous employment of the expression "contrary to reason." He does not really mean that it is not foolish to exchange a momentous for a trivial good or that it is acceptable to overvalue one's own comfort. He means that, strictly speaking, reason and valuation operate on different planes and cannot conflict. Reason is cognitive exclusively and inert without a motivating passion. Passion sets values and puts reason to work for the fulfillment of desires. Reason can only indirectly affect passions by revealing that certain of them are in conflict, thus precipitating a choice of preference; but only a passion can conflict with and defeat another passion. To speak of the conflict of passion and reason, then, would be at best a convenient metaphoric shorthand for a complexly indirect interaction. Unless we understand it as shorthand we are under a misconception. Ambiguity removed, "contrary to reason"

does not mean "foolish," but "revealed by reason to be untrue"; and preferences, trivial or momentous, cannot properly
be called untrue.[24]

This paradox is one of a cluster in this section, all of which
epigrammatically express Hume's tenet of the dependence of
reason upon the motivating force of passion. Of course Hume
is perfectly aware of the sense in which passion depends upon
reason for guidance concerning the possibilities, means, and
consequences of fulfilling desires. (His system itself can be described as an attempt of reason to apprise curiosity of the limited possibilities for knowledge and of the best means to acquire it.) Why then does he lean so hard in his paradoxical
expression in the direction of irrationalism? Partly it is amus-
ingly shocking to do so, but also, one suspects, he is thereby
resisting the common-sense reaction to the causal determinism that he had expounded in the two preceding sections (2.
3. 1, 2). To any who, predictably, will insist that our actions
can be undetermined because reason is free and can control
our passions, Hume now responds by showing that only passion can incite action, including in fact the action of reasoning
itself. This does not mean that reason cannot be efficacious,
for it might be motivated sufficiently by a sincere desire for
truth so as not to be twisted by other passions. Hume is just
identifying the place of reasoning in the causal sequence that
constitutes willing an action. To say, in accordance with ordinary language, that reason can rule passion is a harmless
shorthand until it misleads us into supposing that reason is
somehow mysteriously uncaused and self-activating. So the
tenet of the inertness of reason is not merely a verbal quibble
over arbitrary definitions of "reason" contrived for its shock
value. The tenet arises of itself from Hume's naturalistic approach to the mind. It is because reason is a caused, natural
phenomenon, and not a spiritual entity observing nature from
an external, supernatural station, that it must follow natural
laws and hence be limited: the limits of possible knowledge
are set by the natural laws of the mind. In Hume's "logic," to

---

[24] See Mackie, *Hume's Moral Theory*, 44–47.

be lowly wise is to acknowledge and confine one's inquiries within the natural limits of mind. This insight, the central irony in the "logic," we shall consider further in the next section.

Yet though the irony implicit in Hume's anatomy of reason is no mere literary conceit, the compression of it into epigrammatic paradoxes like the one quoted above creates exceedingly strong flashes of wit. One cannot help thinking of such paradoxes in the *Treatise* when Hume faults the *Esprit des lois* for the "Glare of its pointed Wit."[25] Whatever may be the merits of the witticism quoted above, it does not elicit from us wonder that we had never ourselves thought of the sentiment it expresses. Hume shows himself to have been aware of the rhetorical potential of paradoxes for backfiring. His comments on the rhetorical disadvantages of paradoxicality in general apply by extension to epigrammatic paradoxes. He admits that "of all the paradoxes" he had occasion to advance in the *Treatise*, the derivation of the idea of causal connection exclusively from subjective impressions "is the most violent." This paradoxicality makes him fear that readers will dismiss his tenet: "There is commonly an astonishment attending every thing extraordinary; and this astonishment changes immediately into the highest degree of esteem or contempt, according as we approve or disapprove of the subject" (*THN* 1. 3. 14 [166]; cf. 1. 2. 1 [26]). When in his letter to John Home in dedication of the *Four Dissertations* Hume wrote, "My enemies, you know, and, I own, even sometimes my friends, have reproached me with the love of paradoxes and singular opinions" (*Wks.* 4: 440), he was looking back at the harm that paradoxicality had done to his reputation. The danger of arousing contempt must be amplified when paradoxical tenets are compressed into epigrammatic paradoxes, into paradoxes delivered through paradoxes. Even without the epigrammatic turns of the *Treatise*, it would be an amazing performance indeed for someone to deliver error theories so that they seem natural to readers. On the face of it such a

---

[25] 1 Apr. 1767, *LDH* 2: 133.

compromise between philosophy and elegance would seem impossible; yet such is what Hume attempted in the *Enquiries*, with more success in the second *Enquiry*, he felt, than in the *Philosophical Essays*.

We have noted that Hume's erratic performance in the *Philosophical Essays* is related to whether he is at the moment proposing elements of his own system or confronting philosophical adulteration. In the former instances he suppresses his propensities to strong flashes of wit as well as to peremptoriness; in the latter he gives them both some rein. Only two of the witticisms quoted in the last chapter reappear in the *Philosophical Essays*, and they appear at the conclusion where Hume apportions knowledge between the a priori and the experiential, proclaiming all philosophy violating this division to be adulterate and fit for kindling. He refashions these witticisms so as to reduce their paradoxicality; but curiously, at the same time he adds a paradox not to be found in the *Treatise*, of precisely the same rhetorical construction as one of those that he had toned down. To "Whatever *is* may *not be*" (*EHU* xii. 3 [134]), the same reading may be applied as the following for "Any thing may produce any thing" (*THN* 1. 3. 15 [173]).

Referring to the context, we translate the latter thus: "[If we were to reason as to cause and effect without consulting experience, we could not predict anything more satisfactory than that] anything may produce anything." The accurate formulation is as a subjunctive conditional, but Hume deliberately misstates it as a declarative, creating a momentary ambiguity as to his meaning. Eliot might say that here Hume "dislocates" language for a striking effect.[26] The recasting of this witticism is, in contrast, an unambiguous conditional: "If we reason *à priori*, any thing may appear able to produce any thing" (*EHU* xii. 3 [134–35]). Hume cautiously emphasizes here that the world would not actually be chaotic, but only would appear so to reasoning severed from experience. What-

---

[26] "The Metaphysical Poets," *Selected Essays*, 289.

ever paradoxicality remains is in the tenet, not in the turn of expression.

There is no apparent reason why "Any thing may produce any thing" should be softened and not "Whatever *is* may *not be*." The latter is just an exception in a gradual development in Hume away from epigrammatically condensed paradoxes. When next we encounter the point of logic expressed in "Whatever *is* may *not be*," it is in the prosaic form, "Whatever we conceive as existent, we can also conceive as non-existent" (*DNR* ix [189]). Instead of in epigrammatic turns, Hume's irony is coming to be expressed in a generalized coyness quite different in effect from a strong flash of wit, a coyness that he reserves for religious subjects. Most of the paradoxicality in the *Philosophical Essays* is of this more reticent kind, which we shall examine later.

The second paradox to reappear was originally "Morality . . . is more properly felt than judg'd of." Of course Hume does not really believe that moral questions should be left to the arbitration of passion. The context allows us to translate the paradox into "Morality is [,] more properly [speaking, rather] felt than judg'd of." That is, morality consists at bottom of feelings of approbation and disapprobation rather than of judicial insight into the eternal fitnesses of things. It is not an objective feature of the world, but a subjective one of our passional nature, which, however, we can and do organize under the pressure of social necessity into general rules of conduct and judgment (see *THN* 3. 3. 1 [581–84]). There is such a thing as moral judgment; but when we judge of morality we do not discover the truth or falsity of ontological propositions. In moral choices we pit calm passions, like the pangs of conscience, against other passions, like desire.

Hume's new version of this paradox is not a success. "Beauty, whether moral or natural, is felt, more properly than perceived" (*EHU* xii. 3 [135]) does eliminate the shocking suggestion of the original that there neither is nor should be moral judgment. But to replace "judg'd of" with "perceived" is unintentionally confusing, since in Hume's terminology feelings, being impressions, are a species of perception (see

*EHU* ii [13–14]). How then can we feel rather than perceive morality when, as Hume says preceding the original witticism, "[o]ur decisions concerning moral rectitude and depravity are evidently perceptions" (*THN* 3. 1. 2 [470])? But Hume is being maladroit rather than illogical, having without warning dropped his own terminology in the recasting in favor of ordinary language. To perceive here means "to apprehend with the mind; . . . to observe, understand."[27] Hume means that moral beauty, being a subjective impression, is felt rather than objectively apprehended. While eliminating in this recasting a rhetorical ambiguity from his witticism, Hume inadvertently introduces another ambiguity. Such lapses justify Selby-Bigge's complaint that Hume "is often slovenly and indifferent about his words and formulae."[28]

Another level of paradox in the original witticism Hume leaves untouched altogether. In both versions he ostensibly makes an illegitimate and impertinent value judgment, seeming to recommend a proper way of acquiring moral knowledge when actually his position is that there is no choice. His real point is that "Beauty, whether moral or natural, is felt, more properly [speaking,] than [apprehended]." Since moral beauty cannot be apprehended, advising against apprehending it is only a rhetorical device of emphasis, a paradoxical dislocation of language. The same dislocation underlies the famous paradox "Reason is, and ought only to be the slave of the passions," in which the appearance of the "ought" in this "is"-statement is logically unaccountable but rhetorically striking.[29] (In a passage nearly as famous [*THN* 3. 1. 1 (469–70] Hume had protested against unaccountably educing "ought"- and "ought not"-judgments from "is"-statements.) But in these instances it would be impertinent as well as unaccountable. In the context of Hume's system, to say that moral beauty ought to be felt and that reason ought to be sub-

---

[27] "Perceive," I.1, *OED*; as in Johnson's remark to Adam Fergusson: "Sir, I perceive you are a vile Whig" (31 Mar. 1772, *Life of Johnson* 2: 170).

[28] *Enquiries*, vii.

[29] This paradox can be translated as "Reason is, and ought only to be [regarded as,] the slave of the passions."

servient to passion is rather like saying that the earth ought to be spheroid and ought to revolve around the sun. In the last analysis, though, Hume is neither illogical nor impertinent in these statements because they are just witticisms that he expects us to see through. But he *is* violently paradoxical. In this respect the paradox in the *Philosophical Essays* is as violent as its original.

Such half measures mark the vagaries of the evolution of Hume's wit from a peremptory tone and from epigrammatic paradoxicality to a more subtle ironic coyness. In the second *Enquiry* not a single such flash of wit is to be found. We have noted that Hume's paradoxical tendencies assert themselves for the most part when he attacks the adulteration of philosophy and that when he deals with religion this combativeness manifests itself in an ironic coyness. Not surprisingly, he was less concerned to be polite when he was trying to disabuse us of the pretensions of rationalists and theologians. It is not unusual for someone to be more diffident in submitting his own proposals than in attempting to quash someone else's.

Students of Hume's epistemology might object here to our finding ironic ambiguity almost exclusively in his handling of the opposition. Was not Hume notoriously ambiguous or, worse, equivocal with regard to whether he espoused empiricism or scepticism? We shall see in the next section that he attempted to clarify the relation of his scepticism to his empiricism, and in the following section that he deliberately cast his discussions of religion into ironic ambiguity.

## SETTING THE RECORD STRAIGHT WITH REGARD TO SCEPTICISM

> Imagination has no limits, . . . but where one is
> confined to Truth (or to speak more like a human
> creature, to the appearances of Truth) we soon find the
> shortness of our Tether. Indeed by the help of a
> metaphysical chain of idæas, one may extend the
> circulation, go round and round for ever, without

> making any progress beyond the point to which
> Providence has pinn'd us. . . .
> —Pope, 19 Dec. 1734, *Corr.*

It is difficult to imagine a reconciliation between perspicuity and irony or paradox. In philosophical writing the latter look more like vices than virtues, and even in creative literature they need to be employed well and to good purpose. Eliot, for example, probably would complain that although Hume does dislocate language as poets do, he does not dislocate it *into* his meaning, but *out* of it. Hume's epigrammatic paradoxes involve a distortion of his meaning that we must overcome, momentarily deflecting us from his true course. They are, in a double sense, diverting.[30]

The indeterminacy of Hume's position concerning scepticism has caused confusion that Hume might have prevented had he been less ironic and paradoxical. He failed to provide an assessment of his scepticism in satisfying detail; and to many readers Hume's inability to refute scepticism seems to have meant its *de facto* victory in his system. A stalemate does not seem possible, and the absence of a victory for reason is taken for its defeat. But a victory for scepticism seems to provide no answers to the philosophical problems in which Hume has aroused our interest. Although readers can enjoy an expedition into an epistemological wilderness, they do not enjoy being left there by their guide. And they want Hume eventually to take an unequivocal stand on scepticism.

Hume did take steps in the *Philosophical Essays* to remove the ambiguity from his position concerning scepticism and to provide a sense of resolution. He had not changed his mind: in his view scepticism was still cogent but incredible, a genuine paradox to which philosophy leads ineluctably. Sceptical arguments *"admit of no answer and produce no conviction."* Their effects are "momentary amazement and irresolution and

---

[30] When Eliot said that "parts of Hume" can be called art, he did not have the dislocation of language in mind, but rather "clear and beautifully formed thought" ("The Possibility of a Poetic Drama," *The Sacred Wood*, 7th ed. [London, 1950], 66).

confusion" (*EHU* xii. 1 [127 n. 1]), but never full or sustainable acceptance. This paradox Hume did not contrive out of a desire to shine and surprise, but having been led to it the exuberant young wit exploited it fully in his Philosophical Amusement (*THN* 1. 4. 1–7), giving it a disproportionate prominence. A more sober Hume was in the recastings no longer willing to exploit the paradox, though he could not dispose of it. He could not change his tenets, but he could his emphasis; and he could make his allegiances explicit. Whereas in the *Treatise* he had only mentioned "moderate scepticism," now he devotes his concluding essay to distinguishing between Pyrrhonian and mitigated, or Academical, scepticism. The latter, to which he subscribes, is compatible with, indeed ultimately is an aspect of, empiricism.

Hume adjusts his emphasis by broaching Pyrrhonian paradoxes, paradoxes without solutions, only in the last essay, and there only within the context of a plain repudiation of excessive scepticism. They are raised only as counterexamples to what he espouses, not as a "Trial of *Wit* and *Subtilty*," as they had been in the *Treatise* (*LGent.*, 20). Mitigated scepticism, on the other hand, pervades the whole book.

Briefly, the distinction between the two scepticisms is as follows. Mitigated scepticism is (1) the subscription to what C. S. Peirce later called "contrite fallibilism," to the tenet that "people cannot attain absolute certainty concerning questions of fact."[31] As well as being true, fallibilism recommends itself as working against our natural tendencies to dogmatism. Mitigated scepticism is also (2) the policy of establishing, and keeping our investigations within, the boundaries of possible knowledge. It is the "limitation of our enquiries to such subjects as are best adapted to the narrow capacity of human understanding" (*EHU* xii. 3 [133]). Since the limitations of the mind are set by the natural laws by which the mind functions, we can figuratively call this second aspect of mitigated scep-

---

[31] *The Philosophy of Peirce: Selected Writings*, ed. Justus Buchler (London, 1940), 4, 59. D. C. Stove claims that Hume's development of inductive fallibilism is his greatest contribution to philosophy (*Probability and Hume's Inductive Scepticism* [Oxford, 1973], 91–97).

ticism "cognitive law and order," which itself consists (a) of legislation (the establishment of the natural laws of mind) and (b) of law-abidingness (the restricting of reasoning to what is lawful).[32] Attempting to venture beyond our limitations, we will go astray in one of two ways of widely unequal baneful-ness. Worst, if we are rationalistically inclined we will adul-terate philosophy, intuiting occult properties at convenience and, if in addition we are superstitious, attributing to super-natural agencies everything we cannot explain. Much less ru-inous, if instead we are rigorously empirical we will fall into Pyrrhonian paradoxes and confusion. This eventuality is not so ruinous because a Pyrrhonian state of mind is psychologi-cally unsustainable, whereas human nature will not rescue ra-tionalists from systematically compounding error upon error.

Pyrrhonism, then, contradistinguished from mitigated scepticism and rationalism, is the unadulterated but doomed philosophizing beyond our limits. At best this is a purgatorial phase on the way to mitigated scepticism, a salutary stage of humbling consternation from which one emerges a contrite fallibilist, convinced of the need to be lowly wise. This mor-tification of mind is what the Philosophical Amusement was meant to depict. At worst, Pyrrhonism is "a very extravagant attempt . . . to destroy *reason* by argument and ratiocination" (xii. 2 [127]). Hume does not mention Sextus Empiricus or set forth in any detail the tenets of the school to which he be-longed. Rather he presents arguments of a putative modern counterpart to classical Pyrrhonism, which seem to be of two kinds. In one, described in chapter 2, reason subverts itself through an attempt to estimate the probability of the accuracy of every estimation of probability *in infinitum*, never reaching certainty. This kind of Pyrrhonism makes no appearance in the *Philosophical Essays*. Another kind, which Hume briefly surveys in section 12, has to do with undecidable conflicts be-tween reason and instinct, such as the famous conundrum concerning external reality that puts philosophers into unend-

---

[32] Cf. Peter Jones, *Hume's Sentiments*, 170.

ing oscillation between naive realism, representative realism, and Pyrrhonism.

It is worth noting that mitigated scepticism and Pyrrhonism, though different, are not discrete types of philosophy. They do not involve altogether distinct processes of doubting. One way to mitigated scepticism is to graduate to it after grappling with Pyrrhonism (see *DNR* i [133–34]). Fallibilism and cognitive law and order "may be the natural result of the Pyrrhonian doubt and scruples" (*EHU* xii. 3 [133]). The same arguments may be regarded alternately as Pyrrhonian or Academical, depending upon whether one reacts to them with irresolution and confusion or, more constructively, concludes that one has gotten out of one's depth and turns to less sublime questions. This consanguinity of the scepticisms allows us to explain Hume's curious instancing of an argument as Pyrrhonian that earlier he had advanced as a constructive part of his system. A Pyrrhonist may justly insist, he concedes,

> that all our evidence for any matter of fact, which lies beyond the testimony of sense or memory, is derived entirely from the relation of cause and effect; that we have no other idea of this relation than that of two objects, which have been frequently *conjoined* together; that we have no argument to convince us, that objects, which have, in our experience, been frequently conjoined, will likewise, in other instances, be conjoined in the same manner; and that nothing leads us to this inference but custom or a certain instinct of our nature; which it is indeed difficult to resist, but which, like other instincts, may be fallacious and deceitful. While the [Pyrrhonian] sceptic insists upon these topics, he shews his force, or rather, indeed, his own and our weakness; and seems, for the time at least, to destroy all assurance and conviction. These arguments might be displayed at greater length, if any durable good or benefit to society could ever be expected to result from them.　　　(xii. 2 [130–31])

But these arguments *had* already been displayed, over the length of two essays: "Sceptical Doubts concerning the Operations of the Understanding" and "Sceptical Solution of These Doubts." In the latter essay Hume had ascribed this chain of arguments to Academical scepticism rather than to Pyrrhonism, and the title of that essay indicates that he thought a result was possible other than the destruction of all assurance and conviction. Furthermore, he plainly expected a great deal of durable good to result from these arguments since it is an important part of the science of man to establish the limits of experiential reasoning so that we can make whatever progress is possible within them.

This is not an about-face. When he summarized the chain of arguments as an example of Pyrrhonism, Hume then had in mind a Pyrrhonian reaction to it of astonishment and incredulousness, whereas in sections 4 and 5 he had in mind a more practical reaction, one he advocates. He advocates it because although out of psychological necessity Pyrrhonism must give way to some other state of mind, it does not inevitably give way to fallibilism and cognitive law and order. Although there is no danger that sceptical arguments will leave us permanently in a state of Pyrrhonian dithering, there remains the danger of our rebounding into dogmatic rationalism, as had the Cartesians. Or we might rebound into reactionary antimetaphysics, as had the Scriberlians. Unfortunately human nature does not ensure our graduation to mitigated scepticism. For the benefit of society, therefore, Hume wrote as attractively and persuasively as he could in the hope of leading men toward that graduation.

Hume does not give us all the details necessary to a perfect clarification of his opinion of scepticism. Probably he could not have done so within the scope that he had allotted to the topic. Any number of fascinating questions suggest themselves. One would like, for one thing, an explanation of how experiential reasoning does not dissolve utterly into instinct, losing its authority, when its fundamental premise, the uniformity of the future with the past, turns out to be an instinctive belief not susceptible of reasoned justification. Despite what in Pyrrhonian moments Hume says about reason's being a "wonderful and unintelligible instinct in our souls" (*THN* 1. 3. 16 [179]), there is no doubt that he believed in some mental action that may with propriety be called ratiocination.

One likely answer lies in Hume's paradox of caused free will. If the freedom of the will is, as he believed, compatible with the causation of will, then the willed exercise of reason must be compatible with its causation by calm passions in conjunction with instinctual environmental conditioning, with the operation on us of "custom." A psychological study of the causal process of reasoning does not expose reasoning as illusory; it just identifies the place of reasoning in the causal complex in which everything in the universe takes part, including human actions.[33] It is quite possible within this complex for reason to succeed at what our passions order it to do, in other words, for it to be *effective*: "Our reason must be consider'd as a kind of cause, of which truth is the natural effect; but such-a-one as by the irruption of other causes, and by the inconstancy of our mental powers, may frequently be prevented" (1. 4. 1 [180]). The possibility of fallacious reasoning may prompt the passions to command reason to discipline itself, but this new ratiocinative action is itself part of a causal sequence. And this disciplinary course remains one of ac*custom*ing the mind to work in ways that have desirable effects.

One would like, for another thing, to know precisely what cognitive lawfulness and unlawfulness means. To be law-abiding is to be empirical. But obviously it is not possible, strictly speaking, to break a natural law of mind. When a rationalist is not law-abiding, then, he is just reasoning fallaciously, supposing he has knowledge to work with that he does not have. He is trying to make his mind do the impossible and mistakenly thinks that he is succeeding. Hume wants us to discipline our minds to attempt, as a rule, to do only what they can do. Because what the mind should do depends upon what it can

---

[33] Cf. the following remarks of Tom Beauchamp and Alexander Rosenberg: "[W]e are not arguing that Hume abandons his account of causal and psychological determinism, whereby experience is sovereign. As might be expected of one who holds a compatibilist account of freedom and determinism, Hume finds causal explanations *compatible with and not destructive of* what we now commonly call 'rational justification' " (*Hume and the Problem of Causation* [New York, 1981], 56–57).

do, he calls his epistemology his "logic."[34] Law-abidingness does not insure undisturbed progress, though: an empiricist may push experiential inquiry to the point of Pyrrhonian breakdown. There are two reasons why he might want to do so. Like Hume, he may enjoy wrestling with paradoxes, just as athletes enjoy striving for unattainable feats. So long as he refrains from illicit a priori machinations this amusement is harmless. Another, more important motive to push reason to the end of its tether is that it is only thus that the limits can be established: one cannot know where the boundaries of possible knowledge are until one has tried to break through them and failed. Pyrrhonism is an integral part of the legislative process in cognitive law and order. It cannot be an end in itself, but it can be a means to the ends of mitigated scepticism.

One last speculative clarification may be permissible. Cognitive legislation involves a confrontation with Pyrrhonism. But what exactly would this confrontation be like? It has been convenient to speak of it as a developmental phase, but perhaps this is really a figurative description. Would it be like a nervous breakdown from which one recovers? It looks as though in Hume's considered view it is not a single traumatic event or cluster of events, but rather a chronic condition that a sceptic never entirely puts behind him. Being irrefutable, Pyrrhonism must be confronted anew each time a sceptic thinks through problems like the relationship between our sensory perceptions and external reality: "This sceptical doubt, both with respect to reason and the senses, is a malady, which can never be radically cur'd, but must return upon us every moment, however we may chace it away, and sometimes may seem entirely free from it" (1. 4. 2 [218]). It is something that a sceptic just has to learn to live with.

David Miller says that

[t]his amounts to denying that any intellectually satisfying solution to the dilemma is possible. Instead of arriving at a balanced position, it seems that we are condemned to a perpetual oscil-

[34] See Noxon, *Hume's Philosophical Development*, passim (e.g., p. 14).

lation between scepticism (while doing philosophy) and naive belief (while playing backgammon, etc.). Moderate scepticism must then consist in recognizing the oscillation, retrospectively and prospectively (it cannot just consist in *experiencing* the oscillation, since that happens to Pyrrhonian sceptics too). This is equivalent to recognizing that one is, by turns, a philosopher and one of the "vulgar," but never both at once.[35]

This is helpful but still too simple, for a Pyrrhonian moment cannot be so homogenous as that. No one can even for a moment be completely under the influence of doubt. During a Pyrrhonian moment we are at the same time still naively believing countless things. Suppose that upon reading "Of the Academical or Sceptical Philosophy" someone experiences an illumination and now fully appreciates the force of Pyrrhonism. Yet even as "in a flush of humour, after intense reflection on the many contradictions and imperfections of human reason" he renounces "all belief and opinion" (*DNR* i [132]), he still believes despite himself in the future uniformity of nature with its past. He expects the print before him to continue to signify certain words, the meanings of which will be the same an hour hence. He does not expect it to turn into centipedes swarming across the page. He expects the chair he sits on and the floor beneath it to continue to support his weight. If our newborn sceptic is a convinced Pyrrhonist, he believes Pyrrhonian arguments to be valid, even though these arguments against the authority of experiential reasoning are themselves reasonings concerning matters of fact and therefore subject to self-refutation. Classical Pyrrhonists held that *epoché*, or complete suspension of belief, would lead to *ataraxia*, a state of quietude in which, to lift a strikingly apt expression from Keats, we are "capable of being in uncertainties, Mysteries, doubts, without any irritable reaching after fact & reason."[36] Hume never mentions it by name, but it is plain that he thought such a state was neither possible nor desirable. It

[35] Miller, *Philosophy and Ideology*, 36.
[36] [21 Dec. 1817?] *The Letters of John Keats, 1814–1821*, ed. Hyder Edward Rollins, 2 vols. (Cambridge, Mass., 1958), 1: 193.

would be a reduction of cognition to helpless, unself-conscious percipience: "All discourse, all action would immediately cease; and men remain in a total lethargy, till the necessities of nature, unsatisfied, put an end to their miserable existence. It is true; so fatal an event is very little to be dreaded. Nature is always too strong for principle" (*EHU* xii. 2 [131]). Although Hume often speaks as though momentary triumphs are possible for Pyrrhonism, this is only a manner of speaking about relative strengths at a superficially discursive level of consciousness. If we could pursue the topic in interview with him, he probably would unhesitatingly agree that active doubting can never be more than a fluctuation in a preponderantly naive stream of consciousness.

Mitigated scepticism, then, would not be the recognition of an alternation in us between naiveté and Pyrrhonism so much as the recognition of the experience of Pyrrhonism for what it is: a temporary and minor disturbance in the flow of mind, a ripple on the surface due to the frustrated operation of reason at its extremity. Mitigated scepticism would be a profound self-cognizance, an awareness of the simultaneous coexistence and correlation in ourselves of nagging doubt and compulsive, naive belief. A modern Academical sceptic takes the measure of his own double nature as a willfully critical intellect and a causally determined psychological phenomenon. He recognizes that he is simultaneously a philosopher and one of the vulgar.

Calling his position Academical serves a couple of Hume's purposes. For one, the association is instructive. The proper adjective "Academical" had a wide range of positive associations, as is shown in Dryden's defense of his *Essay on Dramatic Poesy* as being "sceptical, according to that way of reasoning which was used by Socrates, Plato, and all the Academics of old, which Tully and the best of the Ancients followed, and which is imitated by the modest inquisitions of the Royal Society."[37] An association of his scepticism with the

[37] "A Defence of *An Essay of Dramatic Poesy*," in *"Of Dramatic Poesy" and Other Critical Essays*, ed. George Watson, 2 vols. (London, 1962), 1: 123.

Royal Society was not one that Hume would have discouraged, but he chose not to develop it.[38] Perhaps deterred from stressing an association with modern science while the Quarrel between the Ancients and Moderns was fresh in everyone's memory, he focused attention on an earlier form of Academism. He set his own scepticism within the context of the opposition between the classical Academical sceptics and the Pyrrhonists.

As an organized set of arguments with avowed adherents, Pyrrhonism originated in schism from the Academy of Philo of Larissa, Cicero's teacher in philosophy. The schismatics hearkened back to the sage Pyrrho for an epitome of what they took to be an undiluted scepticism not taught in the Academy. By calling his own scepticism Academical, Hume aligns himself with Cicero's scepticism, one that was in Cicero's person notably compatible not only with action, but with eminent public service. (In naming his spokesman in the *Dialogues* after Cicero's teacher, Hume further invites an association of his own scepticism with a particular phase of Academism.) The opposing exemplars that he means to conjure up by putting us in mind of the old opposition are Cicero, the philosopher-statesman, the humanists' paragon of the marriage of study and service, and Pyrrho, the philosophical enthusiast, reputed by Diogenes Laertius to have been rendered by scepticism unable to take care of himself.

Cicero's contributions to Academical scepticism were largely as an embodiment of its tenets in his life and as its disseminator in Latin. Claiming no originality, he adhered to the tenets of his sect. The specific Academical tenets with which Hume aligns himself, then, are those traditionally ascribed to the "Middle" and "New" Academies of Arcesilas and Carneades, as transmitted by Clitomachus to Philo, and thence to Cicero, our principal source of information. There is plenty of opportunity in this sequence of transmission for

[38] For the general association of the Royal Society with Academical scepticism, see Phillip Harth, *Contexts of Dryden's Thought* (Chicago, 1968), 1–31.

distortion and misunderstsanding of what Arcesilas and Carneades espoused, but we need concern ourselves only with what Hume and his contemporaries took Academical philosophy to be. The most important source of information as to the debate between the two scepticisms was then, as now, Sextus's *Outlines of Pyrrhonism* (particularly 1. 220–35). A partisan account of Academical scepticism given by an exponent of a rival school must be suspect, but, once again, our concern is only with the traditional interpretation of the debate that Hume would have expected his readers to hold. His purpose in bringing up the Academy was illustrative, and only an interpretation that was already generally accepted could have served as a backdrop to his own scepticism. This traditional interpretation would have been compounded from Cicero's and Sextus's accounts.[39]

From Sextus we learn that a crucial disagreement was whether a criterion for reasonable action was possible. Both groups held that the gap between appearance and reality was unbridgeable, but they disagreed as to the implications for action of this gap. The Pyrrhonists supposedly held that a criterion for belief and action was unattainable and recommended living without belief, entirely according to appearances and established forms. Resulting from suspension of belief would be ataraxic tranquility. According to the traditional interpretation of Academical scepticism, Carneades responded to the gap by developing a theory of graduated plausibilities. "Our position," Cicero wrote,

> is not that we hold that nothing is true, but that we assert that all true sensations are associated with false ones so closely resembling them that they contain no infallible mark to guide our judgement and assent. From this followed the corollary, that many sensations are *probable*, that is, though not amounting to a full perception they are yet possessed of a certain distinctness

---

[39] David Fate Norton's account of the two scepticisms differs from mine slightly in that he does not confine himself to reconstructing a contemporary, perhaps popularized, version of their opposition (*David Hume: Common-Sense Moralist, Sceptical Metaphysician* [Princeton, 1982], 255–79).

and clearness, and so can serve to direct the conduct of a wise man.[40]

The proposed criterion for action is plausibility. Whether degrees of plausibility were thought to justify corresponding degrees of belief, or instead sceptics were to act according to plausibilities while withholding belief, the traditional interpretation leaves unsettled. But in either case the possibility of error means that the sceptic must always be ready to adjust his calculations of plausibility as appearances change. This is fallibilism, and accords perfectly with the empiricist's readiness to alter his conclusions as new experiential evidence dictates.[41]

The affinities of Hume's mitigated scepticism with this version of Academical philosophy are genuine and instructive. He agreed that in matters of fact we are limited to experiential appearances. His contribution was his tenet that complete suspension of belief is impossible. We must have beliefs, which must be fallible; but we can and should temper our credulity: plausibility, or what Hume called *"moral Evidence"* (*LGent.*, 22), still provides a criterion for belief and action. If we must believe, we can at least proportion our beliefs to the evidence. As new experience contradicts our beliefs, we must be willing to revise our estimates of plausibility. This does not mean that truth changes, only that our best approximations of it are perpetually subject to revision. Although the moral ev-

[40] *"De Natura Deorum"* and *"Academica,"* trans. H. Rackham (London, 1933), 15 (*Nat. D.* 1. 5).

[41] On classical scepticism I am particularly indebted to David Sedley, "The Protagonists," M. F. Burnyeat, "Can the Sceptic Live His Scepticism?" and Gisela Striker, "Sceptical Strategies," *Doubt and Dogmatism: Studies in Hellenistic Epistemology*, ed. Malcolm Schofield et al. (Oxford, 1980), 1–83. Charlotte L. Stough's *Greek Scepticism: A Study in Epistemology* (Berkeley, 1969) has also been helpful. Thomas Stanley thought that the Academical sceptics espoused following probability without belief: "The *Academicks* assert some things to be wholly improbable, some more probable than others, and that a Wise Man, when any of these occur, may answer *yes* or *no*, following the probability, provided that he with-hold from assenting. But the *Scepticks* [i.e., Pyrrhonians] hold all things to be alike indifferent, not admitting Judgment . . ." (s.v. "Arcesilaus," *History of Philosophy*, 217).

idence for belief is always susceptible of falsifying augmenta-
tion, we can fashion our beliefs so as to be consistent with all
the pertinent appearances at any given time. This is not a co-
herence theory of truth, but one of plausibility. It is why
Hume's Philo says that "we may only expect greater stability,
if not greater truth, from our philosophy" (*DNR* i [134]): we
can render our beliefs more stable by bringing them systematically into line with the greatest experience possible, but
we can never get beyond experience to things as they are behind the veil of perception. An Academical sceptic's highest
ambition, then, is "to establish a system or set of opinions,
which if not true (for that, perhaps, is too much to be hop'd
for) might at least be satisfactory to the human mind, and
might stand the test of the most critical examination" (*THN* 1.
4. 7 [272]; cf. 1. 3. 5 [par. 2]).

Accordingly Hume settled for mere experiential appearances when most people would be left deeply unsatisfied. In
anatomizing causal knowledge, for example, he was satisfied
with tracing it to the observable constant conjunction of
events and the attending internal impression of necessary
connection between them that this regularity conditions us to
feel. The more constant the conjunction of the class of events,
the stronger the feeling of necessity becomes, and any refinement in judging of probabilities must work, as far as he is concerned, within the confines of this natural process. It has been
disturbing to many of his readers, though, to think that judgments of probability cannot be validated by somehow getting
behind appearances to reality and ascertaining objective
causal connections. Hume did not bother trying to justify
causal reasoning because he had accomplished his Academical
goals. His object being to establish the limits to possible
knowledge, his focus was not on causation as such, but on
causal reasoning as part of the workings of the mind.[42] He
might have gone on to gauge the plausibility of a hypothetical,
objective causal connection, but this would have been tangen-

---

[42] As has been noted by Mackie (*Cement of the Universe: A Study of Causation* [Oxford, 1974], 4–6).

tial to his agenda and contrary to the spirit of speculative austerity that he wanted to foster. In his own empirical way he was saying, like the Academical sceptics, that we must content ourselves with appearances.

The second purpose served by associating himself with the Academy was to render his scepticism as respectable as possible. We have already noted the advantage of boasting a pedigree including Cicero in countering the suspicion that scepticism must be enervating. By invoking the old debate Hume shows that his distinction between moderate and extreme scepticism is not merely his own contrivance, that the notion of moderate scepticism had all the authority that a classical ancestry could give it. A notion with such credentials could not be dismissed so easily. Pointing up the classical precedents works against the readers' predictable inclinations to view such new-fangled notions distortingly as just the latest salvo in the quarrel between the Ancients and the Moderns. Thus Hume creates an obstacle to his summary dismissal as a duncical Modern.

For the purposes of advocating the science of man, the concluding clarification in the *Philosophical Essays* is much superior to the way that Hume closes his "logic" in the *Treatise*. The Philosophical Amusement is an arresting performance, too arresting, for it brings us to a halt in our progress toward an empirical system. Hume goes on to his "passions" and "morals" but does not carry our full confidence with him, for we are still distracted by the sceptical questions that he had raised. "Of the Academical or Sceptical Philosophy" raises the same issues but ends by nudging us distinctly in the direction of empirical naturalism. As philosophy it may or may not succeed, but, as an intellectual adventure, it does raise complications and bring us around to a sense of resolution.

Did the clarification work? Judging from Hume's reputation we must conclude that it did not. If it had, the commentary in this section would be superfluous. In our day an authority on the history of scepticism, Richard Popkin, has altogether ignored Hume's claim to be an Academical sceptic, concluding from his denial of the possibilities of *epochē* and *ataraxia* that he was more Pyrrhonian than the Pyrrhonists. If one is willing to create a new, improved Pyrrhonism, this is acceptable. Popkin does have a point to make that perhaps justifies this revisionism. He ascribes to Hume an *ad hominem* argument against Pyrrhonism such that the recommendations to suspend belief totally and to follow appearances and natural impulse are mutually contradictory. *Epochē*, were it possible, would plainly be unnatural since man's natural state is to believe in appearances. When appearances are puzzling, it is also natural for us to philosophize and judge of plausibilities. From this argument Popkin concludes that Hume was a "consistent" Pyrrhonist. Kemp Smith would have called this naturalism. Hume himself called it Academical scepticism. Now there is no substantive difference between viewing Hume as a consistent Pyrrhonist and an Academical sceptic. The issue is one of preferred terminology and emphasis. It would be simpler to let Pyrrhonism mean what it has meant and to take Hume at his word when he declares himself an Academical sceptic. Exploring his Academism has fully as much explanatory potential while allowing us to see him as he saw himself. And with this approach we do not end up seeming to imply that Hume was wrong in saying that he was not a Pyrrhonist.[43]

An interesting contemporary response to Hume's claim to moderate scepticism is James Balfour's essay "Of the Academical Philosophy" in his anonymously published *Philosophical Essays* (Edinburgh, 1768), a book that Hume thought "has no manner of Sense in it; but is wrote with tolerable Neatness of Style."[44] The book is doubly interesting to us in that it raises

---

[43] "David Hume: His Pyrrhonism and His Critique of Pyrrhonism," and "David Hume and the Pyrrhonian Controversy," in his *High Road to Pyrrhonism*, ed. Richard A. Watson and James E. Force (San Diego, 1980), 103–47.

[44] 5 July 1768, *LDH* 2: 182. Balfour was then Professor of the Law of Nature and Nations at Edinburgh University, having previously been Adam Fergusson's predecessor as Professor of Moral Philosophy, the post for which Hume had unsuccessfully competed in 1745. He had anonymously published an answer to the *EPM* (*A Delineation of the Nature and Obligation of Morality* [Edinburgh, 1753]), to which Hume had responded with an overture of friendship to the unknown author (see 15 Mar. 1753, *LDH* 1: 172–74, and

objections against Hume based upon the humanist concerns identified above in chapter 1. Balfour, too, espouses Academical philosophy, by which, however, he means the doctrines of the "First" Academy. For him the "Academy" means Plato's Academy. He seems to raise an argument of persuasive definition against Hume, implying that true Academism is not Carneadean scepticism.[45] He rejects the notion that in directing Academical pedagogy into sceptical channels Arcesilas was simply reinstating the Socratic method. Arcesilas's distorting reforms, he thinks, lead to Hume's irreligious scepticism, which Socrates and Plato would have abhorred. Such scepticism eventually leads to dogmatism, just as anarchy leads to tyranny. Balfour's Academism is Platonism as filtered through humanist glasses:

> [W]hilst other philosophers were perpetually disputing about the abstruse nature of things, with regard to which they fell into the greatest blunders, and only exposed their own ignorance, [Plato] brought his philosophy nearer home, and chiefly applied to rectify the minds and reform the manners of mankind; in doing which his more abstract reasonings were corrected or supported by fact and experience; and in carrying on this excellent plan, he employed only the principles of religion, which were entirely suited to the capacities of mankind, and of which the

---

J. V. Price, "David Hume, Thomas Blacklock, and James Balfour: A New Document," *Études anglaises* 41, no. 2 [1988] 186–87).

[45] An argument by persuasive definition is an attempt to redefine a word or phrase so that if it is positive in connotation, its new meaning excludes what the rhetor wants to debunk, or conversely, if its connotation is pejorative, its meaning includes what he wishes to debunk. (Or of course a rhetor could reverse these strategies if he wants to extol something.) An example familiar to literary students is the attempt by nineteenth-century critics to make the public believe that Pope was not a "true" poet. See Charles L. Stevenson, "Persuasive Definitions," *Facts and Values: Studies in Ethical Analysis* (New Haven, 1963), 32–54. Hume adopts this ploy when he talks about "true" religion: "It seems to be almost a general rule, that, in all religions except the true, no man will suffer martyrdom, who would not also inflict it willingly on all that differ from him. The same zeal for speculative opinions is the cause of both" (*Hist.* 3: 436 [A.D. 1555, s.v. "Violent Persecutions in England"]).

vulgar, as well as the philosophers, might feel the influence and
force.

> Plato was, on this account, justly said to have brought philos-
> ophy from heaven to earth; because, instead of employing his
> reasonings upon those objects which are at a distance and above
> our reach, he brought them home to ourselves, and applied
> them to much better purpose, in promoting the real happiness
> of man.[46]

How experience supports the Platonic theory of Forms Balfour does not say. But congruity with experience is much less
important to him than congruity with religion. What is inex-
plicable in God's ways we should accept as beyond our ken
and mind our own business, which is to reform the manners
of mankind. It is to this religious aspect of Balfour's humanism
that Hume responded when he wrote sarcastically, "He supports himself, indeed, by the Authority of Plato, whom I own
to be truly divine."[47] As we have seen, Hume could not agree
more that divinity is beyond us and that we should mind our
own business, but he went further in thinking that religionists
should mind their own business and not adulterate philosophy. "The proper Office of Religion," in his view, is solely "to
reform Men's Lives, to purify their Hearts, to inforce all
moral Duties, & to secure Obedience to the Laws & civil
Magistrate."[48] Religionists should not be insisting that everyone subscribe to their speculations on divinity while at the
same time talking of humbling curiosity concerning mysteries.

Actually it was Socrates, not Plato, whom the humanists
credited with bringing philosophy down to earth. In this, it

---

[46] Balfour, *Philosophical Essays*, 15–16.

[47] *LDH* 2: 182. Cf. 22 July 1768, ibid., 185.

[48] I quote from a manuscript as given in Mossner's *Life*, 306. Cf. *DNR* xii
(220): "The proper office of religion is to regulate the heart of men, humanize
their conduct, infuse the spirit of temperance, order, and obedience." The
clergy "are set apart by the Laws to the care of sacred Matters, and the conducting our public Devotions with greater Decency and Order" ("SE," 617
n.). That is, they are to provide constructive or innocuous channels for religious sentiment to express itself, not to preestablish the findings of philosophy.

will be recalled, they followed Cicero, who assigned the credit in the *Tusculan Disputations*. A parallel passage is Varro's speech in Cicero's dialogue *Academica Posteriora*:

> It is my view, and it is universally agreed, that Socrates was the first person who summoned philosophy away from mysteries veiled in concealment by nature herself, upon which all philosophers before him had been engaged, and led it to the subject of ordinary life, in order to investigate the virtues and vices, and good and evil generally, and to realize that heavenly matters are either remote from our knowledge or else, however fully known, have nothing to do with the good life.[49]

To humanists, sickened by sectarian strife, such a policy must have appeared wonderfully sane. Hume diagnosed this ever-impending social distemper as "zeal for speculative opinions"[50] and prescribed, as we have seen, cognitive law and order to curb theology, and a tincture of scepticism to dampen zeal. Scepticism can turn speculative zealotry into contrite fallibilism. Alone among philosophies it cannot be turned into sectarian zealotry because, being largely critical rather than assertive, "it strikes in with no disorderly passion of the human mind, nor can mingle itself with any natural affection or propensity" (*EHU* v. 1 [35]). Hume does not consider what his critics would say, evidencing Hume himself, that scepticism strikes in with the passion to shine and surprise. But Hume is surely right in thinking that no one could be so fervent in the cause of doubting as to become violent. Zealous doubting is a contradiction in terms. His sceptically tempered empiricism is an important development in, perhaps even a culmination of, the humanist program to direct men away from useless or pernicious investigations. Hume, too, wished to promote the real happiness of men. But Balfour either does not see or refuses to contend with Hume's version of the humanist program. He simply dismisses

---

[49] *"De Natura Deorum" and "Academica,"* 425 (1. 4). But in *Town-Talk* 3, Steele assigns the honor to Seneca (*Richard Steele's Periodical Journalism, 1714–16,* ed. Rae Blanchard [Oxford, 1959], 199–200, 301 n.).

[50] See n. 45 above.

Hume's scepticism and holds up the "First" Academy as a counterexample, reiterating the theme of man's limitations, as though scepticism had no part to play in establishing those limitations:

> [T]he disciples of Socrates made use of the principles of this excellent [Academical] philosophy, not only to govern and direct them in their inquiries after truth, but also to limit and confine these inquiries to the most important objects of it. They observed the large field of science to be too extensive for the weak and limited faculties of man; this reflection naturally led them to give their chief application to what most immediately tended to the perfection and happiness of their nature; and this was undoubtedly the science of morals; a science whose province it was to rectify the heart and regulate the conduct, whilst other sciences were directed to objects of a more external nature.[51]

With giving moral science first priority Hume probably would not have quarrelled. But he was not interested in setting priorities within the different sciences. Balfour was typical in failing to see, or to acknowledge, that Hume wanted to help legislate the limits within which all sciences can proceed successfully. Whether the fault lies with Hume or with his readers or with both, Hume's attempt to show the uses of scepticism in this legislation was unsuccessful.

## IRONIC COYNESS

> [Rousseau] has not had the precaution to throw any veil
> over his sentiments; and as he scorns to dissemble his
> contempt of established opinions, he could not wonder
> that all the zealots were in arms against him.
> —*LDH* 1: 374

Edmund Burke wrote,

> Mr. Hume told me, that he had from Rousseau himself the secret of his principles of composition. That acute, though eccen-

---

[51] Balfour, *Philosophical Essays*, 60–61.

tric, observer had perceived, that to strike and interest the public, the marvellous must be produced; that the marvellous of the heathen mythology had long since lost its effect; that giants, magicians, fairies, and heroes of romance which succeeded, had exhausted the portion of credulity which belonged to their age; that now nothing was left to a writer but that species of the marvellous, which might still be produced, and with as great an effect as ever, though in another way; that is, the marvellous in life, in manners, in characters, and in extraordinary situations, giving rise to new and unlooked-for strokes in politics and morals.[52]

To many it will seem rich to find the great conservative and the notorious infidel animadverting together over Rousseau's resorting to unnatural novelty. The self-promoting sensationalist nonconformism that Hume describes is precisely the vice of which he has always been accused.[53] He did not recognize this vice in himself since his paradoxes and criticism of religion seemed to him to arise naturally from his epistemology. He supposed that to a discerning eye his unlooked-for strokes were naturally novel. From his point of view it was the religionists who looked vulgarly sensationalist, with their dependence for their audience on the supernatural and on exotic, ritualistic behavior. In literary taste Hume was not a nonconformist. We have seen him striving against extravagance in his writing and for neo-Atticism. And not only in literary taste was he not a nonconformist.

[52] *Reflections on the Revolution in France and the Proceedings in Certain Societies in London Relative to that Event*, ed. William B. Todd (New York, 1959), 211. Cf. Smith, 12 Jan. 1763, *Lect.*, 107.

[53] E.g. George Campbell, *A Dissertation on Miracles: Containing an Examination of the Principles Advanced by David Hume* . . . (Edinburgh, 1762), 73–74: "No man was ever fonder of paradox, and, in theoretical subjects, of every notion that is remote from sentiments universally receiv'd. . . . If . . . in respect of the passion for the marvellous, he differ from other people, the difference ariseth from a particular delicacy in this gentleman, which makes him nauseate even to wonder with the croud. He is of that singular turn that where every body is struck with consternation, he can see nothing wondrous in the least; at the same time he discovers prodigies, where no soul but himself ever dreamt that there were any."

The picture of Hume emerging from current scholarship differs widely from his reputation as the iconoclast par excellence. Increasingly his students are revealing him to have been a constructive, even systematic epistemologist. They find that his practical moral and political conclusions were moderately conformist, however extraordinary his steps to those conclusions might seem. And the present study has served to illustrate this view of him. His reputation has stemmed from his readers' disproportionate fascination with his scepticism and from their mistaken notion that scepticism inevitably leads either to nonconformity or, in psychological reaction, to uncritical conformism. Other possibilities for scepticism exist, however. One can no longer simply call Hume a sceptic and suppose that the denomination indicates much of significance about him. We are now more willing to recognize the gradations between mitigated and Pyrrhonian doubt. We are now more willing to entertain the possibilities that to find the origin of causal belief elsewhere than in ratiocination is not to repudiate causation, that to subscribe to causal determinism is not to repudiate moral responsibility, that to reject the Cartesian doctrine of the self is not to repudiate personal identity, that to subscribe to sentimentalist moral theory is not to repudiate morality, and that to regard justice as artificial is not to repudiate it as unnatural. Hume was intentionally sceptical, we now find, only in repudiating accepted accounts of these topics and in denying that a priori knowledge of matters of fact is possible. The possibility remains that his criticisms are successful and his own accounts unsuccessful, that he failed to mitigate his scepticism; but this would not entitle us to discount his intentions and call him a Pyrrhonist. To do so would be rather like calling Newton an atheist because we believe that his mechanistic account of the cosmos conflicts with any possible system of the supernatural. Hume broaches Pyrrhonism to chasten, not discredit, human understanding. He was not, it turns out, some kind of precursory Deconstructionist exulting in his liberation from oppressive rationality. And, in determining the proportions in his system of its two major strains, we find that he is better described as a sceptical empiricist than as an empirical sceptic.

Among the accepted accounts that Hume repudiated, however, was what he called the religious hypothesis, and to many religious people the gradations of scepticism appear insignificant. To them mitigated scepticism is quite sceptical enough. Probably no one would deny that Hume's scepticism led him to nonconformity in religion, except, in his humor and prudence, Hume himself. What he was willing to call "true religion" was with regard to divinity so attenuated by agnostic reservations as to be unrecognizable as religion by most people.[54] While no one, perhaps, has yet been able to codify definitively what exactly it was that Hume called true religion,[55] few readers have not been able to see through his ironic genuflexions. This mixture of obscurity and transparency is undoubtedly just about what Hume intended. Eighteenth-century ironists as a rule intended their ironies to be seen through.[56] But irony by itself is only a negative kind of explicitness. Unless an ironist carefully incorporates into his work an implied positive standard, his irony will communicate to his readers only his repudiation of something. All that can be inferred about what he advocates is that it supposedly does not have the demerits of what he satirizes. To be employed in advocacy, irony needs supplementation. (Swiftian scholars have had so much interpretive reconstruction to do partly because Swift treated his positive standards as self-evident and in no need of specification.) Now Hume did not want to advocate religious tenets. To repudiate obliquely various parts of the religious hypothesis was as far as he could go safely, so

[54] See Kemp Smith's introd. to *DNR*, 9–75.

[55] Notable attempts are Mossner's "Religion of David Hume," *Journal of the History of Ideas* 39 (1978): 653–63; J. C. A. Gaskin's *Hume's Philosophy of Religion* (London, 1978), 159–74; and Terence Penelhum, "Natural Belief and Religious Belief in Hume's Philosophy," *Philosophical Quarterly* 33 (1983): 166–81.

[56] As Irvin Ehrenpreis has argued forcefully in *Literary Meaning and Augustan Values* (Charlottesville, 1974), 1–60.

he was careful not to build into his works a clear standard of "true" religion.

There were reasons for adopting this strategy other than self-interest. For Hume to have expounded his own agnostic alternative to doctrines protected by law would have violated a tacit understanding between free thinkers and the authorities. It would have been to beard authorities who normally were content not to prosecute infidelity and to endanger thereby the large measure of freedom that the press had attained. A prudent friend to liberty knows better than to push it to the point at which a reaction against it is provoked. Hume's fears for liberty in general, and for that of the press in particular, appear more clearly in his letters than in "Of the Liberty of the Press." Describing Wilkes's demagoguery, he wrote, "Here is a People thrown into Disorders . . . merely from the Abuse of Liberty, chiefly the Liberty of the Press. . . . They roar Liberty, tho' they have apparently more Liberty than any People in the World." In his alarm Hume sometimes sounds authoritarian, but it was for the fragile British balance between authority and liberty that he was fearful: "The Misfortune is, that this Liberty can scarcely be retrench'd without Danger of being entirely lost."[57]

Aside from the harm that a prosecution would do to Hume personally, and from the potential risk that it would pose to the liberty of the press, it would bring religious controversy to the attention of the vulgar, something no responsible person would want. And Hume was exceedingly alert to the inflammatory nature of religious controversy. What was apprehensively called "the mob" was somewhat insulated from controversial religious writings by its illiteracy, the average reader by the abstruseness of the exposition; but a public prosecution, with its attending scandal, could provide no such buffers. Although religious contentions were comparatively quiescent in Hume's lifetime, it would have been reckless not to let sleeping dogs lie.

[57] 16 June 1768 and 21 Feb. 1770, *LDH* 2: 180, 216. Cf. 26 Oct. 1772, *NLDH*, 196.

Thus Hume's restraint, or coyness, should not be seen as a strategic limitation in a guerrilla war *pour écraser l'infâme*. Rather it was a wise man's accommodation to social realities. If he was not a conformist in religion, neither was he a revolutionary. In fact Hume went further in this accommodation than just to refrain from advocating his own agnosticism. As a hedge against and discouragement of proceedings against him, he disingenuously made a transparent pretense of being a Christian and selectively advocating one point of orthodoxy: "Our most holy religion is founded on *Faith*, not on reason; and it is a sure method of exposing it to put it to such a trial as it is, by no means, fitted to endure" (*EHU* x. 2 [107]). Of course it was precisely to such a trial that he had been putting religion, and Christianity specifically, when he made this remark. Nominal Christianity was an old and generally recognized free thinker's defense, described as follows by one of Hume's answerers:

> As for the Deists [i.e., the free thinkers], . . . they do not, by any means, do justice to their own cause; they do but in part support it with its own genuine arguments. They stand miserably in awe of fines; they are afraid to speak out their principles, lest they should shock or alarm. It is for these reasons, that they are forced to borrow the name and cloak of Christianity, in order to attack it. . . .[58]

Hume's nominal Christianity is in this way both defensive and offensive. He may not be at war with Christianity, but he is antagonistic to it and deals it some punishing blows, adopting a famous Swiftian tactic. Arguing for faith against reason, he assumes the transparent persona of an inept apologist whose efforts in behalf of Christian theism are utterly disastrous. The persona is ludicrously unaware of the wounds that he inflicts on his own cause, while the readers know perfectly well that Hume is manipulating him into embarrassments.

---

[58] [Philip Skelton,] *Deism Revealed, or, The Attack on Christianity Candidly Reviewed*, 2d ed., 2 vols. (London, 1751), 1: xii.

Such is the offensive aspect of Hume's nominal Christianity. The defensive aspect lies in his supposed rejection of reason, by which he places himself ostensibly within the fideist tradition of Montaigne.[59] Under pressure, he could always invoke that venerable conformist tradition and avow himself faithful. No one might believe these professions of faith, but no one could prove them insincere either.[60] These pious exclamations he interjected where he was in most danger, in the essay on miracles and in the suppressed dissertation on the immortality of the soul. In these contexts they would be effectively undercut by their clashes with the spirit of his arguments; but they would also protect him. To any charge that their contexts belied the sincerity of his professions of faith he could adduce the examples of the Counter-Reformation fideists, whom scepticism had led to faith and conformism rather than to infidelity. Thus he manages to be transparent without yielding any evidence that could be used to prove his infidelity.

It is important to the offensive aspect of this tactic that it be seen through. To feel the full force of the satire the reader must realize that Hume is being satirical. And these ironies, like all ironies, become apparent only when we refer to the context in which they are placed. With regard to Hume's attitudes toward religion, the final context to refer to is not just the essay or even the book in which a particular profession appears; it is the whole of his *oeuvre*. If we thus enlarge the context, we find that the ostensible fideism of the *Philosophical Essays* clashes with the deism ostensibly subscribed to throughout the "Natural History of Religion," in which Hume speaks of "those invincible reasons, on which [monotheism] is

[59] For which see Alan Boase, *The Fortunes of Montaigne: A History of the "Essays" in France, 1580–1669* (London, 1935); Popkin, *The History of Scepticism from Erasmus to Spinoza* (Berkeley, 1979).

[60] George Dempster wrote of Hume, "It seems difficult for me (for me who dotes upon David) to believe that he can have a great regard for even the best mode of religion and the least extravagant if we consider how destitute he is of that only support of it, Faith" (16 Dec. 1756, *Letters of George Dempster to Adam Fergusson, 1756–1813*, ed. James Fergusson [London, 1934], 22).

undoubtedly founded" (*Wks.* 4: 328). On these reasons, on the "argument from design," he *had* cast serious doubts in "Of the Practical Consequences of Natural Religion,"[61] and would again in the *Dialogues*. For the interpreter of the whole *oeuvre*, Hume the fideist and Hume the deist cancel each other out, leaving only Hume the doubting Thomas.

Of course Hume would not have needed this ironic coyness if he had not chosen to attack the established churches' religion. It is possible to conform without belief, as the classical sceptics urged, but Hume was not an incredulous conformist. Since Hume was so notorious a critic of religion, it would be well to balance his reputation with a consideration of just how serious an option incredulous conformism was for him. We might say that he opted for the degree of conformity minimally necessary to avoid serious trouble. He did make a point of disavowing atheism, in private and in publication. (He could do so honestly because he was what we now call an agnostic.[62]) He never renounced his membership in the Church of Scotland. In his letters he speaks of incredulous conformism as a respectable option. Pious hypocrisies may be justified, he writes, for the sake of "Decency and Prudence: And so the World goes on, in perpetually deceiving themselves

[61] *EHU* xi, later renamed "Of a Particular Providence and of a Future State." Also, in app., *THN*, 633 n., Hume says, "The order of the universe proves an omnipotent mind."

[62] E.g. *EHU* xii. 1 (122), and see Mossner, *Life*, 483. Cf. the letter to the Rev. John Roget, 16 Nov. 1781, in *Memoirs of the Life of Sir John Romilly*, ed. by his sons, 3 vols. (London, 1840), 1: 179, in which Diderot reports Hume as having said, *"Pour les Athées, . . . je ne crois pas qu'il en existe; je n'en ai jamais vu."* Henry Lord Brougham wrote: "It is easy to say Mr. Hume was not an atheist; and that neither he nor any man can in one sense of the word be an atheist is certain. If by denying a God we mean believing that his non-existence is proved, there neither is nor can be an atheist, because there cannot possibly be conceived any demonstration of that negative proposition. . . . But we really mean by atheist as contradistinguished from sceptic, one who holds that there exists no evidence of a Deity, as contradistinguished from him who only entertains doubts on the subject—doubts whether there be evidence or no" ("Hume," *Lives of Men of Letters and Science, Who Flourished in the Time of George III*, 2 vols. [London, 1845–46], 1: 202–3).

and one another." When asked about religious hypocrisy he writes,

> It is putting too great a Respect on the Vulgar, and on their Superstitions, to pique one's self on Sincerity with regard to them. Did ever one make it a point of Honour to speak Truth to Children or Madmen? . . . [T]he Pythian Oracle, with the approbation of Xenophon, advisd every one to worship the Gods νόμῳ πόλεως.[63]

He is willing to entertain the notion that this "innocent Dissimulation" is incorrigibly the way of the world, in defying which one would only be the cully of one's own integrity, and that it might even be a noble lie supportive of moral order. But having appeared in print as a free thinker, he could not credibly become a conformist: "I wish it were still in my Power to be a Hypocrite in this particular: The common Duties of Society usually require it."[64]

Despite occasional regrets, Hume must have given a decided preference to free-thinking over conformism: he went on attacking "false" religion sporadically throughout the remainder of his career, and even posthumously in his *Dialogues*. But he certainly appreciated the arguments for conformism. On the one hand he writes that although philosophers who challenge religious doctrines may "be good reasoners," he "cannot allow them to be good citizens and politicians; since they free men from one restraint upon their passions, and make the infringement of the laws of society, in one respect, more easy and secure." On the other hand, "no restraint can be put upon [philosophers'] reasonings, but what must be of dangerous consequence to the sciences, and even to the state, by paving the way for persecution and oppression in points, where the generality of mankind are more deeply interested and concerned" (*EHU* xi [121]). A wise man, we may suppose, chooses between conformism and free-thinking

---

[63] 19 Aug. 1771, *LDH* 2: 248 and Apr. 1764, *NLDH*, 83. The Greek, translated by J. Y. T. Greig (*LDH* 1: 439 n. 4), is "For the good of the state." Cf. 1 May 1760, and [Nov. or Dec. 1760], *LDH* 1: 326–27, 336.

[64] *NLDH*, 83. Cf. 19 Mar. 1767, *LDH* 2: 130.

according to circumstances, according to whether the greater danger to society is presently that lawfulness and morality will decline or that the sciences will stagnate. As we have seen, the present danger that loomed largest in Hume's consciousness was the adulteration of philosophy.

Hume's coyness makes it difficult to reconstruct his positive standard of religion, but a standard just as good for decoding his ironies is available: the science of man that he espouses as the corrective for rationalistically and theologically adulterated philosophy. All of his thrusts at theology clearly support his advocacy of empiricism, and thus his irony escapes ending in mere negation or smug scepticism. With the positive standard of empiricism in mind, we can proceed to examine some of his coy ironies.

We have noted the inherent difficulty in expounding error theories in such a way that they impress the reader as natural. The same difficulty is inherent in criticizing almost universally accepted religious beliefs. Natural novelty would seem to be out of Hume's reach. If, as Selby-Bigge thought, Hume's criticisms of religious belief were gratuitous, Hume could have minimized the difficulty by avoiding the topic of religion, as, in fact, he does in the second *Enquiry*. But in the *Philosophical Essays* the discussions of religion are not gratuitous. One of his professed purposes in that book was to discredit the adulterators of philosophy. Rationalism and theology were so permeated with each other that he could not have criticized one and not the other. Unless he were to give up the critical aspect of his book and concentrate exclusively on expounding his system, Hume would have to deal with religion at the expense of natural novelty. In "Of the Practical Consequences of Natural Religion" he does not even try to mute his criticism of the argument from design. Putting this criticism into the mouth of a paradoxical friend, who himself is pretending to be Epicurus, distances Hume enough from the refutation to protect him; but this device does nothing to make it seem more natural. It might not be *possible* to render natural seeming the logical rules for inferring backwards from effects to putative causes. He does make an attempt, though, in "Of Miracles," in which he presents his criticism of testimony as to miracles in terms familiar enough to his audience. Ostensibly the essay is an attack on popish and other superstitions but not on Protestantism. This discrimination is, of course, ironic, and Hume expected us to recognize the ecumenical applicability of the criticism. This device will yield the effect of natural novelty only to Protestants too blindly partisan to discern the irony. But though the argument does not really discriminate between sects, it is grounded firmly in common sense: ordinarily we do weigh the probability that testimony is false with a view to the unusualness of its content, and miracles are as unusual as anything in human experience can be. Hume wants us to see that when we exempt religious miracles from this test we depart from common sense. To the extent that he succeeds in making us see this, he mitigates the unnaturalness readers will feel when they find their unexamined, life-long held beliefs exposed as baseless. But, after all, he is telling Christians, whose religion is founded upon discipular testimony as to Jesus' miracles, that no such testimony deserves credence. The immediate and lasting notoriety of the essay on miracles shows that pitting common sense against common beliefs cannot yield natural novelty. At best it can reduce the sense of unnaturalness to the point at which people cannot dismiss the criticism as preposterous. And perhaps it is because this particular criticism of credulity is not easily dismissed that it provoked so many answers while that of the argument from design went comparatively unnoticed.

Religious preconceptions also complicate Hume's presentation of his causal determinism. Determinism, as we have seen, is central to his naturalistic account of human nature, so it is not merely to pick a quarrel with religion that he brings it up. But its implications for moral responsibility meant that in his readers' minds it was a topic of religious controversy. Religion just could not be avoided. This topic, then, presented Hume with the compounded difficulty, mentioned above, of rendering natural seeming both his error theory of liberty and his religious scepticism. Accordingly he divides the essay into two corresponding parts, which are sharply different in tone. In the first, in which he deals with our erroneous sense of freedom, he is irenic; in the second, in which he deals with moral responsibility, he is ironic.

His thesis, here as in the *Treatise*, is that all psychic phenomena are causally determined. But whereas in the latter he brusquely rejects the notion of liberty as "absurd" and "unintelligible" (2. 3. 2 [407]), in the recasting he undertakes a "reconciling project with regard to the question of liberty and necessity; the most contentious question, of metaphysics, the most contentious science" (viii. 1 [77]). Now he concedes that the notion of liberty is intelligible in the sense that the will can cause actions: liberty is "*a power of acting or not acting, according to the determinations of the will*" (p. 78). Even so, the will still *determines* the act, and is itself determined by "motives, inclinations, and circumstances" (p. 77). Hume's position has not changed. He just presents it now as an irenic clarification of an issue rather than as a confutation of error. In both places he argues for the paradox of determined will.[65] Before stating his error theory of how we mistakenly come to suppose psychic activity to be uncaused, he explains at length in part 1 that our behavior bespeaks an implicit belief in psychic causation: we continually predict the actions of others as effects of their characters responding to circumstances. Psychic causation, being so fundamental a premise of our everyday thinking, is really unacknowledged common sense. To this explanation Hume allots fourteen paragraphs, as compared to the two allotted to his error theory. His emphasis is upon the commonsensical nature of psychic causation because he does not want us to feel confuted in our error; he wants us to awaken to our implicit agreement with him. The whole vexatious argument, as men of strong humanist sense have always suspected, has never been substantive; and "all mankind, both learned and ignorant, have always been of the same opinion with regard to this subject." "[A]ll mankind," he

---

[65] Cf. *THN* 2. 3. 1 (399): "Of all the immediate *effects* of pain and pleasure, there is none more remarkable than the WILL" (italics added).

repeats, "have ever agreed in the doctrine of liberty as well as in that of necessity" (viii. 1 [66, 77]).

Part 2 contains a similar exercise, this time in minimizing the unnaturalness of the implications of psychic causation for morality and religion. To the objection that determinism annuls responsibility Hume responds that, to the contrary, it would be if our actions were not causally traceable to our characters that we would not be responsible for them. His determinism leaves the character and the will intact. So far so good; but when one traces the causal sequence back beyond our characters, things become awkward for believers in providence. At this point Hume's fideistic persona suddenly appears, saying, "I pretend not to have obviated or removed all objections to this theory, with regard to necessity and liberty" (viii. 2 [81]). As though candidly acknowledging the possible objections to his causal determinism, he lays out in detail its embarrassing consequences: either no action can be evil, since its ultimate cause is god, or actions can be evil and reflect unfavorably upon God's capacities or intentions.

The first, Panglossian alternative he dispatches summarily and then proceeds to the second. How can the fact of evil be reconciled with omnipotent, omniscient providence? Hume has maneuvered us into confronting this ancient question,[66] only to drop the topic abruptly, offering in place of an answer his ostensible faith that an answer exists somewhere above human comprehension:

> These are mysteries, which mere natural and unassisted reason is very unfit to handle; and whatever system she embraces, she must find herself involved in inextricable difficulties, and even contradictions, at every step which she takes with regard to such subjects. To reconcile the indifference [i.e., the indeterminism[67]] and contingency of human actions with prescience; or to

---

[66] "Epicurus's old questions are yet unanswered. Is [God] willing to prevent evil, but not able? then is he impotent. Is he able, but not willing? then is he malevolent. Is he both able and willing? whence then is evil?" (*DNR* x [198]).

[67] "Few are capable of distinguishing betwixt the liberty of *spontaniety*

defend absolute decrees, and yet free the Deity from being the
author of sin, has been found hitherto to exceed all the power of
philosophy. Happy, if she be thence sensible of her temerity,
when she pries into these sublime mysteries; and leaving a
scene so full of obscurities and perplexities, return, with suitable modesty, to her true and proper province, the examination
of common life; where she will find difficulties enow to employ
her enquiries, without launching into so boundless an ocean of
doubt, uncertainty, and contradiction!                    (p. 84)

We must now separate Hume from his persona. Hume the
sceptic and Hume the fideist agree that the problem of evil is
not peculiar to causal determinism and therefore constitutes
no reason to embrace indeterminism: because of God's foresight and abilities, indeterministically willed evil would still
be inconsistent with his moral innocence. But Hume dis-
agrees with his persona in that he thinks (and utilizes the persona to hint) that the problem of evil is not a problem for
causal determinism; it is a problem entirely for the tenet of
providence. Hume the sceptic does not press his advantage,
though. Rather than insist that reconciling adjustments be
made to our conception of God, he agrees with the fideistic
policy of putting speculative theism out of bounds. To induce
us to acknowledge the limits of human understanding in matters of religion, Hume employs a carrot and a stick. In effect
he presents scandalized readers with the choice of a doctrinal
defeat, with the forced surrender of the cherished notion of
providence, or alternatively, with the face-saving retreat to
mystery. To an extent he is mocking the polemical equivoca-
tions of which Locke had complained: "I find every Sect, as
far as Reason will help them, make use of it gladly: and where
it fails them, they cry out, ' 'Tis matter of Faith, and above
Reason.' "[68] But to a greater extent Hume is content for believers to repair to faith, for an exact confinement to faith

[sic], as it is call'd in the schools, and the liberty of *indifference*; betwixt that
which is oppos'd to violence [coercion], and that which means a negation of
necessity and causes" (*THN* 2. 3. 2 [407]).

[68] *Essay* 4. 18, § 2.

would be tantamount to surrendering theology. His object all along has not been, impossibly, to destroy religion, but only to call philosophy down from the heavens to reside in experience. At the same time that he puts religion in its place, he provides a position for theists to fall back upon with which they are familiar and comfortable.

A sense of natural novelty is not to be hoped for in exposés of inveterate prejudices. These efforts toward minimizing the sense of unnaturalness attending religious scepticism are only exercises in damage control. How successful were they? Hume's religious scepticism has always struck readers as unnatural in the extreme, and with a reputation that is over two hundred years old one must be hesitant to quarrel. But two qualifications should be made to any concession to the judgment of posterity. First, Hume only failed to make his religious scepticism *seem* natural to the public, the majority of whom were inveterately prejudiced in favor of supernaturalist religion. It does not follow that his case against supernaturalist belief actually is contrived and that to impartial readers it does not seem to arise naturally from "methodized" common sense. We have been speaking here about rhetorical effects, not validity. Second, when Hume's efforts are seen as suggested above, as making it difficult for the unsympathetic to dismiss his criticisms out of hand, it is arguable that he had a large measure of success.

We should not leave the topic of Hume's ironic coyness without glancing at his persona's most notorious speech, the last sentences in "Of Miracles." Its context is as follows. Hume begins the essay in the character of a sectarian controversialist aspiring to follow Archbishop Tillotson's example in putting down superstition. Tillotson had raised an argument, paraphrased now by Hume, against the popish doctrine of transubstantiation. Hume's persona, too, wishes to provide an argument against superstition, a test for distinguishing between it and true religion, ostensibly Protestant Christianity. His famous test for the credibility of testimony as to miracles is to consult experience, and the scandalous result is that no such testimony has any credibility. The test, it seems, does not produce the desired results. Hume the Protestant apologist, having somehow to rescue from his own test the biblical testimony as to miracles, abruptly invokes faith: "I am the better pleased with the method of reasoning here delivered, as I think it may serve to confound those dangerous friends or disguised enemies to the *Christian Religion*, who have undertaken to defend it by the principles of human reason" (x. 2 [107]). He had started out delivering a method of reasoning for the purposes of discriminating between false and true religion; now he has retreated to delivering a method of reasoning for the purposes of confounding reason. Employing reason to humble reason was a tactic that the fideists had learned from the classical sceptics, but it is entirely unsuited to his sectarian aims since it cannot selectively exempt Protestantism from doubt. Fideism is just a shift to which he resorts because his test cannot corroborate what he wants it to. Claiming alternately the authority and the insufficiency of reason only insofar as it is convenient, he is just that kind of equivocating controversialist about whom Locke had complained. Why faith rescues only the desired testimonies he does not say. Brandishing his test in favor of true revealed religion, he has backed all revealed religion into an irrationalist corner:

> [W]e may conclude, that the *Christian Religion* not only was at first attended with miracles, but even at this day cannot be believed by any reasonable person without one. Mere reason is insufficient to convince us of its veracity: And whoever is moved by *Faith* to assent to it, is conscious of a continued miracle in his own person, which subverts all the principles of his understanding, and gives him a determination to believe what is most contrary to custom and experience. (p. 108)

The apologist for true religion has tied himself into a knot. Now his criterion is faith, which is itself, he claims, a divine intervention into the natural workings of our minds: the criterion for the credibility of testimony as to miracles is personal experience of yet another miracle. What is conspicuously absent is a criterion for this criterion, one for testing the authenticity of our own miraculous faith in particular testimonies. None is offered.

Through his persona's ineptness Hume deftly shifts the question at the end of the essay from the incredibility of others' testimony to that of our own beliefs in the miraculous. The statement that faith subverts all the principles of the understanding is a clear indication of his genuine opinion of supernaturalist religion. George Campbell, who is acute in interpreting Hume's ironies elsewhere in the essay, is oddly obtuse in reading this speech. Accusing Hume of deliberately writing unintelligibly, he produces two construals:

> [I]f any meaning can be gather'd from that strange assemblage of words just now quoted, it seems to be one or other of these which follow: *either*, That there are not any in the world, who believe the gospel; *or*, That there is no want of miracles in our own time. . . . If the second remark is true, if there is no want of miracles at present, surely experience cannot be pleaded against the belief of miracles said to have been perform'd in time past. Again, if the first remark is true, if there are not any in the world who believe the gospel, because, as Mr Hume supposeth, a miracle cannot be believed without a new miracle, why all this ado to refute opinions which nobody entertains?[69]

Campbell is right to say that calling faith miraculous vitiates the proposed test against superstition. But this is embarrassing only for Hume's persona, not for Hume himself, who does not really believe that faith is miraculous. Campbell misses Hume's irony and does not see that Hume is smiling at the notion of self-confirming faith. The alternate construal is also off the mark: Hume does not imply that no one believes in the gospel; he implies that faith, though a kind of belief, is as bogus a miracle as any other alleged miracle. He expects us to see as patently ludicrous the notion that an omnipotent god would perpetrate a back-up miracle to make someone believe in another miracle that is itself supposed to induce credal belief.

---

[69] Campbell, *Dissertation*, 286–87.

There are yet more depths of irony to plumb in this speech. Hume has not only implied his true opinion by ludicrously stating its opposite; he has also positively stated his position by means of deliberate ambiguity in his use of the word "miracle."[70] In the strict meaning, a "miracle is a violation of the laws of nature" (x. 1 [93]; cf. n. 1). The incredibility of testimony as to a violation of natural law is inherent in the notion of such a violation: as we can only descry natural laws through uniform experience of their manifestations, experience necessarily must always favor natural law against testimony as to its violation. This is the crux of Hume's test of credibility. Occasionally, however, Hume mischievously employs a relaxed meaning of the word "miracle." When elsewhere in the essay he admits the possibility of a miracle, it is a hollow concession, for he there employs its relaxed meaning. Possible miracles are only "violations of the usual course of nature" (x. 2 [105]),[71] that is, exceptions in the appearance of regularity in nature that prompt us to reappraise our formulation of the contravened natural law. To reappraise a law in light of new evidence is quite the opposite of looking for supernatural violations of that law. So when Hume calls it a miracle that people believe in miracles, either in the form of a report or of their own faith, he means that their belief is an irregularity in the natural course of psychic events. It is anomalous, not supernatural. It is no more miraculous, in the strict sense of the word, than that people deviate sometimes from their usual standards of reason. "[I]f the spirit of religion join itself to the love of wonder," Hume explains, "there is an end of common sense" (p. 95). To read the speech quoted above for Hume's actual meaning, then, replace the words "miracles" in the first sentence and "miracle" in the second with the expression "freak(s) of mind."

Why do these deviations occur? A Humean error theory of factitious belief can be educed from certain passages in the

[70] See Flew, *Hume's Philosophy of Belief*, 198–203.

[71] Cf. "Miracle," 2. *OED*: "as applied hyperbolically to an achievement seemingly beyond human power, or an occurrence so marvellous as to appear supernatural."

*Treatise* (e.g., 1. 3. 9 [113–15]), but for present purposes we can approach the question better by way of aesthetics. People believe in miracles because it delights them to do so. Miracles satisfy the appetite for the marvelous of which Rousseau spoke. But why then did Hume's paradoxical marvels not satisfy the same appetite? The paradoxicality of priestcraft was for some reason acceptable to the people but that of Academical scepticism was not. Why are the notions of resurrection and virginal maternity pleasing and not those of determined will and cogent incredibility? Hume's answer would be that, as we noted earlier, the astonishment attending paradoxes changes immediately into the highest degree either of esteem or contempt as we approve or disapprove of the subject. Religious paradoxes produce esteem because they are contrived in conjunction with mythologies that strike in with disorderly passions and mingle with natural affections and propensities. These mythologies are approved of because they play upon our fear of death, upon our desire that our enemies be punished and our virtue rewarded, eventually if not in this life, upon our need to feel that there is a purpose to our suffering, and so on. Academical scepticism, in contrast, appeals only to the desire for truth: "By flattering no irregular passion, it gains few partizans: By opposing so many vices and follies, it raises to itself abundance of enemies, who stigmatize it as libertine, profane, and irreligious" (*EHU* v. 1 [36]). Paradoxes arising in conjunction with such an uningratiating philosophy as Academical scepticism are then much more liable than religious ones to produce contempt in the people. We have seen Hume attempting to deal with this problem.

One's aesthetic response to Hume's ironic machinations is bound to be mixed. One admires the rhetorical dexterity and argumentative trenchancy but is displeased with the disingenuousness. Through his character Stephen Daedalus, James Joyce expressed a belief that cunning is one of the attributes an artist needs to keep himself unfettered, but in a philosopher one prefers to find sweetness and light. One wishes that Hume had managed things so as not to have fibbed about his religion. And yet one is chary of holding his conduct up to an

inappropriate standard of candor. Hume's protective disingenuousness was justified by events, particularly by the attempt in 1756 to excommunicate him from the Church of
Scotland. At first glance it may seem fit and proper to remove
his name from the list of members—Hume obviously was not
a good or even indifferent Presbyterian—but an excommunication from the national church, in that time and place, would
have had repercussions far beyond the mere disowning of an
unbelieving member. In all likelihood the scandal would have
meant his ostracism from society, polite or otherwise. Membership in the various clubs and societies in which he figured
prominently would have been unobtainable or forfeit. The
governmental offices that he was given later would have been
unthinkable. And one reason that the excommunication never
proceeded to a trial was that, as Hume's defenders argued, it
would have been impossible to establish to a legal certainty
what Hume's religious opinions were.[72]

## The "Morals" Recast

General propositions are obscure, misty, and
uncertain, compar'd with plain, full, and home
examples: Precepts only apply to our Reason, which in
most men is but weak: Examples are pictures, and
strike the Senses, nay raise the Passions, and call in
those (the strongest and most general of all motives) to
the aid of reformation.
—Pope, 26 July 1734, *Corr.*

The second *Enquiry* is a comparatively straightforward book
and does not invite a close reading of particular passages for
their effects and subtleties of message. This is not to say that
it is a bad piece of work: it is a bland, rather humorless book,
nearly devoid of witticisms and of the ironic duplicities that
make its predecessors so interesting to read quite apart from
their contents; but it is plainly unspectacular by intention. Of
itself it has little to hold the attention of the literary student.

[72] See Mossner, *Life*, 347, 350.

The primary fact about it of interest to us is that despite its prosaicness Hume thought so highly of it as a composition. Prosaicness naturally accompanies the qualities for which he valued it.

Upon his statements of preference for the book Hume did not elaborate, nor is there elsewhere any decisive evidence with which to explain this preference. But if we view the book as a part of the larger developmental picture that has emerged in our study, this preference can be made to make sense. We can suppose that here, as in no previous work, Hume's subject matter, as he understood it, was in harmony with his neo-Attic and humanistic ideals of natural novelty and philosophical usefulness. The literary qualities that make the *Philosophical Essays* so intriguing are not necessarily those that he unambivalently favored, and the absence of them in the second *Enquiry* might indicate an absence of tension between his inclinations and his ideals. The latter book might then represent the fullest realization of Hume's literary ambitions (if not, perhaps, of his talents) and have satisfied him most completely for that reason.

We have seen his taste evolving and his penchant for paradoxes abating. Epigrammatic paradoxes now are gone, never to reappear in his writing.[73] In the *Philosophical Essays* they were largely supplanted by an ironic coyness into which Hume retreated when contravening religious prejudices; but, interestingly, there is little or none of this irony in the second *Enquiry*.[74] Now Hume's efforts are given over entirely to natural novelty.

[73] The one witticism to be found here is not paradoxical: "*Barrenness* in women, being also a species of *inutility*, is a reproach, but not in the same degree [as impotence]: Of which the reason is very obvious . . ." (vi. 2 [227]). Nor is this a strong flash of wit: Hume mutes the innuendo here in pointing us so overtly to the sort of utility left to an infertile woman, making this witticism just a piece of drollery. A stronger turn, such as Dryden could have given it, would have been out of place in a disquisition on morality.

[74] The following surely is disingenuous, but whether it qualifies as irony is doubtful: "Even the general laws of the universe, though planned by infinite wisdom, cannot exclude all evil or inconvenience, in every particular operation" (app. 3 [274]).

This harmony of subject matter (morality), inclination (to be candidly straightforward), and literary ideals (natural novelty and usefulness) was possible because Hume elected here not to confront religion. That he consciously adopted different policies concerning religion in the two *Enquiries* is clear from his letters. To warnings against publishing the *Philosophical Essays* his reaction was "I think I am too deep engaged to think of a retreat. In the second place, I see not what bad consequences follow, in the present age, from the character of an infidel; especially if a man's conduct be in other respects irreproachable." But to Robert Wallace he wrote, concerning the second *Enquiry*, "I hope you will not find my Ethics liable to much Exception, on the Side of Orthodoxy, whatever they may on the Side of Argument & Philosophy."[75] The difference in policy was noticed by at least one reviewer, who predicted that the second *Enquiry* would "considerably raise [Hume's] reputation; and, being free from that sceptical turn which appears in his other pieces, will be more agreeable to the generality of Readers."[76] Hume may not have been a religious conformist, but he was a moral one, and simply by refraining from attacking religion he assumed a respectability that must have been for him a refreshing change.

It is true that Hume's aversion to what he thought were superstitious virtues is undisguised in the second *Enquiry*, but he is perfectly forthright about this rather than satiric, and can be because religion is peripheral to the book. For him morality and religion are entirely separable topics. He deals with morality largely without bringing up religion. The superstitious virtues, presented without any broader critique of religion, were a fairly safe target. The scorn he passingly heaped upon them was commonly enough shared that no appreciable reaction was to be feared. No very considerable portion of

[75] 2 Oct. 1747, *LDH* 1: 106 (cf. 9 Feb. 1748, ibid., 111); 22 Sept. 1751, *NLDH*, 29.

[76] [William Rose,] art. 1, *Monthly Review* 6 (Jan. 1752): 1. Cf. Lord Brougham, *Lives* 1: 206: "Nor is it the least remarkable feature of [the *EPM*], that though preferred by him before all the other productions of his genius, it contains nothing at all even bordering upon sceptical opinions."

that bourgeois society would have been terribly incensed by disdain for "[c]elibacy, fasting, penance, mortification, self-denial, humility, silence, solitude, and the whole train of monkish virtues" (*EPM* ix. 1 [246]). Irony is unnecessary. The complicating factor of his infidelity is not here exerting its influence on Hume's writing.

Still, the separability of morality and religion may in itself seem paradoxical, to many people at least. A number of questions arise concerning the relations in Hume's mind between morality and religion. Why, if he was a conformist in morals and politics, was he not one in religion? If he was willing for sentiment to be the basis of morality, why was he suspicious of it as a basis for religion? Why should religion be exceptional? Sorting out the relationship between Hume's philosophies of morality and religion can help us to account for the literary differences between the two *Enquiries*: one is satirically ironic, the other prosaically earnest, because Hume's approaches to religion and to morality are different. His moral irreproachability in all areas except his treatment of religion puzzled his acquaintances, and it is unlikely that he would not have formulated a rationale for this policy if only for his own peace of mind. That he never explained himself is not surprising, for to do so would have involved an unacceptably explicit discussion of his religious views. But knowing how his mind worked, we can draw up a Humean explanation, one that is not unlikely to approximate Hume's own.

The unsuitability of sentiment as a criterion for true religion is its indistinguishability from enthusiasm, indoctrination, and wishful thinking (see 18 Feb. 1751, *LDH* 1: 151–52). For the same reason sentiment is unsatisfactory as a proof of the religious hypothesis itself, having no weight with those not sharing the adduced sentiment. The question, then, is why sentiment is a satisfactory proof for a corresponding moral hypothesis that the distinction between right and wrong is genuine. Is it not applying a double standard for Hume to countenance moral sentimentalism and not a religious counterpart?

Both hypotheses start with the fact of sentiment. The difference between them is that the religious one moves beyond the fact that people have religious sentiments and illicitly includes occult entities, qualities, and relations. The parallel fallacy would be to infer from the existence of moral sentiment that objective moral relations exist somehow in the fabric of the universe. But Hume's empirical sentimentalism starts and stays with the fact of moral sentiment, drawing from it no ontological conclusions concerning unobservable things. It is an observable fact, Hume insists, that men experience moral sentiments and that they try to compensate for their partiality by codifying and systematizing their sentiments into rules. It is not observable that a supernatural entity, having created abstract moral relations and accompanying rules, has impressed the knowledge of them upon man's mind. Theistically minded sentimentalists like Hutcheson assumed that moral sentiment was built into man when God created him, and to this notion Hume gives lip service: "The standard of [taste], arising from the internal frame and constitution of animals, is ultimately derived from that Supreme Will, which bestowed on each being its peculiar nature, and arranged the several classes and orders of existence" (app. 1. 5 [266]). But he says this only for the sake of "Decency and Prudence." A good empiricist, he contents himself with identifying the psychological principles by which our sentiments operate: utility and immediate agreeableness. That he did not believe in a transcendent moral authority is indicated by the positiveness with which he says, "The general opinion of mankind has some authority in all cases; but in this of morals 'tis perfectly infallible" (*THN* 3. 2. 9 [552]; cf. §§ 8, 11 [546–47, 569]). He looks to no higher appeal in moral questions than to the generalized sentiments of mankind.[77] Even if he were a moral theist, he

---

[77] Cf. "OContr.," 486: "[T]hough an appeal to general opinion may justly, in the speculative sciences of metaphysics, natural philosophy, or astronomy, be deemed unfair and inconclusive, yet in all questions with regard to morals, as well as criticism, there is really no other standard, by which any controversy can ever be decided. And nothing is a clearer proof, that a theory of this kind is erroneous, than to find, that it leads to paradoxes, repugnant to the common sentiments of mankind, and to the practice and opinion of all nations and all ages."

would be behooved on purely procedural grounds to keep his theism to himself, for (as he argues in appendix 1) the standard of observation gives no warrant to hypothesize a supernatural moral cosmology. Sentiment is indeed Hume's standard of right and wrong, but it is itself subject to the standard of observation. So long as moral sentiment is an observable fact and God is not, Hume is innocent of applying a double standard. That sentiment is such a fact Hume spends much of the book arguing.

It does not follow that Hume could not have been a religious conformist, though. (For example, he obviously saw the dubiousness, in the abstract, of prevailing standards of chastity but would not have dreamt of challenging them: such as they were they did serve their purpose, and the sentiments of the populace are not susceptible of fine-tuning.) Moral conformism is to be expected in someone who tends to identify morality with the sentiments of mankind as organized into social mores and laws. But the general opinion of mankind, the infallible authority, has been that piety is a virtue, impiety a vice, that it is a duty at least to refrain from subverting popular religion, which, superstitious or not, is an important support to morality. To a moral conformist, therefore, would not conformity to established religious forms be an obligation irrespective of credal belief or disbelief? Campbell fulminated against those who disregarded the obligation to support the support of morality, calling them "enemies to human nature":

> Let people but cooly ask themselves, If our freethinkers, our speculative and philosophical latitudinarians, should succeed in the dark design they seem sometimes so zealously to prosecute; and if the disbelief of the principles, and the disregard to the rites of religion, which already appear in too many, and plainly show their evil influence on the morals of the age, should, agreeably to the ordinary course of things, descend to the lowest ranks, and become universal, what will be the consequence? Who can hesitate to answer, The utter fall of religion? . . . And if once our faith is subverted, is any so blind as to imagine, that religion will fall alone? Can her disgrace fail to be accompanied

by that of virtue and good manners? In such general ruin,—
what will be safe? Can we be vain enough to imagine,—that our
laws and liberties, or any part of the constitution, will long survive?[78]

Swift put it less hysterically: "The want of belief is a defect
that ought to be concealed when it cannot be overcome."[79]

The moral argument for self-censorship and even for religious hypocrisy was something that was current in Georgian
Britain and that by his own principles Hume had to take seriously. It was to justified hypocrisy that he referred when he
quoted the Pythian oracle; and in minimal ways he engaged
in this hypocrisy. As for self-censorship, Hume publicly acknowledged the possibility of such an obligation, admitting
that

> though the philosophical truth of any proposition by no means
> depends on its tendency to promote the interests of society; yet
> a man has but a bad grace, who delivers a theory, however true,
> which, he must confess, leads to a practice dangerous and per-
> nicious. Why rake into those corners of nature, which spread a
> nuisance all around? Why dig up the pestilence from the pit, in
> which it is buried? The ingenuity of your researches may be
> admired; but your systems will be detested: And mankind will
> agree, if they cannot refute them, to sink them, at least, in eter-
> nal silence and oblivion. Truths, which are *pernicious* to society,
> if any such there be, will yield to errors, which are salutary and
> *advantageous.*                    (*EPM* ix. 2 [253–54])[80]

[78] "The Happy Influence of Religion on Civil Society," *Dissertation on Miracles* . . . , 3d ed., 2 vols. (Edinburgh, 1797), 2: 111–12.

[79] "Thoughts on Religion," *Irish Tracts* . . . , 261.

[80] Cf. *THN* 2. 3. 2 (409) and *EHU* viii. 2 (79). The following anecdote seems
to contradict the passage just quoted. The Earl of Charlemont records: "I
have sometimes, in the course of our intimacy, asked [Hume] whether he
thought that, if his opinions were universally to take place, mankind would
not be rendered more unhappy than they now were; and whether he did not
suppose that the curb of religion was necessary to human nature? 'The objections,' answered he, 'are not without weight; but error never can produce
good, and truth ought to take place of all considerations.' " But this judgment,
if accurately quoted, does not square with what Charlemont tells us later

The closest that Hume ever came in print to designating a truth categorically pernicious is the following reflection on the sovereignty of the people:

> If ever, on any occasion, it were laudable to conceal truth from the populace; it must be confessed, that the doctrine of resistance affords such an example; and that all speculative reasoners ought to observe, with regard to this principle, the same cautious silence, which the laws, in every species of government, have ever prescribed to themselves. Government is instituted, in order to restrain the fury and injustice of the people; and being always founded on opinion, not on force, it is dangerous to weaken, by these speculations, the reverence, which the multitude owe to authority, and to instruct them beforehand, that the case can ever happen, when they may be freed from their duty of allegiance. Or should it be found impossible to restrain the license of human disquisitions, it must be acknowledged, that the doctrine of obedience ought alone to be *inculcated*, and that the exceptions, which are rare, ought seldom or never to be mentioned in popular reasonings and discourses.[81]

Admittedly Hume did not present this argument as his own, but only summarized, though very sympathetically, the reaction of disinterested philosophers to Charles I's execution. But at the least it must be said that the possibility of an obligation to self-censorship was very real to Hume.

So how could Hume in good conscience have published criticisms of popular religion? The precise answer will depend upon which of two criteria for morality we attribute to him. If we take him literally when he calls infallible "the common

---

about Hume's "conviction that infidelity was ill suited to women," which "made him perfectly averse from the initiation of ladies into the mysteries of his doctrine" (*Memoirs of the Political and Private Life of James Caulfield, Earl of Charlemont*, ed. Francis Hardy [London, 1810], 121–22). Boswell records an intriguing reminiscence of Kames's: "He told of Hume resolving never to write against religion" (5 Mar. 1782, *Boswell: Laird of Auchinleck, 1778-1782*, ed. Joseph W. Reed and Frederick A. Pottle, vol. 11 of Yale Eds. [New York, 1977], 430).

[81] *Hist.* 5: 544 (30 Jan. 1649). Cf. *THN* 3. 2. 10 (553–54, 563–64) and "PO," 490–91.

sentiments of mankind, and . . . the practice and opinion of all nations and all ages," then morality for him consists simply in conformity to that standard. History will inform us of what is right and wrong. But Hume sometimes talks as though his criterion is adherence to what the sentiments of mankind *would* be if men were all apprised of the pertinent facts and disabused of prejudices and mistaken beliefs. In this case moral questions are answered not by referring to the history of mankind's opinions, but to the underlying psychological principles that direct sentiment, applied to the particular circumstances of the problem being examined (see *EPM* i [172] and "ST"). Mankind's authority could then be overturned if its opinion is shown to have hinged upon a mistake of fact, such as, perhaps, the belief that morality depends upon religion. I imagine that Hume would apply either or both of these criteria as seemed most suitable to a specific moral problem. As to what policy one is to follow when these two criteria lead to conflicting conclusions, Hume is silent. Temperamentally, though, he probably would be disposed to give the presumption to mankind's opinion.[82]

But in fact the criteria do not result in conflicting conclusions with regard to the morality of religious conformism and self-censorship. Let us suppose first that Hume was a strict moral conformist and did not have the option of saying that mankind has been morally wrong in feeling that popular religions should not be subverted. He might then say that although the prevailing sentiment has been against criticizing popular religion, it has by no means been the general opinion through the ages that religious hypocrisy is virtuous, much

[82] Philip Mercer attributes the latter criterion to Hume, dismissing the former because he finds no support for such a reading in the texts (*Sympathy and Ethics: A Study of the Relationship between Sympathy and Morality with Special Reference to Hume's "Treatise"* [Oxford, 1972], 61–66). Also, like Árdal (*Passion and Value*, 191–93), he is unwilling to attribute to Hume such a (supposedly) preposterous tenet. But I have cited passages indicating that Hume took moral conformism seriously, and this attribution seems much less unlikely when we view him, as he invites, in relation to the classical sceptics, who did advocate conformism.

less an obligation. Furthermore, it *has* been the general opinion that the discovery and dissemination of truth are good. When the truth happens to subvert religion, one good conflicts with another. As with most moral problems, the infallible authority of mankind's opinion offers no clear decision. Mankind is often of several minds concerning moral questions when it considers them in any detail.

In the absence of guidance from mankind, Hume must judge for himself as best he can the morality of religious nonconformism. And this is precisely the situation he would be in if he thought that morality consists in projecting what mankind's sentiments would be if they properly informed themselves concerning the issue. Probably he would now apply the standard of utility, the principle that he thought influences mankind's sentiments when questions of artificial virtue arise. We have already discussed how he would weigh the benefits and detriments of free-thinking and conformism in view of the current state of society, concluding that the greatest present evil was the adulteration of philosophy. He would in addition question the supposed moral utility of religion. Against the incentives and exhortations to morality that religion provides he would adduce the various moral corruptions with which it is associated: factiousness, dogmatism, intolerance, enthusiasm and superstition made possible by the violence that selective credulity does to intellectual integrity, the perversion of morality into the monkish observance of indifferent and arbitrary forms, and so on. Illustrations of and reflections upon these various corruptions abound in the *History*.[83] David Miller says that for Hume the conclusion of these deliberations on the moral utility of religion was that the effects of

---

[83] A couple of the more interesting from the point of view of the present discussion are "Hypocrisy, quite pure and free from fanaticism, is perhaps, except among men fixed in a determined philosophical scepticism, . . . as rare as fanaticism entirely purged from all mixture of hypocrisy" (*Hist.* 5: 572 n. AA), and "The religious hypocrisy . . . is of a peculiar nature; and being generally unknown to the person himself, though more dangerous, it implies less falsehood than any other species of insincerity" (6: 142 ["Manners and arts. 1660"]). See also the characterization of priests in "NC," 199–201 n. 3.

religion in civilized societies are on the whole damaging or at best neutral.[84] When the slightly dubious good represented by truth conflicts with the highly dubious good represented by religion, Hume can consider himself morally justified in plumping for truth.

Hume's sentimentalism, then, does not oblige him, philosophically or morally, to support supernaturalist religion or to censor his doubts. He is free to criticize or ignore it as he deems fit. My own guess is that his reckoning of the benefits and balefulness of religion was either that its moral influence is neutral or that no conclusion is possible one way or the other. A neutral or inconclusive reckoning would be sufficient to account for his treatment of religion, whereas, on the other hand, if he had reckoned the influence to be decidedly bad, one would expect him to attack religion in the second *Enquiry* as he had in the *Philosophical Essays*. That he did not attack religion in his book on morality suggests that he felt no such compulsion and that there was some countervailing reason this time against exposing its adulterating influence on philosophy. An obvious candidate for this reason is the hortatory value of religion.

It is an undeniable fact that, mistakenly or not, morality and religion were intertwined in the minds of the populace. Any attempt to disentangle them would as probably disturb the people's moral convictions as put them on a firmer basis. Equivocal as it is, the moral influence of religion is recommended by the simple fact that it is in place and operating. "[M]orals," Hume believed, "must always be handled with a view to public interest, more than philosophical regularity" (*EPM* iii. 2 [193 n. 1]). True, Hume did tell Boswell "flatly that the Morality of every Religion was bad, and . . . was not jocular when he said 'that when he heard a man was religious, he concluded he was a rascal, though he had known some instances of very good men being religious.' " Years earlier he had told Boswell that "it required great goodness of disposi-

---

[84] Miller, *Philosophy and Ideology*, 116.

tion to withstand [the] baleful effects of Christianity."[85] But such remarks should not be taken too seriously. Boswell continually probed and tested Hume's convictions and was bound to elicit sarcasm. Hume's exasperated railings against the English and against "Whiggery" show how he characteristically fell into sarcastic exaggeration when provoked.[86] And the *Life of Johnson* is a monument to Boswell's talent for prodding people into making colorfully extreme pronouncements. In all probability Hume's considered opinion was that religion was not all bad and that its influence on morality did not merit attack as did its adulterating influence on philosophy. A likely reason the *Philosophical Essays* is satirically ironic and the second *Enquiry* is not is that in his view religion is a definite hindrance to the pursuit of truth but a mixed blessing to the inculcation of morality. In the earlier book Hume was intent on the procedures for pursuing truth, on his "logic." He compromised with the popular taste for easy obviousness insofar as he sought to avoid intricacies and present abstruse truths elegantly, but he did not try to lure men into the paths of virtue (except of course in the sense that reasoning accurately is virtuous). In the later book, however, he was occupied not only with moral theory and the psychology of our moral sentiments, but also secondarily with the inculcation of morality, the primary purpose of easy and obvious philosophy and one he shared with religion. Now his compromise with easy obviousness extends even to painting virtue in her most amiable colors.

This runs counter to what we have come to expect from philosophers, who long ago gave up on advocating the good life. The Analytic movement in its various permutations has been the dominant modern tradition. Until recently, if philosophers descended from second-order topics it was usually to the level of generality of normative ethics. Sometimes they descended further to make ethical judgments on problem

[85] "An Account . . . ," *DNR*, 76, and 2 May 1768, *Boswell in Search of a Wife, 1766-1769*, ed. Frank Brady and Frederick A. Pottle, vol. 6 of Yale Eds. (London, 1957), 177.

[86] See, e.g, 12 Mar. 1763, *NLDH*, 69–71, and 21 Feb. 1770, *LDH* 2: 216.

cases to show how their normative principles could be applied. But even those involved in the currently burgeoning field of applied ethics do not descend to inculcating morality directly. Hume offers neither a normative nor an applied ethics, operating instead at the two most divergent planes imaginable—at the abstruse level, examining the nature of morality, and subsidiarily at the suasive level, presenting virtue to its best advantage. All gradations between he ignores because they do not fit into the plan of the work. He is compromising between the two species of philosophy, making a hybrid. He thinks of the accurate, abstruse kind in terms of mental anatomy, of the easy, obvious kind in terms of literary painting. Normative and applied ethics do not obviously belong under either heading. In obscuring the difference between the two philosophies, Hume declines to choose between teaching what is not known and recommending known truths by his manner of adorning them. Rather he recommends the old moral verities while anatomizing them. The effect for which he is hoping is natural novelty, and it is unlikely that rigorously applying to problem cases any normative standard whatsoever will not produce some startling new moral conclusions. New moral verities are just inappropriate to the hybrid as he conceived it. It would not serve to present morality to its best advantage to show how it is vexed with the uncertainties and controversies of normative and applied ethics. Moreover, as we shall see, it was important to Hume's anatomical purpose (to the establishment of utility and immediate agreeableness as the underlying principles of moral sentiments) that he confine himself to old, uncontroversial virtues: it would hardly lend credence to his principles to infer them from controversial examples.

Hume's attitude toward mental anatomy evidently has changed. In the *Treatise* he designated himself as an anatomist first and last, stating categorically that the anatomist ought never to "pretend to give his figures any graceful and engaging attitude or expression" (3. 3. 6 [620–21]). There he maintained that mental anatomy can only help the cause of moral beauty indirectly by being what it is and not another

thing. Unfortunately the immediate effect of such close scrutiny is, in Johnson's expression, to "shew us the naked skele-
ton of every delight."[87] But it does not follow that philosophy
has to be altogether ugly or even aesthetically neutral. A distinction should be observed between the object dissected and
the process of dissection. Hume says here that an anatomist
should not attempt to prettify the dissected object, but he
does not say that the procedures of anatomy themselves cannot be more or less beautiful. Just as the dexterity and preci-
sion with which an anatomist wields his scalpel can be marvelous, the manner in which Hume philosophized could be
too. Similarly an anatomist's lectures, and Hume's presentation of his findings, could be entertaining as well as instructive. Accordingly in the *Treatise* Hume did not try to beautify
moral sentiments in order to recommend morality to his readers, but he did try to make the anatomizing of sentiment as
marvelous for readers as he found it himself.

Such was Hume's position on the writing of moral philosophy at the time of the *Treatise*. By the time of the recasting
of his "morals" his position had softened. A distinguishing feature of the second *Enquiry*, and a likely reason for Hume's
pride in it, is that in it he had not only anatomized beautifully,
but had beautified and commended moral sentiment as well.
The great achievement is in not beautifying morality at the
expense of accuracy, something previously he had not believed possible. To Hutcheson's objection that in book 3 of the
*Treatise* Hume had lacked "Warmth in the Cause of Virtue,"
he had replied at the time of its publication that an "Anatomist . . . can give very good Advice to a Painter or Statuary:
And in like manner, I am perswaded, that a Metaphysician
may be very helpful to a Moralist; tho' I cannot easily conceive these two Characters united in the same Work."[88] When
Hume brings up this contrast of purposes again in the *Philosophical Essays*, he seems to hint that these characters cannot
be united in one work:

[87] No. 112, *Rambler*, Yale Ed. 4: 232.
[88] 17 Sept. 1739, *LDH* 1: 32, 33.

All polite letters are nothing but pictures of human life in various attitudes and situations; and inspire us with different sentiments, of praise or blame, admiration or ridicule, according to the qualities of the object, which they set before us. An artist must be better qualified to succeed in this undertaking, who, besides a delicate taste and a quick apprehension, possesses an accurate knowledge of the internal fabric, the operations of the understanding, the workings of the passions, and the various species of sentiment which discriminate vice and virtue. . . . The anatomist presents to the eye the most hideous and disagreeable objects; but his science is useful to the painter in delineating even a Venus or an Helen.          (*EHU* i [6–7])

But having said this he proceeds a few paragraphs later to declare his intentions to try to combine politeness with accuracy. He will attempt to write what might be called a mitigated anatomy: without beautifying cognition, the object of dissection, he tries to bring out the beauty of empirical procedures and to make his exposition neat and elegant. The second *Enquiry* represents the next step in the direction of easy obviousness. When he takes up virtue as his object for dissection he beautifies it also, infusing his "morals" with warmth for virtue.

Hume's painterly recommendation of virtue is not usually overt and might easily be missed by readers engrossed, as most are, in his anatomizing. They do not expect it, and because it is not conspicuous it goes unnoticed. One reason for its inconspicuousness is that Hume wished to arouse only calm passions, those that are compatible with wisdom: averse as he is to enthusiasm, he never lets his warmth rise to fervor. It registers in us almost subliminally. Another reason is that Hume is not wildly successful at communicating his warmth. One does not put the book down with an impulse to go out and do a good deed or to make resolutions as to future conduct. Yet few readers will fail to recognize the commendatory aspect of the book once it is brought to their attention. Residing in his tone, Hume's warmth is more easily felt than demonstrated, but a few tangible indications of it can be cited.

The first indication that Hume's jealousy for the autonomy of anatomy has abated is in section 1, in which he paraphrases two opposed accounts of morality with the purpose of reconciling them. The rationalist case is that reason is manifestly fundamental to making moral distinctions since we do dispute over right and wrong as we do over truth and falsity, often with great subtlety. The sentimentalist response is that vice and virtue are manifestly affective qualities and that reason could not descry their affective values before we had learned them from experience of people's feelings. Furthermore, morality must be fundamentally affective if it is to affect our behavior as it does, for only passions can motivate actions. The reasoned insights into morality that the rationalists adduce would be of no practical, and hence no moral, benefit were it not for the antecedent affective values of moral qualities. This case is unmistakably Humean, but in paraphrasing it Hume says something surprising: "The end of all moral speculations is to teach us our duty; and, by proper representations of the deformity of vice and beauty of virtue, beget correspondent habits, and engage us to avoid the one, and embrace the other" (*EPM* i [171]). Accurate, abstruse philosophy seems to have collapsed into the easy, obvious kind. Admittedly Hume is only paraphrasing a prototypical sentimentalist argument here, so possibly this statement does not represent his own position. But it is sympathetically paraphrased, and it accords well with an earlier remark that the passion for philosophy directs us to "the correction of our manners, and extirpation of our vices" (*EHU* v. 1 [35]). At the least, it is significant that Hume makes no attempt whatsoever to qualify the statement as he amends the prototypical argument to reveal his own. Either he agrees with it or does not think it worth the trouble to correct.

Why would it now be not worth the trouble to explain how abstruse philosophy can benefit morality only indirectly? In the *Treatise* and the *Philosophical Essays* Hume had felt constrained to defend abstruse philosophy against the humanist charge of uselessness, but there is no need to be defensive in the second *Enquiry* if while anatomizing he also represents the deformity of vice and beauty of virtue. Sentimentalism allows him to do both. Accuracy does not have to be at cross-purposes with the arousal of disapprobation for vice and approbation for virtue if, according to your analysis, vice and virtue are fundamentally defined by their tendency to arouse feelings of reprehension and approval. It is the nature of virtue to be beautiful, then, and painting it as such is not distorting in the least. As Hume asks rhetorically, "[W]hat philosophical truths can be more advantageous to society, than those here delivered, which represent virtue in all her genuine and most engaging charms, and make us approach her with ease, familiarity, and affection?" (*EPM* ix. 2 [254]).

An abstract discussion of a virtue will not by itself elicit approbatory sentiments. For the arousal of feeling, particular situations are required. A striking change from the *Treatise* is that now Hume generously serves up such particulars, drawing mostly upon classical history and literature. Blair thought historical illustrations helpful in moral philosophy because

> they relieve the mind from the fatigue of mere reasoning, and at the same time raise more full conviction than any reasonings produce: for they take Philosophy out of the abstract, and give weight to Speculation, by shewing its connection with real life, and the actions of mankind.[89]

And Hume's quotations and anecdotes undoubtedly do serve these functions. The more important in a philosophical work is of course the corroboration of speculations. History, as transmitted to the present through literature, is an important source material for an empiricist's research. Surveying history is the only way he has to extend his observation of humanity beyond his own time. Through it he can

> discover the constant and universal principles of human nature, by shewing men in all varieties of circumstances and situations, and furnishing us with materials, from which we may form our observations, and become acquainted with the regular springs of human action and behaviour. These records of wars, in-

[89] No. 37, *Rhet.* 2: 292.

trigues, factions, and revolutions, are so many collections of experiments, by which the . . . moral philosopher fixes the principles of his science; in the same manner as the physician or
natural philosopher becomes acquainted with the nature of
plants, minerals, and other external objects, by the experiments, which he forms concerning them.    (*EHU* viii. 1 [68])

Hume's anecdotes and quotations are the signs that he has
done his research and that his observations are not sociotem-
porally parochial. They substantiate his claim to be basing his
conclusions upon the sentiments of mankind rather than eth-
nocentrically upon those of eighteenth-century Europeans. At
the same time, however, they depict characters and situations
that can stimulate calm passions in us as abstract discussion
cannot. As Hume says elsewhere,

When a philosopher contemplates characters and manners in his
closet, the general abstract view of the objects leaves the mind
so cold and unmoved, that the sentiments of nature have no
room to play, and he scarce feels the difference between vice
and virtue. . . . The writers of history [on the other hand], as
well as the readers, are sufficiently interested in the characters
and events, to have a lively sentiment of blame or praise; and,
at the same time, have no particular interest or concern to per-
vert their judgment.                    ("SHist.," 568)

Through his allusions in the second *Enquiry* Hume incorporates into his accurate investigations some of the affective
value of history. Nowhere else are his anatomical procedures
and belletristic purposes so seamlessly joined.

In examining benevolence Hume draws on Plutarch, Cicero, and Juvenal in quick succession, and then pulls himself
up short:

But I forget, that it is not my present business to recommend
generosity and benevolence, or to paint, in their true colours,
all the genuine charms of the social virtues. These, indeed, sufficiently engage every heart, on the first apprehension of them;
and it is difficult to abstain from some sally of panegyric, as often
as they occur in discourse or reasoning.

Hume goes on to say that the present object is "more the speculative, than the practical part of morals" (*EPM* ii. 1 [175–76]). Initially this seems a plain denial of any hortatory intentions. But on the other hand it is also plainly an admission that he has just been engaged in recommending a virtue and painting its charms. Hume is being arch. He has not really caught himself in getting carried away; he is just imitating, as eighteenth-century prose stylists tended to do, the casual discontinuities, hesitations, afterthoughts, and backpedallings of actual conversation. If his commendatory painting of benevolence were really a deviation from his intentions, he could easily have struck it out. The only reason for failing to revise the discussion of benevolence is that it did indeed reflect his intentions. And Hume only says here that his object is *more* speculative than practical, indicating that practical morals is in fact a subsidiary part of his intentions.

The structure of the book allows Hume to paint the charms of benevolence and other virtues unobtrusively while going about his anatomical business. But as we cannot talk about this structure without referring frequently to the ideas expounded within it, we had better first briefly identify the tenets of Hume's recast "morals." These can be classified conveniently as either abstruse or obvious.

It is an easy, obvious truth that (1) the distinction between vice and virtue is genuine. To develop this point Hume sets up as his foil the amoral egoism then associated with Mandeville. He not only refutes, but disparages it, calling it more of a satirical affectation than a philosophy. Preferring to attack a movement rather than an individual, he never mentions Mandeville by name; but it was Mandeville's egoism that would have come to readers' minds when Hume speaks of those "who have denied the reality of moral distinctions" (i [169]).[90] Another old verity is that (2) we are obligated to be virtuous and not to be vicious. Hume does not put the idea of obliga-

---

[90] Cf. Smith, *Theory*, 308: "There is . . . another system which seems to take away altogether the distinction between vice and virtue, . . . the system of Dr. Mandeville."

tion under his meaning-empirical microscope because to do so would reveal, scandalously, that he believes in neither categorical nor divine imperatives. And scandal would work against his hortatory purpose. Instead of anatomizing, he proposes only to consider briefly our "interested *obligation*" to virtue and "to enquire, whether every man, who has any regard to his own happiness and welfare, will not best find his account in the practice of every moral duty" (ix. 2 [253]). What follows, though, is not an inquiry, but an assertion that we should be virtuous because it is good for us. Hume recommends virtue in terms of enlightened self-interest. In the general course of life, he claims, vice is naturally attended with unwelcome repercussions, virtue with rewards. When exceptions occur, the honest man still enjoys a good character with himself and with the world, while the dishonest man suffers low self-esteem and reputation. As Cicero says, honesty and profitability ultimately cannot conflict.[91] Stated baldly as propositions, these arguments seem inadequate as incentives to virtue. But Hume does not simply state them; he waxes eloquent:

> How little is requisite to supply the *necessities* of nature? And in a view to *pleasure*, what comparison between the unbought satisfaction of conversation, society, study, even health and the common beauties of nature, but above all the peaceful reflection on one's own conduct: What comparison, I say, between these, and the feverish, empty amusements of luxury and expence? These natural pleasures, indeed, are really without price; both because they are below all price in their attainment, and above it in their enjoyment.

The proper valuation of these natural pleasures, and the understanding of their incompatibility with immorality, are the results "of just calculation, and a steady preference of the greater happiness" (pp. 257, 254).

This brings us to the abstruse question of the roles of reason and sentiment in morality. Hume's most discussed abstruse

[91] *Offices*, bk. 3.

tenet of moral theory is that (1) morality, strictly speaking, is felt rather than apprehended. That is to say, morality is not a complex of abstract relations, like arithmetic, about which we apprehend necessary truths instinctively or deductively. It is a matter of contingent fact traceable to our sentiments of approval or disapproval. Just calculation enters into morality superveniently when we project the full consequences of actions, weigh the prospects and comparative utilities of competing goods, and generalize our sentiments into rules to offset our partiality. A careful review of circumstances often prompts a change of feeling; but feeling remains the motivating factor. A choice to honor a rule in a particular application that is contrary to our immediate desires is, interpreted deterministically, the victory in us of a calm passion for the distant but greater goods accruing to the honest: self-approval, maintenance of the socially indispensable reputation for trustworthiness, encouragement of others to reciprocate honest dealings, and so on. The steady preference for the greater happiness is a calm passion aroused by the view of one's own true self-interest. This sentimentalism is important to Hume's answer to Mandevillean egoism, which is that it is an undeniable fact that we do have sentiments of approval and disapproval, upon which we do distinguish virtue from vice.

A Mandevillean would retort that such sentiments cannot support moral distinctions because they are always selfishly directed. To this retort Hume's answer is his tenet that, to the contrary, (2) we do have disinterested moral sentiments, resulting from "sympathy," the natural tendency to feel what we perceive others to feel. In the second *Enquiry* Hume handles this tenet with such a light touch that perhaps in the present context it should be regarded as an old verity. It is certainly an easy, obvious moral truth that we do sympathize with others and normally are inclined therefore to wish them well. Since he employs "sympathy" here interchangeably with "humanity," his point seems at face value to be simply that there is such a thing as humane behavior. But in the *Treatise* he presented sympathy as an abstruse point of mental anatomy, relating it to the principles of association and using it to exemplify the transferability of impressional vivacity (2. 1. 11 [316–20]). All of these complexities now he leaves merely implicit in his description of the communicability of emotions as "a contagion or natural sympathy" (*EPM* vii [231]).

Another anatomical finding is that (3) our moral sentiments are related to the agreeableness of personal qualities to ourselves and/or to others. Hume unintentionally obscures this point by speaking of virtue as being either *"useful or agreeable"* (ix. 1 [245]), but in his system utility is just a type of agreeableness:

> It is the nature, and, indeed, the definition of virtue, that it is *a quality of the mind agreeable to or approved of by every one, who considers or contemplates it.* But some qualities produce pleasure, because they are useful to society, or useful or agreeable to the person himself; others produce it more immediately. . . .                    (viii. [239 n. 1])

Hume's anatomy of virtue, then, can be schematized as follows.

I. Agreeable qualities
   A. Immediately agreeable
      1. To ourselves (e.g., cheerfulness)
      2. To others (e.g., wit)
   B. Indirectly agreeable (i.e., useful)
      1. To ourselves (e.g., discretion)
      2. To others (e.g., integrity)

Particular virtues can of course be agreeable in several ways. Benevolence, for example, is useful to others and immediately agreeable to everyone concerned (vii [236–37]). All virtues, however, must be agreeable in one or some combination of these ways.

The last abstruse point, following from the sentimentalist definition of virtue, is that (4) the usual distinctions drawn between virtue and natural ability, vice and disability, are trivial. Traits like sagacity or physical attractiveness, though involuntary, still arouse agreeable sentiments just as honesty does. This distinction between voluntary and involuntary behavior has significance only for forensic deliberations, in which reward or punishment are to be assigned. But in practice, though we do not mete out rewards and punishments for talents and disabilities, we do approve or disapprove of them. The anatomist of human nature has much more to consider than forensic logic. Delving into forensic logic, moreover, would involve Hume in normative ethics and problem cases, which he has reason to avoid.

These abstruse tenets he delivers as simply and unparadoxically as he can. We have already noted how he refrains from entering into the mechanism of sympathy. In addition he is careful this time not to be provocative in distinguishing between instinctive and cultivated virtues. Terming them "natural" and "artificial" in the *Treatise* had caused problems, and even to Hutcheson he had had to explain, "I have never call'd Justice unnatural, but only artificial."[92] Now he dispenses with the terminology as not worth the confusion it engenders, dealing with the topic briefly in one paragraph and a note (see app. 3 [275–76 and n. 1]). Likewise he is careful this time not to depreciate the role of reason in morality (see i [172] and app. 1 [258–59]). His philosophy has not changed: he always knew the importance of reason. It is just that now he is unwilling to exploit the potential of double-faced philosophy for paradox.

Hume's advancement of the old verities is well integrated into the exposition of his abstruse tenets. His emphasis is on anatomy, but he makes his findings support the old verities in the ways explained above. However, this is the recommendation of virtue by argument. What about painterly recommendation, and how is this activity integrated into a series of arguments? We have already noted that his use of historical illustrations both substantiates his points and serves to arouse the desired calm passions. Moreover, he sets these illustrations within a particular literary structure that serves both the purposes of expositing tenets and of portraying the charms of virtue. Hume presents the virtues to us systematically by

---

[92] 17 Sept. 1739, *LDH* 1: 33. Cf. *LGent.*, 30–31.

means of a catalogue running through most of the book, with the virtues set in capital letters. We commonly associate the catalogue as a literary form with ancient poetry, but it shows up even in modern poetry and is a familiar enough feature of seventeenth- and eighteenth-century writing.[93] It is a form especially well suited to encomiastic writing, and in the second *Enquiry* allows Hume to embed within his Anatomy of Morals a Praise of Virtue. But it is suited also to empirical analysis. At the same time that he is enumerating the virtues and painting their charms, as a sonneteer enumerates and paints those of his beloved, he is proceeding inductively, accumulating specimens of what he wants to study. For this reason the book imparts a greater sense of unity in progression than the *Philosophical Essays*, the sections of which appear less closely related to each other.

Plainly Hume wanted very much for us to understand his procedure, for he explained it three times, at the beginning, middle, and end of the book. Thus disposed, these explanations could serve as signposts for the reader, reminding him at intervals of the investigative procedure being followed. Unfortunately the work lost the symmetry of these intervals when for the 1764 edition of *Essays and Treatises* Hume moved what had been section 6, part 1 to the back. Now one must look to appendix 4 for the second explanation.

Less fortunately still, Hume is unclear in these explanations. In fact, in the present state of my understanding of Hume I cannot acquit him of being a little unsure himself about what his procedure was. In the first explanation he rejects the rationalist practice of "beginning with exact definitions of virtue and vice," proposing instead to

> consider the matter as an object of experience. We shall call *every quality or action of the mind*, virtuous, *which is attended with the general approbation of mankind*: and we shall denominate vicious, *every quality which is the object of general blame or censure*. These qualities we shall endeavour to collect; and

---

[93] See [Roger A. Hornsby,] "Catalogue Verse," *Princeton Encyclopedia of Poetry and Poetics*, enl. ed. (Princeton, 1974).

after examining, on both sides, the several circumstances, in
which they agree, 'tis hoped we may, at last, reach the foundation of ethics, and find those universal principles, from which
all moral blame or approbation is ultimately derived.

(i [173 n. 2])

There are three stages of inquiry described here: the designation of virtue and vice by approbatory and disapprobatory
sentiments, the examination of specimen virtues collected according to this designation, and the inferences drawn from the
specimens. But calling virtue any characteristic that arouses
approbation looks very much like the sentimentalist thesis itself. In what sense is Hume not beginning with definitions? It
will be recalled that what Smith named the Newtonian
method of exposition, in which diverse phenomena are ac-
counted for with few principles, could be either empirical or
rationalist. Both approaches please by revealing an underlying unity in diversity. Like Smith, Hume prefers empiricism.
Rather than commence with axiomatic definitions, he prefers
to collect data as Bacon prescribed. Now there are two possibilities for his designations consistent with empiricism. One
is that these designations, at this point, are a provisional hypothesis to be verified, amended, or discarded as examination
of the specimens progresses. In this case the designations *are*
definitions, but hypothetical ones rather than "exact": they
are propositions to be tested empirically rather than axioms
from which to deduce necessary truths. The other possibility
is that they are not offered as definitions, at least yet, but as
rough working criteria for choosing qualities that will be accepted uncontroversially as virtues. Having accumulated a list
of what everyone takes for virtues, he could proceed to examine them for the circumstances in which they agree and
then to formulate a definition. His sentimentalist designations
could well serve as such rough criteria since the only sure indication that a quality is uncontroversially a virtue is that it
universally arouses approbation. As Hume says elsewhere,
"There are certain terms in every language, which import

blame, and others praise; and all men, who use the same tongue, must agree in their application of them" ("ST," 227).

Now these two possibilities are incompatible. Hume cannot consistently both be submitting a provisional definition for consideration *and* applying rough criteria toward building his catalogue. As has been noted above, the authority of any inferences drawn from the catalogue depends upon the items being uncontroversially acceptable as specimens of virtue and vice. To fulfill their purpose, rough criteria must allow Hume to collect samples that will not be challenged. But a hypothetical definition submitted for testing is necessarily proposed as challengeable. Which is Hume's procedure?

It appears from his second explanation that he thought of his catalogue as a means of avoiding controversy. If he had begun with "exact" definitions, he says, he would have been plunged at the outset into "disputes of words," such as whether a virtue should be defined so as to include natural abilities. These disputes would stop the inquiry before it got started. "It was in order to avoid altercations so frivolous and endless," he writes,

> that I endeavoured to state with the utmost caution the object of our present enquiry; and proposed simply to collect on the one hand, a list of those mental qualities which are the object of love or esteem, and form a part of personal merit, and on the other hand, a catalogue of those qualities, which are the object of censure or reproach, and which detract from the character of the person, possessed of them; subjoining some reflections concerning the origin of these sentiments of praise or blame.
>
> (app. 4 [278–79])

As Locke and Berkeley emphatically said, we cannot hope to get anywhere unless we argue about things rather than words. But Hume might be anxious here only to avoid purely abstract, and hence irresolvable, semantic disputes. It is only axiomatic definitions that he is expressly avoiding here, not hypothetical ones, any disputes over which empiricism can resolve. This explanation is as ambiguous as the first as to whether Hume is beginning his inquiry with rough criteria or hypothetical definitions.

The third explanation at least appears to be unambiguous. Hume here calls his designations a hypothesis:

> The hypothesis which we embrace is plain. It maintains, that morality is determined by sentiment. It defines virtue to be *whatever mental action or quality gives to a spectator the pleasing sentiment of approbation*; and vice the contrary. We then proceed to examine a plain matter of fact, to wit, what actions have this influence: We consider all the circumstances, in which these actions agree: And thence endeavour to extract some general observations with regard to these sentiments. (app. 1 [261])

This seems clear enough. But it is puzzling that Hume says nothing about verifying his hypothesis. Moreover, the procedure that he describes could not verify or falsify the specified hypothesis. To collect specimens of virtue according to a provisional sentimentalist definition, and then upon examining them to infer that virtue is derived from sentiment, would be to build the inference into the premise. And in fact after examining his catalogue Hume does not quite claim to have verified sentimentalism. He humbly confesses

> that this enumeration puts the matter in so strong a light, that I cannot, *at present*, be more assured of any truth, which I learn from reasoning and argument, than that personal merit consists entirely in the usefulness or agreeableness of qualities to the person himself possessed of them, or to others, who have any intercourse with him. (ix. 1 [253])

This proposition is a refinement upon the original sentimentalist designation, so that the "*general approbation of mankind*" resolves into usefulness and agreeableness (i.e., into indirect and immediate agreeableness). Hume reverts here to his old habit of representing the positiveness of the particular instant, cautiously balancing this, however, with a depiction of the following moment when he loses confidence. And well he should lose confidence at this point. A refined sentimentalist conclusion, drawn from evidence selected according to a sentimentalist definition, begs the question of whether approbatory sentiment is the defining feature of virtue. Indirect and immediate agreeableness are the underlying principles of morals only *if* the sentimentalist premise from which they are educed is true, and Hume has not yet proven that. To do so, he needs to get out his meaning-empirical microscope and trace the original impression of morality to sentiment, something he does not do until appendix 1 after finishing with his catalogue. By itself his catalogue can play no part in testing a sentimentalist hypothesis; nor in the third explanation does Hume suggest that it does.

For the 1764 edition of *Essays and Treatises* Hume replaced the first explanation with one that seems to indicate that he did not regard his designations as hypothetical definitions. Perhaps he saw that in the earlier version he had rejected preliminary definitions only to offer what at least strongly resemble them. This time he says that

> we shall endeavour to follow a very simple method: We shall analyse that complication of mental qualities, which form what, in common life, we call Personal Merit: We shall consider every attribute of the mind, which renders a man an object either of esteem and affection, or of hatred and contempt; every habit or sentiment or faculty, which, if ascribed to any person, implies either praise or blame, and may enter into any panygeric or satire of his character and manners. The quick sensibility, which, on this head, is so universal among mankind, gives a philosopher sufficient assurance, that he can never be considerably mistaken in framing the catalogue, or incur any danger of misplacing the objects of his contemplation: He needs only enter into his own breast for a moment, and consider whether or not he should desire to have this or that quality ascribed to him, and whether such or such an imputation would proceed from a friend or an enemy.

He goes on to say that having catalogued these qualities we can isolate the common elements and infer these to be "universal principles." This, he says, is the "experimental method" (i [173–74]). If we are to consider this revision to be

Hume's last word on the subject, we should take it that he intended his designations to be working criteria for compiling an uncontroversial body of evidence from which to isolate his two principles of agreeableness. It should be noted, even so, that from the same catalogue the moral rationalists would claim to isolate a different common element. A rationalist universal principle might be either fittingness to the necessary relations inherent in things, or perhaps obedience to God's instructions. Although Hume's catalogue does help him counter Mandevillean egoism by illustrating how we do care about others, it does not help him to disprove rationalism. Only meaning-empiricism does that.

It is interesting, therefore, that in the second *Enquiry* Hume devotes so little space to meaning-empirical impression hunting. Whereas in the *Treatise* he had begun with it and made it the basis for further reasoning, here he engages in it at the end, as an adjunct to his cataloguing activities. One reason for this emphasis on the catalogue might be that now he is contending with Mandevillean cynicism, against which the collection of virtues serves as a sort of ostensive proof. Another may be that this emphasis is appropriate if one's purposes are hortatory as well as anatomical. Hunting original impressions is rather intractably abstruse and not adaptable to the commendation of virtue, whereas the catalogue served both of Hume's purposes. Whichever way Hume actually employed the catalogue as a device for anatomy, it is clear that he thought, and wanted us to think, that it was a collection of specimens for empirical examination. But it also gave him the opportunity to panegyrize virtue as he proceeded through it.

If this is the way in which Hume saw the second *Enquiry*, then his preference for it is understandable. In it he does not merely strike a successful compromise between the two species of philosophy; he approaches nearly to a harmonious marriage, simplifying an abstruse subject by referring constantly to the sentiments that all men understand, vulgar and wise alike. In directing us to the principles by which these sentiments operate he reveals what before we may have only dimly perceived, though we are intimately familiar with our own feelings. This is natural novelty. No one should be startled to learn that his sentiments are directed according to immediate agreeableness and agreeableness through usefulness, though few will have appreciated the fact. And as well as rendering abstruse material easy and obvious more successfully than he ever did elsewhere, Hume was able to take the further step and contribute to the inculcation of morality.

The desirability of a compromise between the two species of philosophy would have been made more apparent by the failure of the *Treatise* with the public. Humanist moral and literary values militated against the acceptance of so formidably abstract and involved a work, at least outside of a select group of philosophers. No such select group of appreciators materialized until as late as 1758, when the "Wise Club" was founded in Aberdeen.[94] Hume had no reason to think that this system would ever be noticed if left to languish in the *Treatise*, with which, moreover, he was himself dissatisfied. Undergoing a brief apprenticeship to Mr. Spectator and, to a lesser extent, to Caleb D'Anvers, he proceeded to re-present his system more elegantly. In the *Philosophical Essays* he delivered his "logic" with much less of the "false wit" of the *Treatise*, suppressing his proclivity for epigrammatic paradoxes and developing in its place a remarkable skill for satiric irony. All of these writings are informed with his desire to keep philosophy from perniciously fomenting contentions and to press it into the service of mankind. This irenic impulse is unfulfilled in the recast "logic" to the extent that the science of man clashes with the established religion over what kinds of inferences are licit and illicit. The recast "morals," on the other hand, would have gratified Hume in being preponderantly positive and unprovocative. He needs no irony when espousing a conformist version of the good life. What one would expect to be unavoidable conflicts between accuracy and elegance, between dispassionate inquiry and earnest instruction, seem in this work to be resolved.

Was Hume right in disliking the *Treatise* and favoring the

[94] See Mossner, *Life*, 273.

second *Enquiry*? He would be the first to point out that value judgments cannot be true or false. Our literary values are not his; but the existence of disagreement does not mean that he or we have a better insight into the closeness of those books to some supposed essence of literature. Social circumstances might evolve in which the literary values of eighteenth-century Britain would become much more important to us. At present, though, natural novelty and moral improvement are too little valued for it to be likely that modern readers will share Hume's preference. Even if we adopt these criteria, the second *Enquiry* compares less than favorably with Smith's *Theory of Moral Sentiments*, which might serve as a good example of what Hume wanted to achieve. As for myself, having no exaggerated notion of the interest of my own critical opinions I have tried primarily to be informative. But in closing I will confess to valuing literature lower which is merely immediately agreeable than that which is agreeable through its usefulness: all other things being equal, I give priority to writings, literary or philosophical, in which things get accomplished over those that aspire to the condition of music or mathematics. To this extent I share the old humanist values. But Hume's greatest strength in this regard is in helping us to clear our minds of cant, and he is better at this elsewhere than in the second *Enquiry* in which he is so intent on respectability. He is not nearly so good at encouraging the social virtues as clear thinking.

It is fitting to end this literary study of Hume with an affirmation of the priority of his philosophical achievements. If his writings were to lose their philosophical importance, if, say, we discovered incontrovertibly that sceptical empiricism is wholly unveridical, undoubtedly most of his works would recede in status to that of Hume's *History*, which, being superseded in content, goes largely unread. Their literary merits, considerable as these are, would not save many of them from becoming mere documents of a dead intellectual movement. But it is not a dead movement. It has only lost sharpness of definition after pervading Western culture. It is, in fact, the basis for literary scholarship.

233–34, 234n; religious, Hume's lack of, 228, 230, 234

Congreve, William: Hume on, 20

Copernicus, 84

copy principle, Hume's, 89

country party, 150; Hume on, 153–54, 155

court party, 150, 151; Hume on, 153–54

Cowley, Abraham: view of schoolmen, 12

*Craftsman, The*, 20, 124, 154; letters in, 118; as model for Hume and others, 8, 113, 115, 121–23, 157–58, 254; and political controversy, 117, 123, 151, 157–58; and women, 121

criticism, in *Treatise*, projected, 84, 86

deism, 24, 211, 212, 213

Dempster, George, 212n

Descartes, René, 11, 31, 67. *See also* Cartesians

design, argument from, 27–28, 29, 164, 213, 215, 216

Desmaizeaux, Pierre, 73

determinism, causal. *See* causation

dialogue (as genre), 129

Diderot, Denis, 213n

diffuse style: defined, 170, 171; Hume and others on, 169–71, 173

*divisio*, 92–93

divorce, Hume on, 131–33

Dryden, John, 151, 196

Edinburgh, 71; and Hume's journalism, 115–16, 118, 122, 126–27

egoism. *See* Mandeville

egotism: Hume's, in *Philosophical Essays*, 180; Hume's, in *Treatise*, 73, 74, 77, 78, 79, 95, 96, 104, 108, 109, 176; *Rambler*, and essay form, 110. *See also* argumentation

eighteenth-century literary values,

23, 54. *See also* clarity; elegance; novelty; perspicuity; simplicity

elegance, 23; Hume's desire for, 36, 51, 148, 184; lacking in *Treatise*, 73, 180; and philosophy, 43–45, 180, 254

Eliot, Gilbert, 175

Eliot, T. S., 111, 148, 184, 188

eloquence, 57; and violent passions, 65

empiricism, 37, 70, 96, 152, 199; aims of, 149; and the essay, 93–94; history's role in, 241–42; Hume's, 36, 187, 201, 205, 209, 255; Hume's, and the catalogue, 248–49, 252, 253; Hume's, and mitigated scepticism, 189; Hume's program of, 51, 148, 177, 215; Hume's, and sentimentalism, 229; and learning, 119; Lockean, 31–32, 37; Pope's attraction to, 28; and Pyrrhonism, 97–98, 194; and rationalists, 13; and scholasticism, 11–12, 13, 19; and science, 54–55; and Swift, 30–32; and theism, 27; and *Treatise*, 99, 147. *See also* meaning-empiricism

enthusiasm: Hume on, 23–24, 50, 66, 239; philosophical, 117, 127; religious, 118n, 228

Epicurus, 174

epistemology, Hume's, 207, 208

*epochē*, 195, 201–2

essay (as genre), 147, 174–75; the Addisonian essay, 125; Hume on, 108–9, 113–14, 168; Hume's experiments with, 8, 162, 174–75; "miscellaneous way," 101–3, 105, 108–9, 113, 174; and *Treatise*, 93–98, 108–10. *See also* periodical essays; *individual titles under* Hume

ethics: applied, 237; Hume on, 227; normative, 236, 237